PRAISE FOR *BUSINESS RESILIENCE*

T0309178

"It's truly refreshing to see PACE culture at the centre of the Business Resilience Framework; it proves beyond doubt that culture is not only critical to survival, but is what makes an organization a great place to work whilst creating progress in a VUCA world."
Gretchen Hallberg, Global Learning and Development Technology Leader, PwC

"The Business Resilience Framework provides an entirely practical approach to improving the organization's resilience, enabling it to make Progress @ Pace. Most usefully, this framework can be adopted and adapted to make sustained improvements in any organization."
Vikram Ramnath, IS Program Director, Providence St Joseph Health

"Business Resilience is a very popular topic in the current climate; but no one has taken the theories and produced such a clear and practical framework that is so easily adaptable in any organization."
Timothy Fulton, former CFO/COO, Jumeirah Group, and Finance Director, Formula One Abu Dhabi,

"Executives can now face the threat of disruption with confidence; *Business Resilience* offers a fresh and eminently practical model for how companies can adapt and succeed in a continuously changing landscape."
Amanda Welsh, Faculty Director, Leadership and Project Management Programs, Northeastern College of Professional Studies

"Every business endeavour starts with a forecast to build on our hopes for success; but by the time we realize it was far too optimistic, it can be too late. Until now we've lacked clarity on how to strengthen business thinking and structures to react and survive unprecedented change. Now we have a blueprint to better position any business for an increasingly VUCA world."
Richard Pharro CEO APMG International

"Guides abound to managing planned changes or identified risks in projects, programs, and portfolios; this book boldly identifies how to take advantage of 'unknown unknowns.' Developing professional resilience practices is key to making systematic progress from events which might otherwise undermine organizational existence."

Peter Johnson, Senior Consultant Peter Johnson Consultants Ltd

"As someone new to resilience I found this book to be an invaluable asset. Complex concepts are explained clearly and in an engaging manner to help you gain a deep understanding by the end of each chapter. It is such practical guide to implementing resilience throughout the organization."

Ben Snell, Project Support Officer, Department of Work and Pensions, UK

"In today's VUCA world, bouncing forward, not simply bouncing back, is core to pivoting at the right moment with the right speed. *Business Resilience* clarifies the importance of utilizing organizational strengths to provide more customer value. Whilst better processes and tools are important, competency for sustained progress crucially depends upon ethical behaviour and enhancing organization culture. *Business Resilience* is full of practical ideas; how to investigate new insights whilst maintaining focus on resilient journeys; it's a book to use and re-use, time and again. How resilient is that?"

Peter Coesmans, Chief Agility Officer, Agile Business Consortium

"Organizations have witnessed significant impact on their business models as a consequence of the pandemic. They have realized the critical need to build back better and the power of developing business resilience within their organizational processes, procedures and culture to achieve success. This book offers great insights and strategies to build resilience within your daily business operations. It includes case study illustrations which add great value."

Dilshad Sheikh (CMgr CCMI), Dean, Faculty of Business, Arden University CMI Chair West Midlands and North-West Regions, UK

"As soon as I learned about the Business Resilience Framework, I started knowledge sharing with current and next-gen PM professionals. Project leaders, delivery experts and change specialists will appreciate the practical know-how that the framework provides - integrating business resilience with existing methodologies. Organizations adopting this framework should see significant improvement in project performance and business results."

Merv Wyeth, Director of Technology & Digital Events, Project Management Institute (PMI UK)

"As delivery consultant working on multibillion digital transformation programmes in major government departments, I found this book to be innovative, clear and able to open pathways to new ideas. It's a must read when applying the tools and techniques needed to successfully build resilience, navigating through challenging times and beyond."
Wahid Ali, Delivery Consultant, Capgemini

"Resilience is now an essential part of any senior software team; adopting the Resilience Professional role, as shown in this book, will add robustness to any programme, change or transformation team, by ensuring that adapting products, services processes or practices makes the organization both stronger and more profitable."
Pip Nelson, Senior Director of Software Engineering, DHL eCommerce Solutions

"This book provides a well-structured and comprehensive approach to ensuring an organization stays current in a rapidly changing world. It is a must for anyone wanting to ensure that their organization remains agile, robust, competitive and profitable. Well done to the team that produced such a good set of guidance."
Steve Messenger, former Chairman of DSDM, author of Agile Programme Management

"In the rapidly changing business landscape we live in, 'resilience' is an essential quality required by all business leaders. This book defines the core principles of business resilience and is an indispensable tool for organizations of any size."
Yaqub Yousef, Chief Brand Ideator, Quadragina

Business Resilience

*A practical guide to sustained
progress delivered at pace*

David Roberts, Islam Choudhury,
Serhiy Kovela, Sheila Roberts
and Jawwad Tanvir

KoganPage

Publisher's note

Every possible effort has been made to ensure that the information contained in this book is accurate at the time of going to press, and the publishers and authors cannot accept responsibility for any errors or omissions, however caused. No responsibility for loss or damage occasioned to any person acting, or refraining from action, as a result of the material in this publication can be accepted by the editor, the publisher or the author.

First published in Great Britain and the United States in 2022 by Kogan Page Limited

Apart from any fair dealing for the purposes of research or private study, or criticism or review, as permitted under the Copyright, Designs and Patents Act 1988, this publication may only be reproduced, stored or transmitted, in any form or by any means, with the prior permission in writing of the publishers, or in the case of reprographic reproduction in accordance with the terms and licences issued by the CLA. Enquiries concerning reproduction outside these terms should be sent to the publishers at the undermentioned addresses:

2nd Floor, 45 Gee Street	8 W 38th Street, Suite 902	4737/23 Ansari Road
London	New York, NY 10018	Daryaganj
EC1V 3RS	USA	New Delhi 110002
United Kingdom		India
www.koganpage.com		

© David Roberts, Islam Choudhury, Serhiy Kovela, Sheila Roberts and Jawwad Tanvir 2022

Kogan Page books are printed on paper from sustainable forests.

The right of David Roberts, Islam Choudhury, Serhiy Kovela, Sheila Roberts and Jawwad Tanvir to be identified as the authors of this work has been asserted by them in accordance with the Copyright, Designs and Patents Act 1988.

ISBNs

Hardback	978 1 3986 0466 7
Paperback	978 1 3986 0464 3
Ebook	978 1 3986 0465 0

British Library Cataloguing-in-Publication Data

A CIP record for this book is available from the British Library.

Library of Congress Control Number

2022931992

Typeset by Integra Software Services, Pondicherry
Print production managed by Jellyfish
Printed and bound by CPI Group (UK) Ltd, Croydon, CR0 4YY

This book is dedicated to the Business Resilience movement to support sustainable organizations which make progress at the right pace for their situation. To those organizations who have gone through the pain of the financial crisis and Covid-19 and kept going. They have supported their staff and built on their RESILIENCE Foundations, created a PACE Culture and used a PROGRESS Cycle to move forward.

This book is also dedicated to tomorrow's ambassadors of Business Resilience. Investment in resilience enables organizations to work through tough times to emerge in better situations. There are many unnamed martyrs and unsung heroes who are, and have been, working tirelessly to sustain organizations, families, communities and the planet through the peaks and troughs of changing environments. We dedicate this to you and thank you for your understanding of the need for resilience.

CONTENTS

ABOUT THE AUTHORS

David Roberts has enjoyed a rich and varied career spanning over 40 years in both corporate and public sectors, including 20 years as a business owner. Today he designs and delivers customized programmes and best practice certifications in transformations and projects facing VUCA situations globally.

David started consulting practice when he was a young Chartered Institute of Marketing member and while teaching university MBA programmes. Following executive positions in automotive, telecommunications, global pharmaceuticals and director positions in UK and overseas health organizations, negotiating, planning and completing major initiatives and transformations, he co-founded the first APMG Consultancy and Training Accredited Organization, leading client initiatives in strategy implementation and continuously adapting services to ever-changing requirements.

David has also been a Director of the Agile Business Consortium since 2019, is a Chartered Project Professional (Ch.PP) and a Chartered Management Consultant (Ch.MC). His main professional interest is in the developing world of Business Resilience and leading initiatives in organizations committed to making it real.

LinkedIn: https://uk.linkedin.com/in/david-roberts-7476b8

Dr Islam Choudhury is Associate Professor in the School of Computer Science and Mathematics at Kingston University, based in Surrey, UK. Islam has been teaching and researching in several universities since the late 1990s. He has successfully supervised several PhDs to completion and has a wide range of journal, conference and workshop publications. He is also a director of the Agile Business Consortium, working on promoting business agility worldwide. He is a certified APMG AgilePM and AgileBA trainer and has been teaching and recommending the agile way of working to students over many years.

He believes in and is dedicated to continually finding better ways for organizations and their leaders and workforce to build an agile and resilient Mindset that can enable them to appropriately adapt so they can survive and thrive in a volatile, uncertain, complex and ambiguous world. He is also passionate to promote a Mindset and a way of collaborative working that will make people in organizations resilient when faced with difficulties, continue to know their purpose in the business and motivated to work to an optimal level while making progress at a sustainable pace of work.

LinkedIn: https://uk.linkedin.com/in/dr-islam-choudhury-77871a8

Dr Serhiy Kovela is Associate Professor in Project Management at New College of the Humanities at Northeastern University, Boston, USA. He is a scholar, practitioner and educator with over 21 years of experience in project management and business IT, consulting and delivering training programmes in the UK and internationally.

Serhiy has a master's degree in electrical engineering, a PhD in computer science, and an MBA. He also has a range of professional qualifications and is an Accredited AgilePM Trainer and Facilitation Practitioner.

As a practitioner, Serhiy provided training and advisory services focused on increasing organizational efficiency with better management of projects, programmes and IT, in private and state-sponsored organizations. Having lived through the collapse of the Soviet Union and the emergence of the newly independent Ukraine, while pivoting from international touring as a dancer to industry and academic pursuits, Serhiy has experienced many aspects of the VUCA world. He developed a profound appreciation of the importance of adapting at pace, at the individual, community and national levels, resulting in his keen interest in organizational resilience.

LinkedIn: https://uk.linkedin.com/in/serhiykovela

Sheila Roberts' interest in resilience started as a Sister leading a team in Intensive Care. Following her study of and move into management, she recognized the need for resilience at all levels of organizations. Sheila provides support to organizations and Teams to become more resilient in volatile and uncertain conditions. The Covid-19 pandemic enabled the team to share an approach to develop greater Business Resilience.

After 20 years in health, she co-founded the first jointly accredited APMG Training and Consulting Organization. She consults and trains in Business Resilience, programme and project management. She has had appointments as a best practice examiner, quality reviewer and member of the PRINCE2 Reference Group. She is currently an APM Assessor for chartered project professionals and chair of examiners for some APM qualifications. Sheila is chair of the industry body, Association for Training Excellence, and has contributed to publications.

LinkedIn: https://uk.linkedin.com/in/sheila-roberts-0462b22

Jawwad Tanvir is a seasoned professional with an engineering background and 20 years of experience spanning ASIC design engineering, software development, welding automation, and welding consumables manufacturing and distribution. He has experience of working with organizations based in the UK, Germany, Belgium, Brazil, Saudi Arabia, China, India and Pakistan, and has a deep understanding of business.

As CEO he is spearheading Metallogen Ltd expansion beyond borders. He offers consultancy to SMEs in implementation of better business cases, management of value, business agility and lean solutions. Jawwad is also an APMG Accredited Trainer for Better Business Cases and Scrum Master and disseminates his experience through training government and software development organizations. His current work is focused on resilience and growth amid VUCA environments, which was expedited by Covid-19. He is also working on using artificial intelligence and data analytics for organizations to keep making progress despite the odds.

LinkedIn: https://uk.linkedin.com/in/jawwadtanvir

QUALIFICATIONS

The Business Resilience qualification is available through APMG International (APMG). The Business Resilience qualification uses this book as the examinable text and candidates will need to become familiar with the content. More information about the APMG Business Resilience examinations and the Accredited Training Organizations that provide the training and qualifications can be found at www.apmg-international.com.

APMG International is a leading global examination institute that manages certifications for professionals across a range of disciplines. It accredits the trainers and training organizations through a robust Assessment process. APMG International is externally accredited by the United Kingdom Accreditation Service (UKAS). The commitment to high-quality standards means that the training organizations accredited and examinations set by APMG International are thorough, consistent and reliable. These enable candidates to offer a qualification that represents an individual achievement at a standard valued by employers.

ACKNOWLEDGEMENTS

The authors would like to thank APMG International for the encouragement they have given to the authoring team. Particularly to Richard Pharro, APMG International CEO, for recognizing the necessity for Business Resilience and suggesting we produce the book, supporting its development and believing in the need for a qualification scheme. APMG International has also ensured we have focused on Business Resilience without straying into other disciplines.

We would also like to express our thanks to the reviewers, who gave generously of their time to identify constructive feedback, leading to improvements. Peter Johnson, who can work at the speed of light, and Ben Snell, who has a mastery of English – we are indebted to you both. A number of other experienced consultants, business people and trainers also acted as sounding boards to clarify specific points. Our thanks to them all.

We are grateful to the 250 master's students who participated in the proof of concept of the Business Resilience Framework, ensuring it makes sense to those currently working in organizations, despite not yet having the book for reference. They not only understood but passed the exam as well.

The editorial team at Kogan Page has guided us through the publication process and patiently answered all our questions. We are grateful for their experience and explanations to compensate for our inexperience of publishing.

Finally, but by no means least, we wish to acknowledge our families, who have lived through the inception of Business Resilience and given us care and support, which has enabled us to deliver the result.

TRADEMARKS

PRINCE2®, PRINCE2 Agile®, MSP®, MoP®, M_0_R®, MoV® are registered trademarks of AXELOS Limited.

PMBOK® and Disciplined Agile® are registered trademarks of the Project Management Institute Inc.

SCRUM™ is a trademark of Jeff Sutherland.

AgilePM®, AgilePgM®, AgilePfM® and AgileDS® are registered trademarks of the Agile Business Consortium.

Accelerating Collaboration Everywhere® is a trademark of Assentire Ltd.

DiSC® is a registered trademark of John Wiley & Sons, Inc. and its corporate subsidiaries.

MBTI® and Myers-Briggs Type Indicator® are registered trademarks of the MBTI Trust Inc.

PERMA™ is a trademark of Martin E.P. Seligman.

Process Iceberg® is a registered trademark of Resource Developing Business by Developing People Ltd.

In writing this book, many best practices, models and techniques have been referenced, as the Business Resilience Framework builds on the excellent work that is already available. We have made every effort to honour all copyright holders. Should there be any which we have inadvertently missed, we sincerely apologize and will correct these in a future edition.

FOREWORD
by Stephen Jenner

Following well-established professional careers in industry, government and academia, the authors established and sustained best-practice training and consulting companies. Their careers have been a journey through widely divergent organizations, but what was common to them all was the constant challenge of adapting to an ever-increasing pace of change.

Adapting and responding were fast becoming essential organizational capabilities in the 21st century. But what the series of seismic socio-economic shocks from the global financial crash to the pandemic have highlighted is that, while still necessary, this is no longer sufficient. Organizations need to look beyond merely adapting and responding to change, to developing the capability and capacity to anticipate and leverage emerging opportunities as well as unanticipated threats - and so a new journey of discovery began.

Researching corporate data highlighted two very important messages. The first was that some organizations showed remarkable resilience, even when faced by a series of VUCA challenges - indeed they not only survived but thrived, while others in less challenging circumstances were consigned to the dustbin of history. The second was that mental well-being was now one of the biggest costs/impediments to business survival and growth. The authors were intrigued - what was it that distinguished these organizations from their less successful competitors? Could the difference that makes the difference be identified, captured and re-imagined into a repeatable framework? The authors set about modelling and testing their insights. The result - a Business Resilience Framework (BRF) and its key domains of RESILIENCE Foundations, PACE Culture and PROGRESS Cycle - practical, accessible, robust and relevant.

This book enables the reader to learn from organizations that have successfully navigated the challenges of unknown/unknowable conditions. That alone would be of value, but the book goes beyond merely telling us what works - by collating the lessons learned into an evidence-based framework of enterprise-level capabilities, structured into five domains and 22 elements, with supporting best practices. Furthermore, organizations are offered four strategic approaches to introducing the BRF, building on current strengths, but with a forward-looking perspective. Crucially, in my view, the authors don't advocate additional specialist resources; rather they see resilience professionals working alongside established leadership or PPM roles, testing and tailoring the BRF to suit local circumstances. This book will also provide the guidance necessary for professionals seeking to gain certifications in Business Resilience.

The book will be of value to organizational leaders at all levels, including those engaged in Portfolio or P3O environments. Business Resilience provides the missing link in ensuring sustainability – not just in business change programmes, but also in relation to the organization's very existence. Finally, the book demonstrates how to assess your existing organization using the Business Resilience Profile, PURE strategies to migrate, whatever the starting condition or business challenge. Business Resilience will help your organization look confidently towards a future that it can create rather than respond to. This really is an exceptional piece of work. Read, apply, learn, repeat.

Stephen Jenner is a best-practice author, business practitioner and academic. His work centres mainly on the fields of project portfolio and benefits management, complex projects and strategic supplier relationship management. He is a Fellow of the Chartered Institute of Management Accountants, with an MBA and Master of Studies degree from Cambridge University. He designs and teaches courses for the Graduate School of Business at Queensland University of Technology, where he is an adjunct professor.

PREFACE

The need for enduring Business Resilience

A great turning point is ahead – a new reality beyond digitization in design and delivery, a future where organizations must raise the quality of Portfolios to embrace next-level personalization, social responsibility and green consciousness in the transition to better 21st-century products and services. Organizations need to achieve higher levels of innovation, harness more Energy and overcome the inertia of established practices and processes. Business resilience enables the Challenge of market chaos to become an opportunity to energize human systems and technologies, to make Portfolio progress at pace and secure success by the proVision of more customer value.

The increasing scale and reach of global technologies had already had a profound effect on the business landscape. As financial pressures grew, leaders responded with shorter lifecycles, lean and value engineering, customer and quality initiatives; but behind this productivity drive, non-financial pressures began to take their toll on working populations through ever-increasing demands. In a business era dominated by low-cost production, information technology revolutions, globalization and financial crises, the worldwide impact of the Covid-19 pandemic has provided a new perspective: some organizations have been overwhelmed, forced to close for good, while others have succeeded in a miraculous fashion. Change has happened fast, but progress has been uncertain.

Some organizations responded to the crisis by spending ever-increasing amounts in adapting current products and services, only to reach breaking point. So, what are the characteristics of resilient organizations? What is it that enabled some organizations to make positive business progress while others simply could not adapt in time under similar VUCA (volatile, uncertain, complex and ambiguous) conditions?

This guide captures the essentials of Business Resilience, presenting what matters most in a straightforward, practical way. It will appeal to leaders throughout organizations wishing to step up, taking advantage of 21st-century VUCA conditions. Business resilience is a complementary management discipline that uses experience and Learning differently,

---

A CONSULTANT'S STORY

Inspiration for this guide grew from many years of seeing people in organizations feeling like they were navigating white water Rapids with only a kayak to protect them. Some colleagues and friends found the kayak was not sufficient, hit the rocks and ended up in the water, either managing to struggle to the bank or very sadly some went under. As a would-be authoring team, discussions commenced in autumn 2019 on how to help professionals and organizations become more resilient, more able to negotiate choppy waters and find their way to the winning post. And then it really hit home – one of the original team had not made it; Chris had a fatal heart attack on the way to work in Switzerland, hundreds of miles away from home and family. Our time for conjecture had passed; we resolved to make professional working life better – not simply smarter ways to make more money, but for organizations to be great places to live and learn, as well as work. Together the authoring team members would share their highs and lows, lessons and ideas for making a better working world.

---

welcoming opportunities for innovation, taking practical steps to re-energize, to realize sustained success in the future.

The pandemic of 2020–21 provided an unexpected opportunity to take stock, with an immediate impact of lockdowns resulting in the need to adapt at pace across the world. We were in an extreme VUCA condition, where travelling to clients or the office was off-limits to all but essential workers. Refreshed insights into family lives, colleagues and friends prompted organizations and professionals to question what really mattered: what was happening in the world of work? Inevitably, the financial and economic pain of the pandemic was shared unequally across families and nations; uncertainty and survival became the new reality for many, while others worked tirelessly to deliver progress at pace. The authoring team resolved to use this time to complete the Business Resilience Framework.

A positive outcome of the pandemic has been time to reflect, and a rich Learning opportunity. In examining the unsustainability of late-20th-century business transformations, highlighted by inefficient work practices, organizational Energy was literally consumed rather than created. Some organizations were fortified by the ability to make a difference in challenging times, utilizing their culture and adapting practices and processes to provide great product or service value in fighting the pandemic – not for them the sense of

REPORT ON GOVERNMENT RESPONSE TO COVID-19 PANDEMIC

Indeed, in conclusions to the *Sixth Report of the UK Health and Social Care Committee and Third Report of the Science and Technology Committee of Session 2021–22*, entitled *Coronavirus: Lessons learned to date* (House of Commons, 2021), there are very important observations possibly applicable to other organizations facing extreme VUCA conditions.

Conclusions

During the first three months of the Covid pandemic, the UK followed the wrong policy in its use of non-pharmaceutical interventions. When the UK moved from the 'contain' to 'delay' stage, there was a policy of seeking to only moderate the speed of infection through the population – flattening the curve – rather than seeking to arrest its spread. The policy was pursued until 23 March because of the official scientific advice the government received, not despite it. Questions remain about whether the containment phase was pursued aggressively enough – we believe it could have been pursued for longer. During this period government policy did not deviate from the scientific advice it received in any material respect. The fact that the UK approach reflected a consensus between official scientific advisers and the government indicates a degree of groupthink that was present at the time, which meant we were not as open to approaches being taken elsewhere – such as earlier lockdowns, border controls and effective test and trace – as we should have been.

Observations

The 'flattening the curve' policy was implemented by introducing new restrictions only gradually and slowly, acting as if the spread of the virus were susceptible to calibrated control. Modelling at the time suggested that to suppress the spread of Covid-19 too firmly would cause a resurgence when restrictions were lifted. This was thought likely to result in a peak in the autumn and winter, when NHS pressures were already likely to be severe. In addition, it was thought that the public would only comply with severe restrictions for a limited period, and so those restrictions should not be applied before they were most needed. This approach should have been questioned at the time for a number of reasons:

- It entailed people contracting Covid in large numbers, with hundreds of thousands of deaths likely to result.

- Other countries, in Asia and in Europe, including some with experience of SARS and MERS, had chosen to implement earlier, more comprehensive strategies of non-pharmaceutical interventions, which were having success.

- Suppressing the spread of the virus in the early period would have bought valuable time to consider what was the best way to manage the pandemic in the medium term.

Explanations

There are several possible explanations for what was a significant error in policy and advice early in the pandemic. These include:

- lack of adequate data on the spread of Covid-19, as a result of the inadequacy of the UK Testing operation;

- over-reliance on specific mathematical models when there were too many uncertainties;

- assumptions about public compliance with rules that turned out to have underestimated the willingness to conform, even for long periods;

- composition of SAGE (Scientific Advisory Group for Emergencies) suffered from a lack of representation from outside the United Kingdom; and

- preference for a particular UK approach may have been favoured above advice based on emulation of what was being pursued elsewhere.

'after the gold rush', where capable people left, products and services were in low demand, and practices and processes in desperate need of replacement. So, to simplify possible implications for other organizations facing extreme VUCA conditions, the findings within this report are mapped to key aspects of this book: the Business Resilience Framework, Progress @ Pace 8-4-8 Model, domains or elements, discussed in later chapters (Table 0.1).

By autumn 2021, vaccination programmes indicated a way forward for many towards survival, but remained the preserve of wealthy countries. In parallel, many organizations responded to a new Vision of organizational life, but more uncertainty and Risks lay ahead; leaders have to rethink and re-evaluate how to succeed. This practical guide looks forward to implementation of what has been learned from this turning point – combining with pre-pandemic lessons and experience to re-invigorate organizational

TABLE 0.1 Mapping onto key aspects of the book

Policy/ advice error	Lessons learned or explanations for ineffective action/inaction	Mitigation benefits of using the Business Resilience Framework in organizations
1	Lack of adequate data on VUCA status	RESILIENCE Foundations and PROGRESS Cycle utilize VUCA Storm Scale Assessments
2	Over-reliance on mathematical modelling when combined with many uncertainties	Rational and behavioural Assessments are combined for decision-making when utilizing the Progress @ Pace 8-4-8 Model
3	Assumptions from the past were incorrect for the new VUCA disruption	PACE Culture encourages champion/ Challenger activity throughout domains when exploiting the Progress @ Pace 8-4-8 Model
4	Lack of diversity in understanding or analysis of the impact of crisis situations	Diversity of thinking is one of 7 Principles to be applied when implementing the Business Resilience Framework in organizations
5	Belief that the best solutions will always be found 'in-house'	Opportunity Assessment and network Collaboration are optimized when external partnering is included in organizations

designs and cultures, and providing greater purpose and value in professional working lives for a brighter future.

Business resilience provides a prospective insight into professional organizations of tomorrow – enterprising, forward-looking, keeping close to customer experiences and the working lives of their people and partners. It will come as a source of great relief to many that in tomorrow's organizations, the focus is way beyond the impact of relentless price competition of globalization; organizational purpose and value can replace naked greed in response to a new global perspective.

Resilience objective

Sustained progress delivered at pace is a laudable objective for all organizations. It offers employees the prospect of a better business world, where the Challenge of increasing customer expectations is met or exceeded by great innovations. When business conditions change, industry threats are seized upon as market opportunities and this Learning ensures the organization becomes even more resilient and it uses this experience to revitalize its products, services, processes and practices.

Leaders in the 21st century are facing even greater VUCA disruption as technology continues to shrink distances between customers and suppliers and competitive advantage from technology leaders assists early adopter organizations to invade new markets, adding uncertainty and complexity to established organizations. In these VUCA conditions, organizations need to move at pace but also to build resilience.

Reference

House of Commons (2021) *Coronavirus: Lessons learned to date*, 21 September, committees.parliament.uk/publications/7496/documents/78687/default (archived at https://perma.cc/2VKW-VDKX)

01

Introduction to Business Resilience

Purpose

The purpose of Business Resilience is to select the appropriate strategy, with firm RESILIENCE Foundations, which would enable organizational energy to be unleashed, realizing initiatives and creating sustained progress delivered at pace. To achieve Business Resilience, the organization needs to know the practices, knowledge, skills, tools and techniques that have proven to be consistently effective, and to develop an organizational culture to continually adapt to the current environment.

The purpose of this guide is to provide a cohesive, practical guide to building Business Resilience, enabling leaders to implement an effective framework in an inclusive and sustainable way. At a 2021 conference on resilience, a speaker said: 'What is missing is not more great ideas, but a practical framework within which to implement them.' This guide provides the missing framework.

This guide defines a five-domain Business Resilience Framework, with a model for progress, and the elements and tools contained within the framework that, when implemented skilfully, ensure organizations will be able to deliver sustained progress, leading to organizational continuity, whatever the prevailing socio-economic conditions.

A scientific perspective on disruption

To make progress at pace, organizations must be able to perform in all conditions and this requires Business Resilience. In this practical guide a framework is established to address working in VUCA environments. At the heart of the framework is PACE Culture (**purposeful mindset; application of** tools; **Capability and Skills;** elevating energy), energizing the direction of the organization.

An interesting analogy and explanation for the Business Resilience Framework – in particular, why this design features a practical PACE culture at its core – can be found by considering scientific modelling.

Hawkins (1998) discusses the concept of entropy, Newton's 2nd law of thermodynamics, explaining that the universe is constantly moving towards disorder, and energy is needed to bring about order. It is also known that energy cannot be created nor destroyed, but can only change from one form to another. Demma (2012) discusses very convincingly that this law can be applied to understand the modern world and particularly to improve organizations. The author gives further examples of this action, such as the inevitability that people's bodies will deteriorate, houses will disintegrate, cars will break down and an organization will go out of business. The only way to counteract this is to utilize energy appropriately – to keep a body healthy through correct diet and exercise, a car working well by servicing it, a house liveable by constant maintenance, and an organization viable and valuable through good business strategy and execution.

Demma (2012) asserts that great organizations that want to survive and thrive over long periods of time will need to know how to counteract this inevitable entropy, which manifests as VUCA disruptions. Organizations need leaders to deliberately utilize energy and inspire their workforce; chaotic energy around the organization can then be repurposed to sustain delivery and survive.

The key point here is that change is inevitable due to entropy, whereas progress is not. Progress needs a deliberate input of energy to return order and improve the organization. It is also important that the amount of energy used by the organization must be managed so it uses just enough energy depending on the situation. If too much energy is used during times of relative order and business as usual, the people of the organization will have used up their individual energy supply. So, when there are severe VUCA disruptions and large amounts of energy are required, the people in the organization could burn out quickly.

In many organizations, people at all levels leave because they feel under pressure and their energy is being drained due to a lack of appreciation and value. Leaders must regulate the pace of progress to enable sustained organizational growth, where value is derived from organizational energy, feeling passionate, creative and innovative, rather than pressurized to perform beyond endurance with unrealistic targets. Although organizations can survive in a growing market if they are not energized, they will not thrive, and they will not make progress. Such organizations will become dysfunctional and, although they may maintain the appearance of functionality, the lack of Business Resilience and progress culture will eventually lead to their demise, takeover or merger.

What is the Business Resilience Framework?

The combination of the five Business Resilience domains, as shown in Figure 1.1, provides the way forward for organizations wishing to move beyond traditional company designs, embracing modularity and innovation. It energizes professionals by emphasizing the purpose and value of their work to avoid staff burnout associated with the grinding poverty of seemingly pointless work.

The five domains of the Business Resilience Framework enable teams to establish and exploit 22 elements with a goal of making Progress @ Pace (see Chapter 3). That is, the most appropriate pace (across network partners), whether fast or slow. This book provides a practical guide to understand and implement the 22 elements of the Business Resilience Framework. It is not intended to dictate the processes or practices to be followed or, indeed, the tools to use, but to provide a framework in which these decisions can be taken in order to strengthen the Business Resilience of the organization.

FIGURE 1.1 Business Resilience Framework

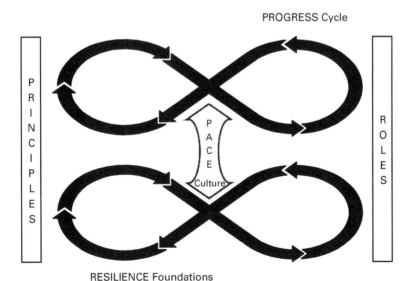

Where organizations have existing practices and processes that are relevant to one or more of the 22 elements, these could supplant those shown in the Business Resilience Framework when adapting it for operational use, using the plug-and-play approach described in Chapter 8. Nonetheless, the purpose of the elements must remain intact following whatever practices or tools are substituted.

In Business Resilience, the importance of investing in culture and people is explored through the PACE Culture domain, which will make a positive impact on operational practice. Developing a distinctive organization culture is characterized by implementation of four PACE elements. It provides a unique culture to sustain an organization through disruptive or VUCA conditions; and when merged with RESILIENCE Foundations and the PROGRESS Cycle, a high-performance zone is created where organizations deliver Progress @ Pace. These three central domains make up the Progress @ Pace 8-4-8 Model and are supported by the Principles and roles domains to complete the Business Resilience Framework.

Five levels of organization are referenced in this guide. Although it is appreciated that organizations will have different numbers of levels, it is important that Business Resilience is both owned and deployed at all levels. Where fewer organizational levels are needed, a more open and connected culture develops and organizations benefit from an ability to make greater Progress @ Pace.

How Business Resilience can help

The Business Resilience Framework and Progress @ Pace 8-4-8 Model provide a great starting point to conduct an assessment of opportunities and threats – the first task being to understand Business Resilience as an approach, and then to baseline the current situation and identify goals for improving steadily. A practical perspective reveals a list of Business Resilience questions (and the guide will enable readers to answer them):

- How can organizations lay foundations to prepare for future turbulent times?
- What can be done to identify and exploit opportunities during VUCA times?
- How can progress be delivered for shareholders, employees and customers during chaotic or complex situations?

- Are the same best practice responsibilities repeatable during times of Calm and chaos?
- Are tools and techniques available for measuring the organization's readiness for VUCA?
- What is the best way to ensure leadership and staff wellbeing amid a chaotic business environment?
- Does Business Resilience reduce fire-fighting activities, ensuring smooth operations by preparing in advance of challenging times?
- As a change manager, what route is there to progress to the next level (individual)?
- Can I recruit a Resilience Professional to support the introduction of Business Resilience (individual)?
- I want to prove my credibility and competence in leading organizations through turbulent times. Is there a Resilience Professional qualification available to prove it (individual)?

The Business Resilience Framework has been designed to be flexible, using a modular design that can be applied at all levels of the organization. Choices can be made to build on experience or move rapidly to a standard solution. It lends itself to piloting and testing within organizations and to being used as a framework for development and implementation of initiatives.

In everyday organizational life, key performance indicators (KPIs) provide a temperature check that organizational performance is on target. If there is a departure from expectations, an organization might seek to clarify its wellbeing using the Resilience Profile (see Chapter 10), in the same way a patient might seek a series of blood tests. This enables a leader to take an overview of the organization's resilience, identifying areas that need to be strengthened and leading to action by the Business Resilience Owner.

Organization leaders should be concerned to improve below-expectation performance before examining new business opportunities. A practical way to explore concerns would be to use an audit checklist of the 22 elements in the Business Resilience Framework. More detailed observations and analysis are available using the resilience profile.

Solving the riddle of seemingly competing requirements in organizations is through understanding the value that is significant to customers. If an organization is able to move up the resilience profile levels, productivity can be improved by working on the areas that deliver more value, thus reducing wasteful effort in the organization.

What makes Business Resilience different?

Business Resilience provides an organization with the ability to make progress through both good times and bad. It is more than simply bouncing back after a crisis or being an agile organization. It is more than assessing risk or having business continuity plans in place. It is more than ensuring cyber security or ecological sustainability. It is more than technical innovation or great service. All these aspects are linked and are needed by organizations. Business Resilience happens as a result of investing in a culture that is as much about a state of mind as it is about a process and practices.

In many businesses, culture evolves haphazardly from the work practices of the past; it is not planned or purposeful, becoming a daily burden to people in the organization. The phrase 'Culture eats products for breakfast, strategy for lunch and everything else for dinner' is often attributed to Peter Drucker, and made famous by Mark Fields, when president of Ford Motor Company in 2006 (Rick, 2020). It is used to highlight how poor culture can destroy a company! His message was simple: 'don't leave culture unattended'. Culture reflects spirit, and ultimately management's ability to lead at any level.

In Business Resilience the importance of actively managing organization culture is clear, as it impacts everything that will be achieved. RESILIENCE Foundations provide the functionality, PACE Culture the spirit and energy to move through the PROGRESS Cycle in times of relative Calm or the confidence to pivot, to respond to chaos, in unexpected conditions.

FIGURE 1.2   Progress is the high-performance zone where PACE Culture works with RESILIENCE Foundations and PROGRESS Cycle

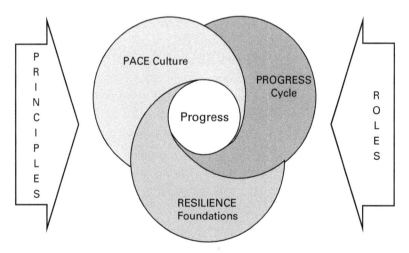

PACE Culture elements connect RESILIENCE Foundations to the PROGRESS Cycle, bringing the organization to life; it generates energy among professionals and value to customers; it also brings optimism that the organization can realize its future vision. PACE Culture is the lifeblood of the organization, taking time to grow and develop across network partners and customers. Ultimately, a high-performance zone emerges, where Progress @ Pace becomes achievable; working in this zone will have a profound impact on the products, services, practices and processes in the portfolio, on progress to develop or improve them, and consequently on Business Resilience.

Benefits, costs and risks of implementing the Business Resilience Framework

Business Resilience has the distinctive benefit of optimizing relative organizational progress, regardless of socio-economic or VUCA conditions. So in implementing Business Resilience, a business culture is established across all levels of the organization, with adaptability at the forefront of new capabilities.

Key benefits to implementing Business Resilience and improving it in an organization are:

- increased productivity – by unleashing energy and innovation at all levels of the organization;
- operational effectiveness – through a one-team approach to optimizing all the areas of operations;
- improved customer satisfaction and retention – customers know if there is sincerity about their needs and wants;
- predictable delivery performance – from the use of empirical approaches to development and delivery;
- reduced cost and rework – because a transparent and fail-fast principle is adopted to avoid large volumes of rework;
- talent is retained – as staff feel the sense of purpose and value;
- resilience value flow – investing in the portfolio leads to the right products and services, customers value the organization, staff feel valued and the organization enhances its resilience;
- stronger linkage between strategy and execution – with the purpose understood by all;

- greater market share – due to a continual customer focus in both new product and service development and the maintenance of the current portfolio;
- improved competitive advantage – from the ability to prioritize the aspects most important to customers and that the organization is passionate about.

The level of benefit will depend on a range of factors, including the baseline level of resilience in the organization, the external environment conditions and the approach to implementing Business Resilience that is chosen. Baseline measures for the benefits should be undertaken prior to implementation and then measured at intervals during implementation.

Costs and risks are shown for each Business Resilience domain in the relevant chapters.

Who this guide is for

This guide is for professionals with purpose, and a strong desire for progress. Individuals may work within organizational leadership teams, PMO staff, change management teams, business development teams, or consultants and Business Advisers. In all cases, these are people who see great opportunities to inspire others and realize the value of greater business security and success. In short, they are tomorrow's Resilience Professionals.

In writing this guide the authors wish to pay tribute to all those chief executives, directors, heads of departments, programme or project management office leaders, project and change managers, among others, who have been sacrificed at the altar of changes of strategy, stakeholder malfeasance or adherence to unattainable or unachievable plans. The authors have listened to the obituaries of such earnest men and women, people who made great efforts in striving for better products, services, processes or practices, but ultimately could not.

Business Resilience paints a much brighter future, one which noble people past and present would be proud to inhabit. Much has been learned from observations in recent VUCA situations and how the best organizations adapt to them. Unpredictable, large-scale changes in the business environment will inevitably mean organizations will have a stronger appetite for innovation, to discover new and novel ways to provide tomorrow's products and services. The winds of change point to a need for resilience professionals to create the resilient organizations. This guide is for today's organizational leaders at every level who share this vision – a belief in great organizations who will make a great contribution to a better working world, where progress is defined in terms of innovation and customer value and benefits are shared by partners, leading to sustained business success.

Summary

In this practical guide to sustained success in organizations, there is a focus on where future value lies, with firm foundations, a culture to unleash energy and to be prepared to adapt so progress is achieved. A quote often attributed to Charles Darwin, British naturalist, but also to Professor Leon C. Megginson of Louisiana State University, a Fellow of the Academy of (US) Management, states: 'It is not the most intellectual of the species that survives; it is not the strongest that survives; but the species that survives is the one that is able best to adapt and adjust to the changing environment in which it finds itself' (Blinklane Consulting, 2020). Stephen Hawkins also emphasized this by saying, 'Intelligence is the ability to adapt to change' (Mission.org, 2019). So sustained progress requires an organization to intelligently adapt to changing environments.

Forward-looking organizations embrace fresh thinking ideas about work, what is valued and how to provide a better environment, while others continue to focus on squeezing costs and productivity. Business Resilience is the result of working on and observing initiatives in different industries around the world, over many years. The modular Business Resilience Framework is designed to accommodate what is known, respond to unknowns and deliver better performance. It is a robust format for businesses to become authentic organizations in the 21st century.

The chapters in this guide describe how to implement Business Resilience. The chapters and focus are shown in Table 1.1.

TABLE 1.1 The book chapters and content

Chapter	Contents
1 Introduction to Business Resilience	An introduction to Business Resilience, its purpose, framework and benefits
2 Principles of Business Resilience	The 7 principles that underpin and are essential to Business Resilience in any organization
3 Business Resilience Framework and Progress @ Pace 8-4-8 Model	The 5 domains and 22 elements of the Business Resilience Framework and the Progress @ Pace Model
4 Roles for Business Resilience	The 3 core Business Resilience roles and key responsibilities, with the optional roles and those which interface
5 RESILIENCE Foundations	The 8 building blocks to create firm foundations for the organization to support the PACE Culture and PROGRESS Cycle
6 A PACE Culture for sustained progress	The 4 elements to utilize a Purposeful Mindset, releasing organizational energy with the capability to apply the right tools
7 PROGRESS Cycle	The 8 steps to make progress, from defining progress to celebrating success and learning for the future
8 PURE Business Resilience implementation strategies	The 3 recommended approaches to implement Business Resilience in organizations as Progressive, Urgent or Responsive
9 Tools for Business Resilience	The tools that are unique to the Business Resilience Framework, described so that they can be applied
10 Resilience profile	The measurement of Business Resilience across the 5 domains at 5 levels, enabling a baseline and improvement to be seen
11 Adapting the Business Resilience Framework	How to adapt the 5 domains and 22 elements of the Business Resilience Framework
12 Insights	Insights of how organizations have used the elements or domains of the Business Resilience Framework
Appendix A: Business Resilience role descriptions	Descriptions of the responsibilities, capabilities and mapping of the 3 core Business Resilience roles to existing roles
Appendix B: Popular best practice tools complementing the unique tools	Mapping of existing tools to the elements of the Business Resilience Framework to build on existing practices

(continued)

TABLE 1.1 (Continued)

Chapter	Contents
Appendix C: Mapping to international standards	Mapping of Business Resilience to recognized international standards
Appendix D: Progress @ Pace 8-4-8 Model	Diagram of the PROGRESS Cycle, PACE Culture and RESILIENCE Foundations domains, with 20 elements to deliver sustained Progress @ Pace
Appendix E: Business Resilience Framework overview	A diagram of the Principles, PROGRESS Cycle, PACE Culture, RESILIENCE Foundations and roles domains, with 22 elements to develop Business Resilience
Glossary	Definitions of the key terms of Business Resilience

Terms used in the guide

In this guide the authors have used some terms which cover a range of options. These are:

- 'Business' is used for any organization, whether commercial, public or third sector.
- 'Customer' is used irrespective of whether there is any financial transaction. For example, a hospital patient is termed a customer because there is a service being provided.
- 'Organization' is used irrespective of the size or make-up of the entity, from a start-up to a global multinational.

Other terms are defined in the Glossary.

QUESTIONS TO THINK ABOUT

- Is a new culture of business authenticity emerging among customers, and if so, how can organizations in an uncertain world adapt their businesses to make sense of it, let alone benefit?
- Has today's complexity overwhelmed yesterday's business certainties or can human factors be energized within global technological environments?
- Some organizations are able to respond to unexpected situations, while many cannot find a new way forward. Why is this?

References

Blinklane Consulting (2020) *Covid 19: Survival of the fittest or adaptability to change?* [blog] https://www.blinklane.com/insights/covid-19-survival-fittest-or-adaptability-change/ (archived at https://perma.cc/NJM9-G6H9

Demma, J (2012) *Entropy Always Increases – The second law of thermodynamics applied to business management*, 15 July [blog] johndemmablog.com/2012/07/15/entropy-always-increases-the-second-law-of-thermodynamics-applied-to-business-management (archived at https://perma.cc/NW3U-8X9H)

Hawkins, S (1998) *A Brief History of Time: And other essays*, Bantam, New York

House of Commons (2021) *Coronavirus: Lessons learned to date*, 21 September, committees.parliament.uk/publications/7496/documents/78687/default (archived at https://perma.cc/DX5A-XYDT)

Mission.org (2019) *Intelligence is the Ability to Adapt to Change*, 14 March, medium.com/the-mission/intelligence-is-the-ability-to-adapt-to-change-9f22ec3cdaa6 (archived at https://perma.cc/NJM9-G6H9)

Rick, T (2020) *How and Why Organizational Culture Eats Strategy for Breakfast, Lunch, and Dinner*, 27 February, www.supplychain247.com/article/organizational_culture_eats_strategy_for_breakfast_lunch_and_dinner (archived at https://perma.cc/GLP7-DZLC)

02

Principles of Business Resilience

Purpose

The purpose of the Principles is to support organizations in developing Business Resilience without being overly prescriptive and acknowledging that each situation is unique and may require a tailored approach. If the Business Resilience Framework is tailored to the specific organizational situation and the Principles remain clearly in place, the organization will continue to make Progress @ Pace. If any of the Principles are not satisfied, progress may be incomplete, or at a slower pace than desirable for the organization, due to resistance to change. The Principles provide high-level governance confirmation to the Business Resilience Owner that the framework is fit for purpose.

Introduction

This chapter describes the Principles that underpin the Business Resilience approach. The Principles are intended to be universally applied to act as

FIGURE 2.1 The seven Principles of Business Resilience

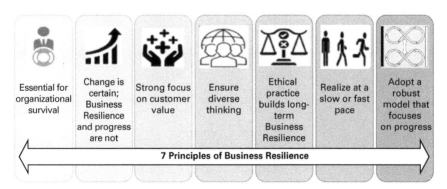

guidance to influence the Business Resilience processes, practices and culture. The adoption of these Principles characterizes whether an organization is implementing the Business Resilience Framework to make Progress @ Pace. The Principles are applied throughout the Business Resilience Framework and are present in the RESILIENCE Foundations, PACE Culture and PROGRESS Cycle.

The Business Resilience Principles (Figure 2.1) are based on empirical learning and understanding of best practices available for managing organizations, operations, projects and teams. They are interdependent and are essential to be in place for organizations to make progress, not just change. Together these Principles underpin the Business Resilience Framework, and Progress @ Pace 8-4-8 Model (see Chapter 3) for everyone involved in organizational success, and therefore are relevant throughout all levels of the business.

It is acknowledged that other Principles may also be in place in organizations; Business Resilience Principles should complement them, representing a minimum viable set. Collectively, Principles provide the basis for effective operation, development or improvement of the Business Resilience Framework and resulting organizational performance. Without them, organizations may lose their way, serving themselves rather than their customers. Principles act like a compass, helping everyone to make the right decision, or understand why something is needed. Ultimately, Principles guide Business Resilience, and Business Resilience sustains progress in any VUCA (volatile, uncertain, complex or ambiguous) condition.

The Business Resilience Principles

The seven Business Resilience Principles are:

1 Business Resilience is essential for organizational survival.

2 Change is certain; Business Resilience and progress are not.

3 Strong focus on customer value enhances Business Resilience.

4 Ensuring diverse thinking builds Business Resilience.

5 Ethical practice builds long-term Business Resilience.

6 Business Resilience and progress can be realized at a fast or slow pace.

7 Adopting a robust model focused on progress strengthens Business Resilience.

Principle 1: Business Resilience is essential for organizational survival

An organization is resilient if it can withstand the troughs and crests of the waves that it will face. The Principles of Business Resilience are present to reduce the troughs and optimize the crests. Continual assessment of the organization's ability to manage initiatives using tools such as the VUCA Storm (external environment) and Adaptive Enterprise (internal environment) scales enables progress through Business Resilience by recognizing the external and internal environmental factors (see Chapter 7). The more adaptive the enterprise, the higher the level of VUCA Storm it will be able to manage.

In the 2020/21 Covid-19 pandemic, organizations had an enormous Storm to deal with and many pivoted to address the challenges. For some this meant that resilience was simply to bounce back, for others it was to bounce along and for others this meant an opportunity to bounce forward. And for some organizations there were limitations being placed by the government that stopped their operations, decimated revenues and resulted in going backward. For others the halt to operations meant an opportunity to think creatively about other ways to provide their services. Good instances of creative actions include art and gym classes online, drive-in cinemas, marathons completed in hybrid environments, online wine tastings, and so the list goes on.

There are many examples of innovative ways in which the delivery models were changed to enable organizations to continue to make progress at the pace that was possible given the high VUCA Storm Scale at the time. When the VUCA Storm Scale is low, the focus is to have products and services that are on the upward part of their lifecycle balancing those that are on the downward slope. This can include ensuring products and services are updated to continue the upward trend.

ORGANIZATION WITHOUT BUSINESS RESILIENCE NOT SURVIVING

In 2004, Blockbuster was bringing in $6 billion in revenue and Netflix was a scrappy start-up. Netflix is now a multi-billion-dollar company and Blockbuster went bankrupt. Blockbuster's leadership failed to recognize how quickly the video rental market was changing due to disruption (Lepsinger, 2017).

> ### ORGANIZATION WITH BUSINESS RESILIENCE SURVIVING
>
> The mobile phone market has survived by updating products to maintain upward demand as technology changed. Phones have been continually updated from the original 'carry in a (mini) suitcase' models of a basic telephone to today's smart phones, which have enormous capacity and functionality, as a small easily portable device. The Principles of Business Resilience support this activity by adopting the right pace of progress to deliver more customer value as opportunity arose.

Supporting factors

- Leadership should acknowledge that Business Resilience is essential for survival.
- Leadership should put in place processes, practices and the culture to enable Business Resilience to be part of the DNA of the organization.

If this principle is applied, the following behaviours will be observed:

- The Principles of Business Resilience will be utilized at all levels of the organization.
- Leadership and teams use continuous professional development to enhance their Business Resilience capabilities.
- Leadership and teams undertake resilience profiling as a routine part of business reviews.

Principle 2: Change is certain; Business Resilience and progress are not

Change is certain because the environment, technology, expectations and people change all the time and organizations must adapt to survive. Without adapting, organizations may not survive. Organizations need to use the energy of change to bring about Business Resilience desired progress rather than simply responding to any specific change or series of changes.

It is therefore essential that business objectives are clear, and that the strategy for creating and realizing customer value and measurable benefits is aligned within a PROGRESS Cycle; adapting the organization to change should result from defined progress. It is not only that the benefits of adapting to change must be defined, but that the change proposal benefits also identify how progress links to Business Resilience. When working within the Business Resilience Framework it is essential to consider how changes can be implemented: they should not only maintain current positions or limit taking an organization backward; they should adapt and innovate to enable the organization to progress forward, whenever possible.

CHANGES WITHOUT BUILDING RESILIENCE

An organization that creates monetary products from specialist papers decides to sell its paper mills to align to a development strategy and improve cash flow. This strategy results in a requirement to purchase specialist papers at higher prices. The CEO responsible made the change and in the short term the balance sheet was improved with a cash injection. Almost inevitably, the CEO moved on, but the organization has a long-term detriment. In this situation, a Business Resilience focus would be on how to use Enterprising Investment to ensure progress in the medium and long term while financing technological development, rather than implementing change for short-term benefit.

CHANGES WITH BUILDING RESILIENCE

A motor dealership organization responded by making their current products available virtually, ensuring the staff who had the most experience and expertise were retained to add value through virtual presentations to customers. This enabled continued sales, investment in online technology and recovery in Stormy VUCA conditions, maintaining progress.

Supporting factors

- Senior management should focus on organizational resilience and progress more than simply delivering changes to satisfy immediate needs.
- Progress for the organization should be defined and shared across network partners.

If this principle is applied, the following behaviours will be observed:

- There is vision-led leadership to ensure organizational progress and build resilience.

- Capability and Skills, and application of tools are recognized and built to enable resilience.
- All levels of the organization have the energy needed to make progress and build resilience.

Principle 3: Strong focus on customer value enhances Business Resilience

Customer focus is at the heart of Business Resilience. Key customer interests (KCIs) need to be understood and any customer pains addressed. Many organizations state that their customers are at the heart of what they do, but fewer identify and track what the organization could do to resolve the customer pains in the system and meet the customer interests. Even when customers like the service or products provided, they may not use them most effectively if there is a pain point, such as a lack of convenient public transport/car parking. This may not be able to be addressed in the current locations but should be taken into account when considering new locations or when a lease is coming to renewal. Progress is achieved when it delivers value for customers. If little value is added to customers, the organization becomes internally focused, which will, in turn, lead to decline. Value can be defined in different ways, but the most important aspect is to understand what the customers consider to be of most value and adapt accordingly.

LACK OF FOCUS ON CUSTOMER VALUE

An organization had feedback that their newly launched online services had issues due to firewalls of their largest customers blocking the site. Therefore, the organization decided the customers needed to amend their firewall protocols to allow the services to be utilized. This resulted in some large customers changing provider of services and not returning.

Some motor dealerships spent the time during Covid-19 making senior staff redundant and changing the governance structures rather than considering how to improve products or deliver more value. As competitors placed products online and simplified customer buying processes, these organizations are now in the situation where the short-term cash situation is good but remaining staff are all too busy and inexperienced to be able to deliver new initiatives or improve services, with limited learning opportunities.

ADDING CUSTOMER VALUE

Early in the Covid-19 pandemic, a supermarket started to prioritize their vulnerable customers as soon as the delivery slots for home deliveries had higher demand than the resource available to deliver. This provided value not only for those customers directly but spread value to the families and carers of these vulnerable customers, creating loyalty from all these groups to build Business Resilience. Delivering value for customers can also be done within the public sector, such as providing breakfast clubs at schools to enable parents to work.

Supporting factors

- Everyone in the organization should be focused on the customer.
- Innovation should be supported by the organization, so that there is always new value to offer customers, based on the customers' perception of value.

If this principle is applied, the following behaviours will be observed:

- There is collaboration across the network that is focused on meeting customer needs and addressing customer pains.
- There is innovation that is targeted at customer needs and removing customer pains.
- Leadership aligns to customer value and empowers decision-making at appropriate levels.

Principle 4: Ensuring diverse thinking builds Business Resilience

Business Resilience relies on good decisions for it to be effective. If the decisions taken in an organization are usually reached by easy consensus, it could indicate that the organization is in danger of groupthink prevailing. There is increasing research which shows that including diverse thinking in decision-making leads to greater success. Diverse thinking is achieved by having people who have diversity of backgrounds, experience, knowledge, skills and preferences working together and collaborating with a variety of perspectives.

The way individuals think is influenced by their unmet needs and behavioural preferences. These ideas have been considered by many psychologists and models are available to understand how to learn, develop and respond to others in organizations, in the most productive ways. These aspects are considered in PACE Culture.

In the champion/challenger technique, the champion supports the current approach (or most favoured innovation) and the challengers put forward alternative approaches or ideas. Only if an alternative is shown to have greater benefits, following analysis, is a change of direction or innovation agreed. By encouraging diverse thinking there is the greatest likelihood that the right way forward will be identified and, through examination of the alternatives, be supported. A simple decision-making formula can be shown as:

Diverse people + Appropriate information + Right time = Good decision (2.1)

Breaking this down, the 'diverse people' are those that bring different perspectives and ways of thinking; the 'appropriate information' includes alternatives to the current situation or favoured proposal; the 'right time' is as soon as possible after the requirement for a decision is identified. Good decisions are required for Business Resilience to be developed in the organization, as discussed in the *Harvard Business Review* (Reynolds and Lewis, 2017).

LACK OF COGNITIVE DIVERSITY DOES NOT BUILD RESILIENCE

Swissair was the national airline of Switzerland. As it was powerful, profitable and successful, the board became overconfident. The number of board members was reduced and much of the management team's industrial expertise was lost. Those remaining on the board shared similar backgrounds and assumptions, which made it harder to spot bad decisions. Swissair filed for bankruptcy in 2002 (Hermann and Rammal, 2010).

DIVERSE THINKING IMPROVES RESULTS

3M introduced a lead user (LU) idea-generation approach, including a research project to reduce infections from surgery. A wound-healing expert, an animal surgeon and a make-up artist specializing in adhering materials to skin were involved. The cognitive diversity of the make-up artist was crucial to creating a breakthrough product to reduce surgical infections.

Empirical evidence from the 3M LU projects showed forecast sales in year 5 were more than eight times higher, had significantly higher customer needs addressed, novelty and forecasted market share in year 5, than those from more conventional methods. All benefitted from cognitive diversity (Gary *et al*, 2002).

Supporting factors

- Leaders should build teams that include diverse thinking with individuals who take different approaches and have different views.
- Challenge is welcomed within a structured framework to ensure decisions lead to Business Resilience.

If this principle is applied, the following behaviours will be observed:

- Individuals in the organization are energized by having their views considered.
- Decisions are taken that improve Business Resilience.
- Challenges are raised at all levels of the organization.

Principle 5: Ethical practice builds long-term Business Resilience

All the Principles should be implemented ethically to deliver long-term Business Resilience. Making progress by disadvantaging people, polluting the environment or providing goods or services that are not delivered honestly and with integrity would not create lasting Business Resilience. Usually, such practices do not gain traction in the long term and may result in substantial harm, either to organizational reputation or financially. Ethical implementation means that the Principles are delivered with honesty, integrity, non-discrimination, fairness, equality, dignity, diversity and upholding individual rights. This should also be carried out within the regulatory and legal framework in place for the industry and country where activities are taking place and that the customers would expect. Ethical practice should be part of the culture of the organization and all initiatives should be identified, planned and delivered in this way.

In an era of global trade and global connectedness, the need to review all parts of the partner network has never been more necessary. There are significant differences in cultural expectations of ethical behaviour and these need to be carefully considered to build resilience. Business Resilience for organizations that operate in areas where bribes are standard practice to get things done will need to identify how to create a situation where the organization can still achieve without needing to provide bribes. This could be by using alternative incentives, such as recommendations when good service is received. Most organizations have an ethical code, whether in the culture or written. This will support the implementation of the Progress @ Pace Principles. According to Ethisphere, an organization that identifies strong business ethics and rates companies based on their ethical standards, the most ethical companies historically outperformed others financially by 7.1 per cent over a five-year period (2016–2021), demonstrating the connection between good ethical practices and performance that's valued in the marketplace (Ethisphere, 2021).

NOT USING ETHICAL IMPLEMENTATION

When it became known that an international coffee shop chain had paid very little tax, a campaign not to use the chain was started, resulting in both reputational and financial consequences. Another example is in producing goods for the European market, customers would not accept child labour even when it is legal in the country of production.

USING ETHICAL IMPLEMENTATION

Electronics retailer Best Buy (NYSE: BBY) was named 'America's most sustainable company' in February 2019 and ranked in the top five in the last four years (Liu, 2020). They earned their place by a commitment to ethical practice, including a reduction of environmental impact by reducing waste. This is by driving hybrid cars to save petrol, encouraging electronics to be repaired rather than scrapped and recycling 2 billion pounds of unwanted electronics and appliances. In addition, it teaches basic technology skills to disadvantaged teenagers, reducing unemployment and creating skilled employees of the future. Ethical implementation has contributed to Best Buy being the only national electronics chain left in the United States.

Supporting factors

- There should be clarity of what is expected in the organization to demonstrate ethical behaviour, usually by having a code of ethics.
- There should be clear reporting and escalation routes to provide support to maintain the highest ethical standards.

If this principle is applied, the following behaviours will be observed:

- Ethics is part of decision-making in the organization.
- Individuals report behaviours or decisions that do not align to the code of ethics.

Any suggestions for gain that are not ethical do not receive support.

Principle 6: Business Resilience and progress can be realized at a fast or slow pace

The appropriate pace is the speed of progress that is appropriate for the organization and external environment prevailing at the time to realize Business Resilience. Each part of the Business Resilience Framework using Progress @ Pace improves organizational success, but as a whole they work together to optimize Business Resilience and enable progress, which, in turn, allows the organization to outpace the competition. The pace to build resilience could be to walk slowly, as this will achieve the appropriate level of success defined by the organization. The organization may need to run when the environment is changing Rapidly, to respond to a customer or to a specific VUCA disruption. The organization may need to pivot to react and then play out the adaptation and review again. Pivoting causes a complete change of direction, such as a new technology being introduced that threatens the existing model, requiring a Rapid response to continue to progress. The right pace can vary between initiatives as well as for the wider organization.

NOT DEVELOPING AT THE APPROPRIATE PACE

A voluntary organization planned to implement new procedures and implemented training for all the team members and volunteers. The changes were introduced within a week of the training and applied to all areas. Some volunteers were not confident of using the new procedures and did not feel they had time to absorb the new procedures. As a result, volunteers were lost and the organization had to reduce their services. Business Resilience would have been improved if the changes had been introduced incrementally, allowing the volunteers to adapt to one change at a time.

DEVELOPING AT AN APPROPRIATE PACE

When a welding consumables manufacturer needed new chemistry in a product for a customer, the product development team needed time for research and development. In contrast, the sales team needed to respond quickly and provide the product 'yesterday'. The organization needed to balance ensuring the product was both fit for purpose and delivered in time for the customer. This was achieved by purchasing the initial customer order from another source and then developing their own product in time for the second order, so building resilience through the partner network.

DEVELOPING FAST

When Uber started to operate in London, the existing London black taxi drivers created Taxiapp (Sheffield, 2017) so that the features which customers liked, such as knowing how far away the closest taxi is, could be offered in addition to their traditional features.

Supporting factors

- Senior management provides support for different parts of the organization progressing at different paces to suit the needs of the customer, team, department or division and build Business Resilience. There is acceptance that a change of speed will be needed at times and the reasons are clearly communicated.

If this principle is applied, the following behaviours will be observed:

- Pace is determined by the organization responding appropriately to the external environment or events that impact the organization.

- All levels of the organization influence the pace of progress to optimize customer value and team cohesion.
- Leadership recognizes that different teams or parts of the organization need to be enabled to progress at different paces.

Principle 7: Adopting a robust model focused on progress strengthens Business Resilience

Using a robust model that has a focus on progress strengthens Business Resilience. The Progress @ Pace 8-4-8 Model (see Chapter 3) provides all the elements that are needed to make progress and build Business Resilience. The Business Resilience Framework and Progress @ Pace 8-4-8 Model is demonstrated to implement Business Resilience. Using a robust model provides the organization with the structure and discipline to introduce or implement Business Resilience with all the elements that are required. Business Resilience complements and reinvigorates other disciplines, practices and methods, rather than replacing them. It builds on what is working. The most important thing is to understand how to harness approaches for optimal progress (see Chapter 8). Most organizations will use a hybrid of approaches and so identifying the practices that will provide optimal benefit will bring the best progress.

NOT USING A ROBUST MODEL

An organization decided to implement a new system to all its departments and divisions with implementation undertaken using a 'big bang' approach without a recognized model for progress. They made staff with expertise on the old systems redundant and new staff did not have corporate memory of the old system. The new system had a few gaps and, when they needed to respond to customers, or when it was necessary to revert to the old system, there were issues as staff were not familiar with the procedures. Customers felt the change and some did not renew their contracts.

USING A ROBUST MODEL

During the 2020 Covid-19 pandemic a ventilator challenge was launched in the UK. Existing manufacturing organizations, of other products, developed ventilators for intensive care use in Covid-19 patients in record time. They used existing product development and manufacturing practices with a model with a focus on progress. This enabled the delivery of 400 devices per day at the peak. DHL used existing best practice to acquire 42 million parts and electronic components, with the supply chain established in 10 days. The Medicines and Healthcare Products Regulatory Agency approval was obtained within three weeks and went on to supply the National Health Service in the UK (Cabinet Office, 2020).

Supporting factors

- There is an identification of when and how to introduce a reputed model, such as Progress @ Pace, with the Principles, processes and practices to optimize value and build resilience.
- Empowered teams and the organization implement a reputed model at the right time, choosing the right elements, to enable progress and develop Business Resilience.

If this principle is applied, the following behaviours will be observed:

- Resilience profiling of the organization, using a recognized model, will be undertaken.
- The profiling will be shared to agree the required innovations that add most value to the organization.
- Network Collaboration is used to implement the reputed model elements that will add value to the network partners.

Using the Business Resilience Principles to adapt Business Resilience

The Business Resilience Principles enable the framework to be tailored, or adapted, to the unique business in which it is implemented. The framework may need to change in terms of the way it is applied to meet specific circumstances. The Principles provide the basis for the adapting to be undertaken. The framework processes and practices can be adapted, using the principle that the framework is modular, as long as the change upholds the relevant Principles.

Adapting organizations reflect changes in the VUCA Storm Scale and the Adaptive Enterprise Scale. As the organization becomes a more Adaptive Enterprise, it will be able to pivot more easily to changing situations.

The Principles can be applied differently in one smaller part of the organization versus across the whole organization, or for a smaller organization that operates less formally. Changing the way a principle is applied does not mean that the Principles are optional. They should all be seen in the organization, but how they are expressed will vary. For example, a start-up that wishes to use the Progress @ Pace Model will not have existing practices or initiatives and so will not be preserving existing good practices, products or services. However, as soon as the organization is operating, it will quickly need to consider what is working and should be preserved and what initiatives should be progressed in a Rapid approach.

Roles for the Principles domain

The Principles should be implemented by everyone in the organization and, where appropriate, the network partners using the Business Resilience Framework. Principles will guide the processes and procedures in place to ensure they enable progress rather than create an unintended barrier to progress. The specific Business Resilience Roles that are responsible for implementing the Principles are:

- **Business Resilience Owner** – ensures the organizational Business Resilience Framework is aligned to the seven Principles. Gains support of the organizational leadership team. Sets the direction and acts as a role model for the behaviours and practices of staff at all levels. Takes responsibility for provision of advice and coaching to implement the Business Resilience.

- **Progress Master** – provides in-house workshops to explain how and why Principles form part of the Business Resilience Framework. Maintains conformity of entries in the lessons log relating to Principles. Communicates Principles to partners in the context of the Business Resilience Framework. Reviews the robustness of Principles in achieving Progress Definitions, and advises the Business Resilience Owner of potential changes.

- **Initiative Leader** – adheres to the Principles on their initiatives. Seeks and provides feedback examples of good practice and alignment into the Progress Master. Provides suggestions for improvement to Principles, using the champion/challenger model. Ensures Principles are reviewed with partners at the start of the BRIT workshop process (see Chapter 5).

When these Principles are applied across the organization, the application should include the partner network, including suppliers and customers. Without suppliers, progress will stop through lack of raw or developed materials. Without sales channels and customers, revenue will cease. The partner network may not be using the full Business Resilience Framework, but, nonetheless, can still benefit by adopting the Principles.

Benefits, costs and risks of implementing Business Resilience Principles

Benefits

The benefits of implementing the Principles of Business Resilience will be that the organization will be more resilient than prior to implementation. This can be measured using the Resilience Profile tool (see Chapter 9), which will identify areas that need further improvement. The benefits desired from Business Resilience will need to be clarified with a measured baseline set.

Benefits of Business Resilience Principles are:

- ensuring corporate social responsibility of Business Resilience is visible;
- aligning organizational behaviour to resilience and Progress @ Pace;
- attracting diverse talent, with early recognition of common values;
- clarity in how Business Resilience and Progress @ Pace is implemented;
- guidance and flexibility when creating in-house resilience methodologies;
- making exploration of organizational values meaningful with partners;
- support to all levels making decisions in VUCA environments.

Costs

The costs of implementing the Business Resilience Principles will depend on the starting position and whether they are being implemented using the Business Resilience Framework. If there is a major gap between the baseline and the desired position, the costs could be higher. Costs should, however, be offset by the improvements in Business Resilience and could mean the difference between survival and no longer being a viable organization when the next significant VUCA Storm hits.

Risks

The risks of implementation are few as the Principles underpin good practice in any organization. The risks will include some individuals who may not wish to support improvements in Business Resilience, which will call into question their reasons for being with the organization. There are risks that individuals may vary in their interpretation of ethical implementation, of the pace to proceed, of the PACE Culture and what delivers customer value.

It is recommended that risks are considered and mitigations developed using a BRIT workshop, with the seven Principles forming an agenda, and actions identified to de-risk the implementation and operation of the Business Resilience Framework. Different interpretations are to be expected, but conflict can be proactively mitigated and managed by engaging the Business Resilience Owner in the process; where required, the Business Resilience Owner may involve the organization leadership team to agree their interpretations and give a clear direction.

Risks are considerably reduced if Principles are subject to audit, indicating which elements of the Business Resilience Framework will need to be reviewed and actions prioritized to maintain integrity.

Summary

This chapter has introduced the seven Principles of Business Resilience. They should be seen as underpinning the framework and are the enablers for tailoring or adapting to an organization. There is no such thing as 'one size fits all', as each organization is unique, with its own culture, products, processes and practices. The Principles should integrate with each of the Business Resilience Framework and Progress @ Pace 8-4-8 Model elements and be visible throughout the organization. Organizations are advised to confirm alignment to Principles via internal audit, where possible.

Some organizations may believe they follow the same processes or practices, such as adherence to the clinical guidelines for healthcare organizations; however, how they are implemented may vary considerably, and this applies equally to Business Resilience. Ethical practices implemented at a fast or slow pace with diverse thinking focused on customer value, using a robust model to deliver progress, will provide Business Resilience for any organization. There are choices about how to implement the Principles using the Business Resilience Framework, which will vary with each organization's unique circumstances.

QUESTIONS TO THINK ABOUT

- Are any of the Business Resilience Principles present in your organization already and which are absent?
- Which of the other Principles would be easiest to implement immediately?
- Which of the Principles would add most value to your organization?

References

Cabinet Office (2020) *Ventilator Challenge Hailed a Success as UK Production Finishes*, 4 July, www.gov.uk/government/news/ventilator-challenge-hailed-a-success-as-uk-production-finishes (archived at https://perma.cc/66NV-8YMA)

Ethisphere (2021) *Ethisphere Announces the 2021 World's Most Ethical Companies*, 18 October, ethisphere.com/2021-wme-announcement (archived at https://perma.cc/N6PK-L6RH)

Gary, L *et al* (2002) Performance assessment of the lead user idea-generation process for new product development, *Management Science*, doi: 10.1287/mnsc.48.8.1042.171 (archived at https://perma.cc/3PU6-XHTL)

Hermann, A and Rammal, H (2010) The grounding of the 'flying bank', *Management Decision*, www.researchgate.net/publication/242340874_The_grounding_of_the_flying_bank (archived at https://perma.cc/JBL5-DFRV)

Lepsinger, R (2017) *3 Companies that Failed to Adapt, and Where They Went Wrong*, 14 August, www.business2community.com/business-innovation/3-companies-failed-adapt-went-wrong-01895678 (archived at https://perma.cc/QU8L-AKSM)

Liu, E (2020) The 100 most sustainable companies, reranked by social factors, *Barron's*, 26 June, www.barrons.com/articles/these-companies-rank-best-on-social-criteriaand-could-reward-investors-51593215993 (archived at https://perma.cc/DQ3A-ZWJQ)

Reynolds, A and Lewis, D (2017) Teams solve problems faster when they're more cognitively diverse, *Harvard Business Review*, 30 March, https://hbr.org/2017/03/teams-solve-problems-faster-when-theyre-more-cognitively-diverse (archived at https://perma.cc/7PFL-2MF9)

Sheffield, H (2017) These London taxi drivers have made an app like Uber to save black cabs, *Independent*, 14 August, www.independent.co.uk/news/business/indyventure/taxi-app-uber-black-cab-london-hailing-lyft-a7876051.html (archived at https://perma.cc/WR32-2MZ5)

03

Business Resilience Framework and Progress @ Pace 8-4-8 Model

Purpose

The purpose of the Business Resilience Framework is to build and support Business Resilience within an organization. It comprises five domains: Principles, Roles, RESILIENCE Foundations, PACE Culture and PROGRESS Cycle. These domains form the basis of implementing Business Resilience at pace, for organizations seeking sustained progress.

Introduction

In introducing the Business Resilience Framework, including the Progress @ Pace 8-4-8 Model, this chapter provides an overview of scope, direction and purpose of Business Resilience for an organization. Figure 3.1 shows the framework and Figure 3.3 shows the framework which contains the Progress @ Pace model. In this guide, the three domains of RESILIENCE Foundations, PACE Culture and PROGRESS Cycle are brought together within the Progress @ Pace 8-4-8 Resilience Model (Figure 3.3). These three domains are further broken down into 20 elements, which are the core activities. Progress is optimized when organizations integrate effort in these three domains. The other two domains, Roles and Principles, underpin this framework and are present throughout.

Profiling the organization utilizing the Business Resilience Framework is the basis for a Rapid insight into the vision for Business Resilience. For Resilience Professionals, this provides a key reference point or standard, indicating what is involved and how it could be applied within their

FIGURE 3.1 Business Resilience Framework with five domains

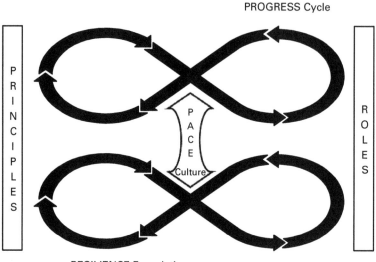

organization or network. Profiling is great as a communication tool and the basis of practical implementation. Profiling enables all individuals to engage, whether as a director or senior responsible owner, a Progress Master or consultant, or an Initiative Leader, contributing to Business Resilience improvement.

The Business Resilience Framework can be used to share the essence of the Business Resilience philosophy and scope. It is also a Rapid guide to how an organization can get things done; and, better still, how to make it right for the organization, its network, customers and markets. So, at first glance, profiling might look like the answer – but in truth, it is really just the beginning, a 'starter for 10'. Introducing Business Resilience to the organization is a two-stage process: first, understand and adopt it; second, adapt and implement it (see Chapter 8.) Understanding Business Resilience is achieved using the framework and improvement takes place following development of an organization-specific framework, built by utilizing and adapting the standard Business Resilience Framework and Progress @ Pace 8-4-8 Model.

The Business Resilience Framework defines the scope in five domains – a cognitive space for Business Resilience Professionals in which to operate the core Progress @ Pace 8-4-8 Model.

The Business Resilience Framework reflects a philosophy of making progress, whatever the conditions, relative to other business coping strategies. Such coping strategies include 'do nothing', 'do minimum' or do some other option which accepts changes in the business environment, rather than exploiting them. It is suggested that these strategies are not sufficient for an organization to survive and thrive in a VUCA world. At the heart of this philosophy is anticipating volatility as part of the business-as-usual environment and creating a culture of readiness for adaptability with the organization and partner network.

Five domains of the Business Resilience Framework

The Business Resilience Framework utilizes the five domains of Principles, Roles, RESILIENCE Foundations, PACE Culture and PROGRESS Cycle. Importantly, it also clarifies the purpose – to make 'Progress @ Pace'. The five domains and the reasons for their inclusion are:

1 **Principles** – the seven Principles that must be followed in order to achieve Progress @ Pace. *Reason: ensures implementation of Business Resilience is valid.*

2 **Roles** – the core responsibilities for ownership, implementation and action. *Reason: ensures resilience framework and progress models are justified and effective.*

3 **RESILIENCE Foundations** – elements that must be in place to support PACE Culture and PROGRESS Cycle. *Reason: ensures the organization is robust, relevant to resilience and functionally complete.*

4 **PACE Culture** – elements that drive behaviours and form a distinctive resilient organization. *Reason: ensures people are empowered to contribute positively within psychological safety.*

5 **PROGRESS Cycle** – a roadmap for development and improvement leading to resilience and progress. *Reason: ensures selected initiatives are aligned and can adapt to Progress Definition goals.*

The PROGRESS Cycle, PACE Culture and RESILIENCE Foundations are guided by seven Principles (see Chapter 2) and implemented by three core Roles, which are the Business Resilience Owner, Progress Master and Initiative Leader (see Chapter 4). The organization's individuals and teams

FIGURE 3.2 Business Resilience and business-as-usual development in the portfolio

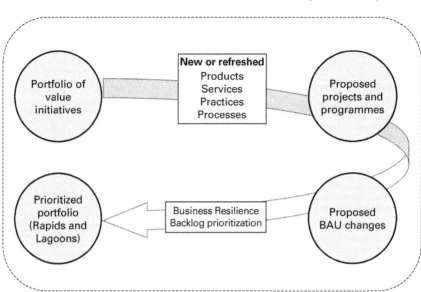

define progress and the priorities for resilience. It is this combination that supports the objective of sustained progress delivered at pace.

In this way, the Business Resilience Framework coordinates portfolio and programme responsibilities, with project and business-as-usual (BAU) changes, sharing responsibility throughout the organization or enterprise network, in matrix management (Figure 3.2). Whether initiatives are large or small, internal or external, they will be examined for their contribution to Business Resilience, in the context of making Progress @ Pace. Opportunity to contribute is open to all within a collaborative PACE Culture (see Chapter 6).

There is an expectation that organizations will have established people working in one or more of the domains in this framework, such as on the seven Principles or RESILIENCE Foundations; however, these individuals may not work together to maximize progress and drive Business Resilience. These five domains also define, by implication, what is outside of these responsibilities; so importantly, core responsibilities for Business Resilience outcomes and how to achieve them are included – not detailed functional expertise, though, as this responsibility remains within dedicated departments, teams or individuals (see Chapter 4).

The three core Roles for Business Resilience are Business Resilience Ownership, Progress Master and Initiative Leader. Business Resilience Owners will be at a senior level, typically a director or partner; Progress Masters will be at a manager (or senior manager) level, and Initiative Leader responsibility will be at team level. Any or all of these Roles could be undertaken by a Resilience Professional.

While these three Roles are core to the delivery of Business Resilience objectives, the three responsibilities could be added to existing Roles, or introduced as stand-alone ones, where Business Resilience Profiles of a department, business unit, organization or network indicate there is much to be done. When required, consultants or practitioners would be hired to provide professional support to core teams in realization of 'to be' Business Resilience objectives.

The Business Resilience Owner is responsible for the effectiveness of the framework. Depending on the organization design, this role could be located in the general management, transformation and change, innovation, programme or portfolio office functions within the organization. Indeed, it is quite conceivable that Business Resilience Owners will develop into this senior role from a number of disciplines, and it will appeal to those with ambition to take on wider organizational responsibility.

Importantly, because Business Resilience permeates throughout the organization and its partner network, what matters most is that Business Resilience Owner, Progress Master and Initiative Leader resources are drawn from across the organization; in this way, the effectiveness of the Business Resilience Framework becomes everyone's business (see Chapter 4).

Principles domain

It is important to recognize the contribution of the seven Principles. Collectively, Principles are a test – eg, following adapting the model, if all Principles are in place, then so is Business Resilience. This control should be applied at all organizational levels.

The seven Principles are:

1 Business Resilience is essential for organizational survival.

2 Change is certain; Business Resilience and progress are not.

3 Strong focus on customer value enhances Business Resilience.

4 Ensuring diverse thinking builds Business Resilience.

5 Ethical practice builds long-term Business Resilience.

6 Business Resilience and progress can be realized at a fast or slow pace.

7 Adopting a robust model focused on progress strengthens Business Resilience (see Chapter 2).

RESILIENCE Foundations domain

RESILIENCE Foundations (Figure 3.3) provide the platform for a robust organization, one with the ability to become and maintain a resilient organization in changing social and economic conditions. Eight elements comprise the capability set. Relevant skills need to be developed in each element to contribute to the common purpose, which is to enable the PACE Culture and PROGRESS Cycle to be executed with efficiency and effectiveness; indeed, a true test of RESILIENCE Foundations is the capability to fully establish these domains, at all five levels of the organization (these are shown in Chapter 4). The domain and organizational elements should be tested regularly, as determined by the Business Resilience Owner. Functional capability within each of the eight elements will impact the organizational goals within RESILIENCE Foundations and in turn the PACE Culture and PROGRESS Cycle domains; it is for this reason that this domain is termed RESILIENCE Foundations: it impacts all three domains within the Progress @ Pace Model. To this extent, investment in this domain is pivotal in determining the functional horizons of the organization – its ability to build robust capability and capacity to realize sustainable returns. The eight elements of RESILIENCE Foundations provide a platform from which the dynamic organization is developed in the PACE Culture; this in turn enables the creation and maintenance of customer value from improved products, services, processes and practices, through commitment to right-paced delivery and progressive portfolio evolution in the PROGRESS Cycle.

The eight elements of RESILIENCE Foundations work as shown in Table 3.1.

FIGURE 3.3 RESILIENCE Foundations infinity loop showing the eight elements

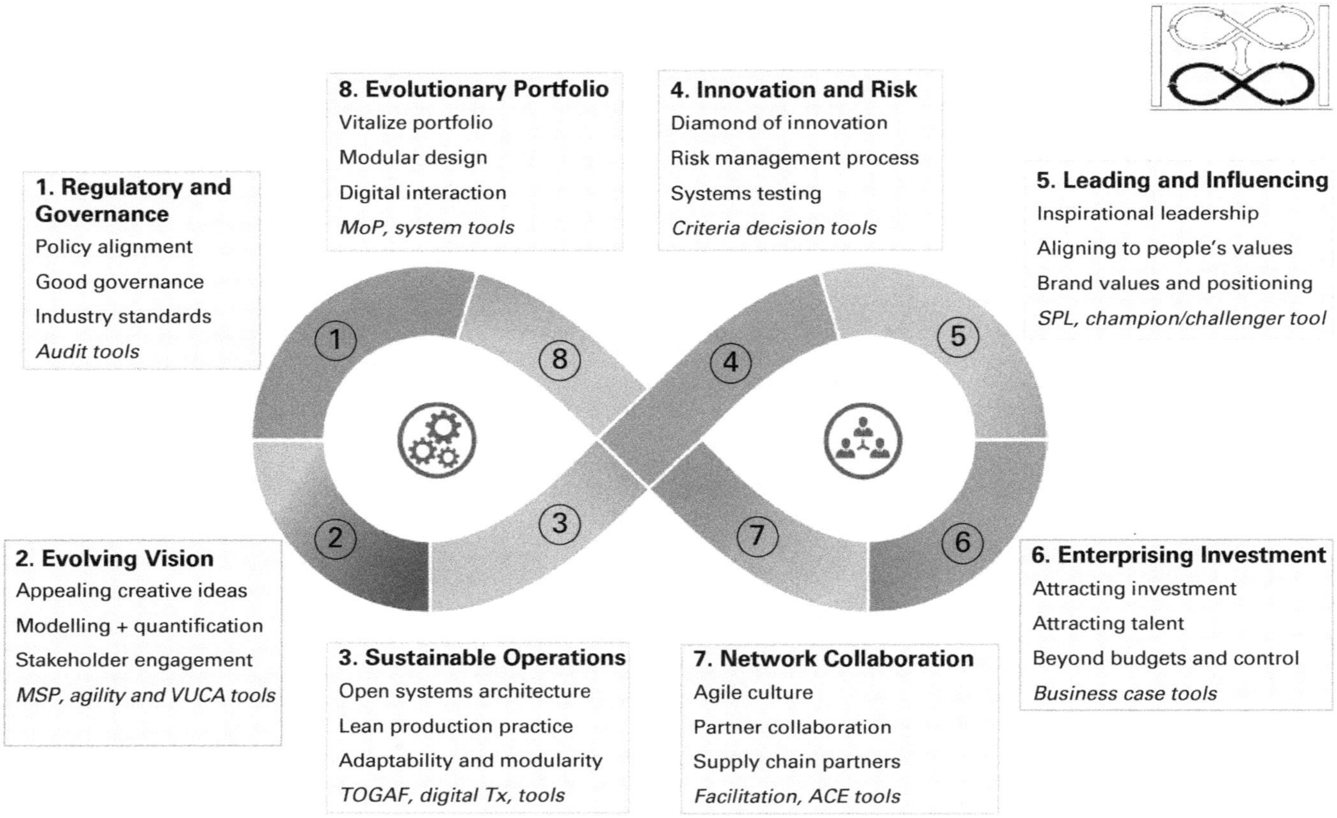

1. Regulatory and Governance
Policy alignment
Good governance
Industry standards
Audit tools

2. Evolving Vision
Appealing creative ideas
Modelling + quantification
Stakeholder engagement
MSP, agility and VUCA tools

3. Sustainable Operations
Open systems architecture
Lean production practice
Adaptability and modularity
TOGAF, digital Tx, tools

4. Innovation and Risk
Diamond of innovation
Risk management process
Systems testing
Criteria decision tools

5. Leading and Influencing
Inspirational leadership
Aligning to people's values
Brand values and positioning
SPL, champion/challenger tool

6. Enterprising Investment
Attracting investment
Attracting talent
Beyond budgets and control
Business case tools

7. Network Collaboration
Agile culture
Partner collaboration
Supply chain partners
Facilitation, ACE tools

8. Evolutionary Portfolio
Vitalize portfolio
Modular design
Digital interaction
MoP, system tools

TABLE 3.1 RESILIENCE Foundations elements

RESILIENCE Foundations element	Description
1. Regulatory and Governance	Clarify industry standards – and that organizational policies are aligned to them – using auditable practice from which learning and improvement takes place
2. Evolving Vision	A series of incrementally better organization design ideas where people collaborate within social and technological future environments to deliver benefits for all
3. Sustainable operations	Adaptable, digital and modular operational capability supporting lean practices with refined tools for the implementation of learning within networks
4. Innovation and Risk	Balancing the desire for portfolio innovation with resource availability from an enlightened value perspective on technological and financial risk assessment
5. Leading and Influencing	Understanding and inspiring others; creating belief in a future where organization brand values and positioning reflect the aspirations of the network
6. Enterprising Investment	How to attract talent and investment into the organization by building believability in next steps and sharing the benefits of vision realization
7. Network Collaboration	A spirit of collaboration and partnership, built upon application of an agile culture, where facilitation of stakeholders, testing and customer value predominates
8. Evolutionary Portfolio	An abiding belief in market focus, digital by design and modularity combine to deliver lifecycle desirability with confidence to pivot due to VUCA conditions

Business Resilience Owners will take a lead role in reviewing that the eight elements remain sufficient and valid, by ensuring network partner feedback and audit lessons are scheduled, and experiences are captured and analysed. Where there are implications for improving RESILIENCE Foundations, these may arise from performance or outcomes from the elements or impacts on this or other domains with the Progress @ Pace Model.

All proposals are added to the Progress Backlog and reviewed as part of the regular review of the Progress Definition within the PROGRESS Cycle. Positive attitudes to audit and an adherence to learning lessons is made possible by delivery of the PACE Culture, which provides the dynamic drive throughout all five levels of the organization and is addressed in the next domain.

PACE Culture domain

Getting things done well used to involve professionals gaining considerable experience in a relatively small set of products, services, processes or practices (the portfolio) and providing these to customers. But the digital world has truly changed traditional ways of getting things done; and the green agenda is doing it again. Today's technology giants produce products to be sold at scale; returns to global capital investments are ever higher; returns to in-country labour, ever lower. And so service organizations and professionals must respond faster than ever to sustain their business or practice.

In this practical guide to sustained success in organizations, an alternative way is suggested to address this global phenomenon, which is to refocus the organization on where future value lies and be prepared to adapt. A quote often attributed to Charles Darwin, British naturalist, but also to Professor Leon C. Megginson of Louisiana State University, a Fellow of the Academy of (US) Management, states: 'It is not the most intellectual of the species that survives; it is not the strongest that survives; but the species that survives is the one that is able best to adapt and adjust to the changing environment in which it finds itself.' So sustained progress will require an organization to adapt to changing environments, possibly many times.

Machine learning and AI holds out the prospect of learning from experience, and increasing efficiency; but by comparison, it is human capital that remains the most adaptable – at least for now! So, organizations looking to sustain success will need to invest in driving value from human capital; and the way forward is to focus upon the second of our domains, the PACE Culture (Figure 3.4).

The whole world is living through an era of increasing pace, as the power of technology enables science fiction of the post-war era to become everyday reality; in fact, technology is probably outpacing that too! Across generations, whether raised on deferred gratification or instant gratification, the

FIGURE 3.4 PACE Culture

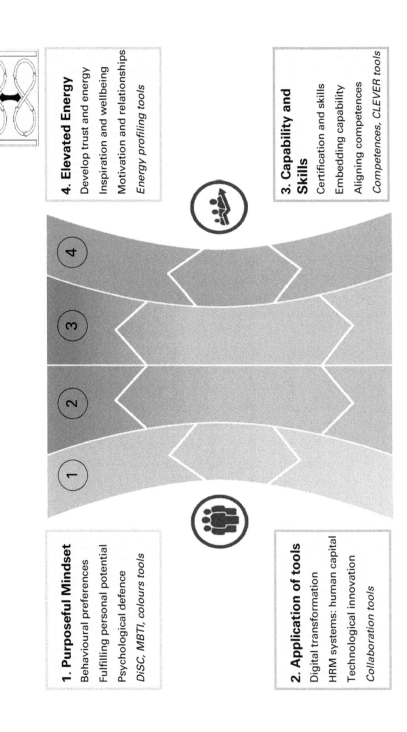

1. Purposeful Mindset
Behavioural preferences
Fulfilling personal potential
Psychological defence
DiSC, MBTI, colours tools

2. Application of tools
Digital transformation
HRM systems: human capital
Technological innovation
Collaboration tools

3. Capability and Skills
Certification and skills
Embedding capability
Aligning competences
Competences, CLEVER tools

4. Elevated Energy
Develop trust and energy
Inspiration and wellbeing
Motivation and relationships
Energy profiling tools

appeal of pace cannot be overstated. Organizations exist to serve customers, to satisfy ever-changing needs. And while the desire to respond both quicker and better may seem daunting, to others it is simply an opportunity. In this section, we can consider how organizations can empower their people to deliver Progress @ Pace. This is what we have called the PACE Culture.

Imagine a four-lane highway connecting two great cities: one is an exemplar of resilience, the other of progress. The purpose of PACE Culture is to provide such a highway for the two-way flow of innovative ideas.

Four PACE Culture elements

The culture highway comprises lanes, or four PACE elements; these work together to build adaptability and generate passion and Elevated Energy for innovation. Considered individually, these four elements are the drivers of the PACE Culture, and successful organizations will find smart ways to invest in these (Table 3.2).

TABLE 3.2 PACE Culture elements

PACE Culture element	Description
Purposeful Mindset	Creating a sense of individual self-worth and belief in the value people bring to the organization in delivery and development Roles at all levels, and partnership networks, through better understanding of ambition, behavioural preferences and psychological defence
Application of tools	Exploration and evolution of the right tools for digital transformation, human systems and technological innovation. The resulting effectiveness, efficiency and economy of tools should be addressed from an outcome perspective of collaborative delivery of customer value
Capability and Skills	Ensuring the right capabilities and skills are sought, taught or learned so that teams will feel proud of their performance starts with understanding 'why' we do things, as well as 'how' to do them. Certification and aligning of competences focuses on better capability
Elevated Energy	By focusing on customer relationships and agreeing priorities, individuals feel part of a team, where 'we can!' Achieving visible increments can support collective wellbeing. Cross-checking organizational motivation results in redirecting effort towards more positive energy

Realizing a PACE Culture will be the work of the whole organization; Business Resilience Owners will take responsibility for developing it, but Progress Masters, initiative owners and their teams must 'live the dream', whether as individuals, in teams, business units, organizations or partner networks. The fusion of these capabilities is what will enable organizations to respond purposefully to changing situations and make progress. PACE Culture goes beyond learning capabilities and how to optimize tools, with skills to adapt the organization under VUCA conditions. Underpinned by a Purposeful Mindset, customer feedback and team lessons, leaders create a culture of confidence. Innovation and Risk, preparedness to adapt and positive approaches to progress (see champion/challenger technique) ensure the four PACE drivers continually evolve and remain valid. And in more challenging VUCA times, positive team energy enables paradigm shifts to be tested, implemented and to realize radical organizational progress.

PROGRESS Cycle domain

The PROGRESS Cycle (Figure 3.5) is the second of the two infinity loops, which defines eight elements within a continually improving process for development of the organization's portfolio of products, services, practices and processes. For an initiative to be selected, it should be achievable, attractive and align to one of the four portfolio areas (product, services, practices and processes) referenced in elements 1–4 of the cycle. Qualifying value initiatives are then taken forward at the right pace – through elements 5–8 of the cycle.

Two decision gates (Table 3.3) will filter initiatives to 'go live'; the first follows Good Alignment, which confirms a development should be done, and the second follows completion of development, and Success and Learning, when a final decision is taken on release to production or commercial release.

FIGURE 3.5 PROGRESS Cycle

1. Progress Definition
Value initiatives (PSPP)
Gap to progress position
Roadmap to progress
MCA, SWOT/TOWS tools

2. Recognize Challenge
Capacity loading
VUCA sensitivity
AE capability
Urgency
VUCA scale, AE, load tools

8. Success and Learning
Portfolio review
Learn from experience
Celebrate success
Resilience Profile, CPD tool
Decision Gate 2

4. Good Alignment
Resilience profile (from Step 1)
Partner network
Contribution to progress
Resilience value
Decision Gate 1

3. Opportunity Assessment
Benefits assessment
Value to partner network
Delivery confidence
BM, MoV, DICE tools

5. Rapids and Lagoons
Consolidate PSPP backlogs
Rapids/lagoons backlogs
Define prioritized portfolio
Agile/classic KPI tools

6. Enabling Teams
Self-managed teams
Collaboration methods
Facilitation methods
Governance and ACE tools

7. Selecting and Testing
Quality tests/reviews
Market assessments/UX
Contribution to progress
MoP, success factor tools, Kanban

TABLE 3.3 PROGRESS Cycle elements and decision gates

PROGRESS Cycle element	Description
Progress Definition	This forms a reference point for delivering value to both organization and its customers, and defines the gap to progress target elements
Recognize Challenge	Assessment of prevailing business conditions leading to challenge to deliver the target progress level (measured using capacity-loading, the VUCA Storm Scale, Adaptive Enterprise capability and urgency)
Opportunity Assessment	Attractiveness of the customer requirement or proposed opportunity (measured as a benefits assessment, value to partnerships and delivery confidence)
Good Alignment	Alignment of opportunity to Progress Definition – using the business alignment scale; it considers all elements of contribution to the organization and partner network
Decision Gate 1	Completion of the first four elements provides the basis for a go/no-go decision to proceed to development. The risk and return of value initiatives must be attractive to customers and contribute to progress of the organization, and ideally its partners
Rapids or Lagoons	Value initiatives are prioritized according to negotiated requirements and planned using the most appropriate tools – typically agile or traditional project or programme methods
Empowered teams	Initiatives are owned and executed by self-managed work teams, working in collaboration with customers and/or users, through a facilitated process of iterative development
Selection and Testing	Selection of product or service versions and variants, following quality and market or user testing, is a key part of the PROGRESS Cycle
Success and Learning	A review of the portfolio to confirm that the products are ready for release or failure provides learning opportunities to refine the PROGRESS Cycle; retrospectives may lead to the adoption of new (or replacement) PROGRESS Cycle elements or refinement
Decision Gate 2	Decision to release the outputs of the value initiatives, for production or live use, which have successful testing and portfolio review outcomes

Roles domain

The Roles domain has three core Roles and one supplementary role of Business Resilience. The Business Resilience Owner, Progress Master and Initiative Leader are the core Roles that lead, facilitate and implement the Business Resilience Framework and value initiatives. As a supplementary role, the Resilience Professional can advise, support, coach, facilitate or deliver the responsibilities of one of the core Roles. The role is particularly helpful when introducing the framework and it is recommended for organizations to engage a Resilience Professional to aid implementation. Additionally, there are Roles such as finance, marketing or operations that interact with the core Roles to deliver improved Business Resilience.

The Business Resilience Roles are discussed in Chapter 4, with role descriptions in Appendix A.

Three domains that comprise the Progress @ Pace 8-4-8 Resilience Model

There are three domains of the Business Resilience Framework (RESILIENCE Foundations, PACE Culture and the PROGRESS Cycle) which combine to make up the Progress @ Pace 8-4-8 Resilience Model. Each domain contributes to the organizational capability to achieve sustained progress, whatever the conditions or environment. Business Resilience is therefore a live and changing capability that is optimized when the three domains are combined across the organization and its partner network, for the purpose of making Progress @ Pace.

Importantly, without RESILIENCE Foundations, a PACE Culture cannot be realized; without a PACE Culture progress cannot be realized; and without PROGRESS the business or organization cannot be sustained.

The design of the Progress @ Pace 8-4-8 Model has evolved from the authors' practical experience of working in organizations, as well as from reviews and retrospectives of challenging times – in particular, the importance of purpose, clear ownership and collaboration to get things done, at pace. In the Business Resilience Framework, the Principles and Roles both underpin and support the RESILIENCE Foundations, PACE Culture and PROGRESS Cycle domains. The three domains of RESILIENCE Foundations, PACE Culture and PROGRESS Cycle (Figure 3.6) contain 20 elements that reflect organizational capability to make progress and define what needs to

FIGURE 3.6 Progress @ Pace 8-4-8 Model: designing for success

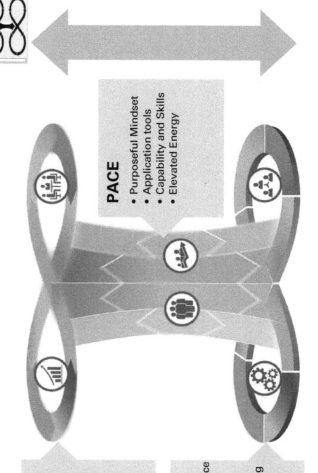

PACE
- Purposeful Mindset
- Application tools
- Capability and Skills
- Elevated Energy

PROGRESS
- Progress Definition
- Recognize Challenge
- Opportunity Assessment
- Good Alignment
- Rapids/Lagoons
- Enabled teams
- Selection and Testing
- Success and Learning

RESILIENCE
- Regulatory and Governance
- Evolving Vision
- Sustainable operations
- Innovation and Risk
- Leadership and influencing
- Enterprising Investment
- Network Collaboration
- Evolutionary Portfolio

be addressed to realize progress. The Principles and Roles act as a magnetic force to maintain the effectiveness of these core domains.

This chapter shows what is included in the standard model and the reasons why each element contributes to progress. Chapter 11 shows how to adapt the model to the organizational situation. Practitioners can take advantage of the easy 'plug and play' modularity to achieve a unique organizational solution, building on prior experience or excellence in the domains.

Implementing the Business Resilience Framework

A programme for Business Resilience will follow development and approval of a business case, in which adoption of the framework and 8-4-8 model and its adaptation to the unique organization-based networks will be explored, many options considered, and the preferred implementation approach for stakeholders identified.

How to adopt and adapt Business Resilience is considered further in Chapters 8 and 11. The business case approach ensures the organization and all network partners are included as stakeholders, raising awareness, understanding and opportunity to participate in Business Resilience activities, developing with the PACE Culture and making progress.

The Business Resilience Owner must ensure the business case is vision-based, focusing on closing Resilience Profile gaps, managing implementation risk in terms of both threats and opportunities. Ultimately, a cost-effective and affordable programme of Business Resilience must be identified.

The programme should also be inherently flexible, as implementation of initiatives, in-year, will be determined by prevailing VUCA conditions, the level of challenge and progress in developing other priorities. For this reason, business case critical success factors should take into consideration impacts at portfolio and programme level of the organization in addition to analysing individual initiatives.

Setting the right pace for progress

Finding the right momentum, cycle speed or portfolio refresh rate is essential to sustained success. The design of the Progress @ Pace 8-4-8 Model captures the three domains as two infinity loops, one for resilience and one for progress, with the third domain being the PACE organization culture, shown as highway flows between the RESILIENCE Foundations and PROGRESS Cycle domains. The three domains form a lifecycle model for continuous business development in the context of all VUCA conditions and partnership networks. Implicit to the application of the model are concepts of business agility and adaptability, and maintenance of a backlog to capture improvements to practices and processes within the organization, and for products and services – reflected in the PROGRESS Cycle (Chapter 7). It is a value-focused model reflecting organizational passion for improvement and enablement of technological evolution (Chapter 5).

Building collaborations by contributing value is key to strong and resilient innovation in a complex world, and sharing partnership ideas is a great way to commence initiatives. Progress @ Pace modelling is designed to empower teams throughout a business network – communicating ideas and focusing on adding value. It is also a smart tool for sharing lessons with partners and improving/refining Progress @ Pace Model application in changing market sector conditions to focus on opportunity and the road to success.

Building momentum has been seen as the holy grail of many 'agilists', a desire for development velocity. Some managers focus on 'just do it' cultures, reflecting a desire for greater delivery; similarly, accountants are driven to option evaluation in terms of shorter payback periods, supporting 'quick wins'. But whatever business Roles are considered within an enterprise, winners achieve momentum from sustained investment in people and ideas: a culture of innovation and testing, across network partners. Learning organizations build on service failures, repurposing the feedback to opportunities for practice improvement and momentum. But the insatiable desire for faster development, more delivery and quicker returns can lead to dysfunction, breakdown and failure of individuals and organizations. This guide focuses upon the realization that sustained progress is what is truly desirable.

Remaining static or indeed losing momentum to market leaders is clearly also undesirable; products become older and less competitive, less customer value is delivered, margins wither away. Organizations that fail to innovate will ultimately fail, and the price is paid by all investors, employees and customers. So sustained progress is in everyone's interest – everybody wins.

In Business Resilience this organizational cadence is referred to as 'pace'. As social and economic conditions change, it is crucial that progress continues to be made at pace. (See the VUCA Storm Scale in Chapter 7.) Progress might take an alternative form or be quantifiably different, but the business focus remains – to deliver customer value and make progress at the right pace for the organization.

The ability to achieve this remarkable outcome is built from RESILIENCE Foundations, and development of an organization culture that supports all levels of the organization: individuals, teams, departments or divisions, the organization and its wider network. Making use of relevant planning tools (eg Diamond of Innovation in Appendix B), exploring customer value improvements for potential market situations and defining multiple strategic pathways creates options for strategy implementation. Importantly, this enables organizations to keep connected to customers and partners, through a willingness and ability to pivot implementations, promotions or portfolio investments to meet ever-changing, possibly Stormy VUCA conditions.

In this way, the three domains of the Progress @ Pace 8-4-8 Model work together with the Principles and the Roles in the Business Resilience Framework to create resilience, strengthen trust throughout all parties in the partner network, and provide value to customers. In the following chapters, the 20 elements of the Progress @ Pace 8-4-8 Model are introduced in outline for each of the three domains.

Benefits, costs and risks

The benefits of the Business Resilience Framework are that:

- Empirical evidence and experience are utilized and built upon for the organization.
- The time to develop and implement Business Resilience is reduced, leading to benefits being realized more quickly.
- Standardized processes and practices are used that enable the organization to ensure the Capability and Skills are available to deliver.

Costs of the Business Resilience Framework arise from the ambition of senior leaders and what internal and external resources can be available to work on initiatives: what timescales are realistic to close gaps between the current and target level of the Resilience Profile and where do current priorities lie within the portfolio? With answers to these questions, a cost estimate for the Business Resilience programme can be prepared.

Implementation of the chosen option(s) will determine when the costs are incurred and when benefits might expect to be received. However, benefits of the resilient organization will accrue due to the organization's ability to manage risk and adapt to changing conditions. Therefore, relative performance or sustainability of the products and services portfolio, in light of VUCA conditions over the medium term, may be a better guide to benefits realization than narrower measures of individual product or service line success – as well as improvements to practices and processes.

Risks are reduced through the use of the Business Resilience Framework to improve Business Resilience. Implementable risk mitigation strategies and the organization's ability to migrate activities towards achievement of the Progress Definition should be captured; and these should be reviewed when undertaking learning from experience at the end of the PROGRESS Cycle. These insights form the basis of an assessment of risk mitigation and benefits realization, achieved as a result of Business Resilience initiatives across the portfolio.

Summary

The Business Resilience Framework shows how organizations can create sustained progress delivered at pace by building RESILIENCE Foundations, adopting a purposeful organization PACE Culture and focusing on the PROGESS Cycle. It is an approach that enables teams to innovate at any level, delivering customer value, whatever the conditions, when it is needed. Roles and Principles of the framework maintain organizational direction, empowering progress towards objectives. Resilient organizations empower staff to adopt practices and adapt processes to ensure customer value is delivered, where rigid adherence to preconceived practices or processes cannot.

Business Resilience is an inclusive approach. The Business Resilience Framework provides a guiding hand for all stakeholders in the enterprise, raising the spirit, whatever one's level. By clarifying and refining market niches while maintaining a focus on progress, organizations create advantage, building more customer value into products, services, practices and processes. Desired outcomes are customer satisfaction in the near term, outpacing less passionate competitors over the medium term, and survival in the long term.

Whether in public, private or third sectors, the Business Resilience Framework will enable organizations to maintain a focus on great public service or responsible commercial or other activities. Above all, people will experience a feel-good factor and unity of purpose will flow from implementing this framework.

In the following chapters Business Resilience is examined from a practitioner perspective. Many questions may arise: will business functions or teams support its introduction? Which people in the organization might take up resilience Roles? Would existing Roles need to change? What degree of readiness for Business Resilience is required? Can PMOs be repurposed as change agents? Have experiences occurred that mean it would be attractive to adapt or adopt it now? These practical concerns are considered further in the chapters that follow.

QUESTIONS TO THINK ABOUT

- To what extent does the Business Resilience Framework consider the full scope of activities for Business Resilience?

- What is the best way to Rapidly assimilate the Business Resilience Framework in your organization?

- Can you obtain the benefits of the Business Resilience Framework without addressing the five domains that make it up?

04

Roles for Business Resilience

Purpose

The purpose of the Business Resilience Roles and team structure is to enable and facilitate sustained progress to be delivered at pace. Business Resilience teams can be created, developed and retained, with elements of the Business Resilience Framework contributing to this process.

Introduction

To achieve the objective of embedding Business Resilience, specific core Business Resilience Roles should support teams within the organization in the implementation of Business Resilience and value initiatives. The Roles should be trained in relevant Business Resilience practices, focus on delivering organizational objectives identified in the Progress Definition, and do so with clarity about value for their customers. The core Roles ensure that the teams apply tools, processes and practices appropriately to optimize value from the implementation and maintenance of Business Resilience.

The organization may already have resources who are appropriately skilled and trained to appoint to the Business Resilience Roles. Examples of Roles that potential candidates for Business Resilience Roles may already be in, along with their desirable attributes and specific responsibilities, are outlined in Appendix A. The Roles should integrate and interact with the existing organizational structure and responsibilities, as Business Resilience covers all aspects of the organization. It is only when Business Resilience is being introduced to an organization that does not currently have any of the Business Resilience elements that the Roles will need to be new appointments.

There are three core Business Resilience Roles and one supplementary role: the Business Resilience Owner, the Progress Master, and the Initiative Leader are the core Roles, and the Business Resilience Professional is the supplementary role. In addition, there are Roles that are expected to routinely interact with the Business Resilience Roles. It is important to note that the Business Resilience Roles are not in competition with the functional Roles of the organization but complement and enhance the functions so that there is an understanding of and focus on Business Resilience that underpins the sustained progress of the organization.

As Business Resilience can be introduced at different levels of the organization, the Roles should be considered for the level at which they will operate.

Business Resilience Roles ensure that:

- progress is realized by Business Resilience teams, mainly through the interactions between Roles and stakeholders, supported by appropriate processes, practices and tools;
- progress is delivered and quantified with documentation sufficient to support progress;
- Business Resilience Roles actively collaborate with network partners to deliver progress instead of negotiating to have contract superiority;
- Business Resilience teams respond and adapt to the changing business environment instead of adhering to a static plan.

Business Resilience Roles have a focus on effectiveness to deliver sustained progress.

Five levels of organization to implement Business Resilience

The organization structure for Business Resilience can take many forms. These can include functional, matrix, projectized or others. Business Resilience recognizes five levels within the organization. These levels are:

1 Individual – a single individual implementing one or more Principles or elements of Business Resilience.
2 Team – a team implementing one or more Principles or elements of Business Resilience.
3 Department or division – a single department or a division of a large organization implementing one or more Principles or elements of Business Resilience.

4 Organization – the whole organization implementing one or more elements of Business Resilience.

5 Network partners – the whole organization plus the network of partners working with the organization, including customers, suppliers, development partners and others such as volunteers.

These five levels represent the levels at which the Business Resilience Roles can be drawn from and operate. The level at which Business Resilience is implemented will impact the level of Business Resilience that can be achieved for the whole organization. Similarly, the organizational level at which Business Resilience is implemented will impact the choice of individuals to be appointed to the Business Resilience Roles.

Figure 4.1 shows an example of how the Business Resilience Roles can be spread across the five levels. This will depend on the strategy implementation approach that is being utilized.

Business Resilience core and supplementary Roles

Business Resilience teams are made up of competent, experienced and skilled professionals who are empowered to deliver Business Resilience by implementing the framework or elements. The Business Resilience Roles do not

FIGURE 4.1   Five levels of organization to apply Business Resilience

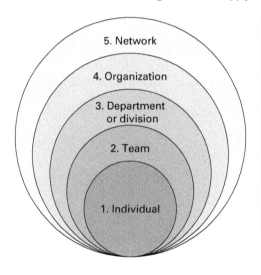

need to be new Roles created for the purpose but could be achieved through changes to existing Roles. See Appendix A for possible existing Roles that could become Business Resilience Roles.

The responsibilities of the core and supplementary Roles are:

- Business Resilience Owner (core): responsible for embedding sustained resilience in an organization by implementing Business Resilience through enabled teams;
- Progress Master (core): an expert in Business Resilience best practice and entrusted with advising and facilitating Business Resilience initiatives;
- Initiative Leader (core): functional experts responsible for executing Business Resilience value initiatives according to their areas of expertise;
- Business Resilience Professional (supplementary): a subject matter expert qualified in Business Resilience – a Resilience Professional could be a Business Resilience consultant and take on the Business Resilience Owner, Progress Master or Initiative Leader role; they will support organizations that lack in-house expertise in Business Resilience and could be engaged to implement Business Resilience.

Figure 4.2 shows Roles forming the core Business Resilience team.

FIGURE 4.2 Core Business Resilience Roles

Business Resilience Owner (core role)

The Business Resilience Owner is the individual with overall responsibility for ensuring that Business Resilience is implemented and maintained in the organization. They choose the strategy implementation approach and ensure the decisions to proceed to implement or release a value initiative at Decision Gates 1 and 2 are taken with the appropriate information and individuals.

DESCRIPTION OF THE ROLE

The Business Resilience Owner is an experienced leader who establishes Business Resilience, and in doing so enables progress through both Calm periods and crisis. The Business Resilience Owner role should be allocated to one person, not shared between professionals, to promote a sense of responsibility, focus and accountability. When adapting the Roles in a very large organization, there may be a Business Resilience Owner for each division to enable localization.

In order to establish Business Resilience during Calm periods, the Business Resilience Owner ensures the RESILIENCE Foundations and the PACE Culture are embedded across the organization to build the ability to make progress. As the VUCA Storm Scale increases, the Business Resilience Owner will maintain the integrity of RESILIENCE Foundations, expedite PACE Culture and drive the PROGRESS Cycle, adhering to Business Resilience Principles. This is explained further in the RESILIENCE Foundations and PACE Culture chapters.

The Business Resilience Owner will identify and understand the Business-critical components vital for Sustained Operations. The Business Resilience Owner may also appoint Resilience Professionals to assist them with strategy implementation, assessing VUCA events, advising on actions or training staff in Business Resilience practice.

The Business Resilience Owner encourages the use of standard early warning procedures, most appropriate to the industry, to ensure there are few surprise events. An example would be early warning notifications in the construction industry, whereby any indication that the work may diverge from plan is immediately notified. With the help of the Progress Master, they watch for political, environmental, social, technological, legislative, economic (PESTLE) events that at first might not seem significant but on further analysis might impact on the business-critical aspects. When a VUCA disruption occurs, they ensure the challenge, opportunity and alignment are analysed to justify any value initiative required to respond. A 'state of resilience board' displaying events categorized according to their proximity, probability and impact on key business components can serve as a visual information source for stakeholders. The Business Resilience Owner would ensure that it is maintained so that all events that can impact beyond a threshold would be highlighted, along with any corresponding value initiatives.

The Business Resilience Owner needs to have a thorough understanding of the Business Resilience process and possess the leadership qualities and influence to bring the organization (and the network partners) with them on the resilience journey.

SUEZ CANAL BLOCKAGE

In March 2021, the Suez Canal was blocked (BBC, 2021) when a huge container ship owned by Evergreen that was taking goods from China to the Netherlands became wedged across it. The event meant not only that that ship wouldn't reach the destination in time, but it also blocked the canal for several days, impacting 12 per cent of global trade and affecting companies in both Europe and Asia.

Before the blockage, the Business Resilience Owner of a company based in Europe, who was reliant on Asia for the supply of medical goods during the Covid-19 pandemic, monitored potential logistics disruption events and had a value initiative ready, along with funds allocated. The value initiative meant supplies were available by air at short notice and that shortlisted Europe-based quality-assured suppliers were in place for the disruption in the supply chain. This saved precious human lives and also the company's reputation. The Business Resilience Owner ensured they were implementing the RESILIENCE Foundations and PACE Culture and were driving the PROGRESS Cycle through this event.

Progress Master (core role)

The Progress Master is the person who is responsible for advising the Business Resilience Owner on the Business Resilience Framework and facilitating the implementation and maintenance of Business Resilience by supporting the Initiative Leaders as they implement value initiatives in the Progress @ Pace model and facilitating the processes and procedures for Business Resilience, as detailed in the RESILIENCE Foundations and PROGRESS Cycle.

DESCRIPTION OF THE ROLE

The Progress Master is at the heart of Business Resilience, ensuring that sustained progress is delivered by adhering to Business Resilience Principles, domains or elements. They are responsible for advising on, adapting and implementing processes and practices for Business Resilience and can get involved in more than one value initiative. Depending on the size, nature and complexity of an organization's business, it can have more than one Progress Master advising on and facilitating resilience value initiatives at any point in time, reporting to the Business Resilience Owner.

The Progress Master should have extensive experience and in-depth understanding of all RESILIENCE Foundations, PACE Culture and PROGRESS Cycle elements. They therefore advise and assist the Business Resilience Owner through strategy implementation to adopt, adapt and embed the domains or elements across all five levels of the organization, or part thereof, depending on the strategy implementation approach chosen. It is pertinent to mention that the four aspects of PACE Culture – Purposeful Mindset, application of tools, Capability and Skills, and Elevated Energy – need to be particularly supported by the Progress Master to ensure the PACE Culture is in place to optimize the value of the RESILIENCE Foundations and apply them to the PROGRESS Cycle. The Progress Master therefore should not only have Business Resilience expertise, but should also be a good collaborator with a wide understanding of best practices.

The Progress Master supports the Business Resilience Owner through the PROGRESS Cycle by ensuring each element is undertaken and supported at the appropriate organizational level. This support could be in the form of training, coaching, facilitation, advice or quality assurance.

MEDICAL SUPPLIES

The Progress Master of the European medical supplies company – referenced in the Suez Canal blockage VUCA event above – had already prepared a value initiative from discussion with the Business Resilience Owner, who had logistics disruptions added to the 'state of resilience board'. When the event happened, the Business Resilience Owner re-assessed the event and triggered the initiative where the Progress Master facilitated implementation of the initiative as a 'Rapid'.

The Progress Definition had already been agreed with the challenge and opportunity levels assessed plus the alignment. This meant that when the event happened, these elements only needed to be checked. The initiative was allocated as a Rapid and the Initiative Leader (from the commercial team) implemented the plan using their partner collaboration experience. The initiative was successful, with many lessons that were shared, and it meant that the company was more resilient through the further logistics problems caused by Covid-19.

Initiative Leader (core role)

The Initiative Leader is the person responsible for implementing and executing the value initiatives to deliver products, services, processes and practices. They will manage the value initiative on a day-to-day basis, with the support and facilitation of the Progress Master, where needed.

DESCRIPTION OF THE ROLE

The Initiative Leader is a functional expert aiding the Progress Master and the Business Resilience Owner by sharing their functional expertise and leading value initiatives supported by the Progress Master.

The Initiative Leader works with an initiative team to successfully execute the value initiatives using relevant best practices, technology accelerators, techniques and industry standards. The specific implementation methods will depend on the organization, industry and initiative to be implemented.

They will lead the initiative team through the forming, Storming, norming and performing phases by focusing on team-building and empowering them to deliver progress. They will manage all risks and issues at the team level using appropriate processes.

SUPPLY CHAIN VALUE INITIATIVE DELIVERY

In the same Suez Canal event described above, there were Initiative Leaders who were assigned in the medical supplies company to ensure that production and supply met demand. The Progress Master identified Initiative Leaders from account management, production and distribution to deliver Rapid initiatives to provide supplies at short notice. The Initiative Leaders used best practice methods to deliver the initiatives, empowering their teams and testing prior to release. There were lessons from each initiative that were used to improve Business Resilience and make progress during the remainder of the Covid-19 pandemic.

Resilience Professional (supplementary role)

The Resilience Professional is a professional who is qualified and experienced in Business Resilience and can be appointed to work alongside organization colleagues to undertake any of the three core Roles, subject to their experience.

The Resilience Professional can be particularly helpful when an organization is adopting or adapting Business Resilience. They can provide advice on the most appropriate strategy implementation approach, assist or undertake adapting the Business Resilience Framework or elements, or coach staff to take on the core Roles. If the organization does not have a suitably experienced Business Resilience Owner or Progress Master, the Resilience Professional can either be appointed in this role or support the person appointed to the role until they have the level of knowledge and experience required.

A Resilience Professional should be engaged as early as possible by the organization or Business Resilience Owner, if there is no in-house expertise, so that Business Resilience Roles can be trained and supported. If in-house expertise is available, the Progress Master and the Business Resilience Owner might still need the help of a Resilience Professional to undertake the Resilience Profile or improve an organizational Business Resilience Framework, in which case they can act as consultants, advisers or coaches.

Importance of Business Resilience Roles working with existing organizational Roles

The Business Resilience Roles do not act in a vacuum. They interact with others in the organization. There will be interactions across many functional areas and network partners, depending on the value initiatives being implemented. There are some organizational Roles that will interact more closely with the Business Resilience Roles, which are:

- initiative team(s): teams assembled to execute value initiatives led by Initiative Leaders;
- Business Adviser(s): responsible for advising the Business Resilience Owner and Progress Master on business-level matters such as policies, strategies, regulations and prospective changes in the business environment; they can be internal or external to the organization;
- Functional Lead(s): responsible for advising Initiative Leader and teams on initiative-related aspects such as marketing, human resource management and technology.

Initiative teams

The initiative teams deliver value initiatives under the guidance of Initiative Leaders with expertise in one domain and collaboration with other team members who have knowledge in additional domains. They deliver value initiatives using their Capability and Skillsets to succeed as a whole team and not as individuals. It is possible to deliver one iteration of the initiative with one team and another with a different team or with changes in team members. They will consult Functional Leads for subject-matter expertise on a need basis.

INITIATIVE TEAM IN ACTION

The general practitioner teams commissioned by the NHS to deliver Covid-19 vaccinations comprised teams with different skillsets. Under the leadership of an Initiative Leader, the initiative team delivered vaccinated communities. The general practice manager was the Initiative Leader and the team members identified the most vulnerable people, contacted them to allay their concerns about the vaccine and booked their vaccinations, received, stored and administered the vaccinations as prescribed, then updated the health records of vaccinated people while booking their second appointment at the same time.

Business Advisers

It is impossible to have all the skills, knowledge and experience available in a single team, which is where Business Advisers (and Resilience Professionals) are helpful. Business Advisers are specialists in a particular area of knowledge or operation who can support the Business Resilience team.

The Business Advisers can be engaged at any time and can be drawn from a wide range of areas, both internal and external, with some being very specific. The objective is to help the Business Resilience Owner and Progress Master gain an in-depth understanding to make informed strategic and implementation decisions.

Depending on the type of advice required, the Business Resilience Owner can arrange it or delegate to the Progress Master. At the initiative level, these could include advisers on enabling technologies and relevant best practices that will help the initiative team deliver the outputs and realize outcomes.

FIGURE 4.3 Core and supplementary network engaged in a value initiative

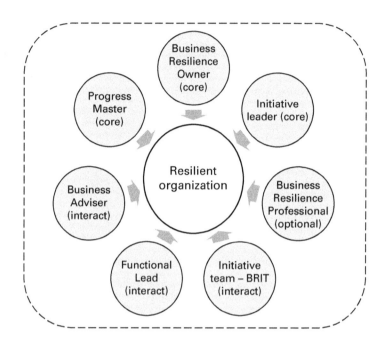

Functional Leads

The functional areas of the organization will need to provide input to enable Business Resilience to be implemented and maintained. This is so that the existing processes and practices are inputs for both the Resilience Profile and value initiatives. Functional Leads may act as Initiative Leaders for value initiatives in their functional area, such as finance, IT or HR, or as subject-matter experts to provide input to an Initiative Leader or Progress Master.

With the core and supplementary Roles it is possible to map current Roles within the organization against these, so that a plan to build foundations for a resilient enterprise can be supported with appropriate experience and skills.

Partnering

Partnerships have become a key extension to organizational capability, enabling greater value to be delivered to customers. Supporting team inter-actions within a spirit of partnership energizes teamwork, benefiting pace throughout the PROGRESS Cycle; partnering should result in more benefi-cial opportunities taken and greater portfolio evolution of higher-value products, services, processes and practices. So, in addition to satisfying internal or external customers in the PROGRESS Cycle, Business Resilience is reinforced through sustained partnerships, resulting in a more Adaptive Enterprise.

For this reason, the Business Resilience strategy should consider engaging both the organizational teams and network partners in collaboration when implementing the PACE Culture and PROGRESS Cycle.

The right people are an organization's best assets

Selection of individuals for Roles is made with the understanding that the success or failure of value initiatives depends on the quality of the people in these Roles. It is important to ensure:

- The most capable and trustworthy people are assigned to the Business Resilience Roles.

- The biggest opportunities are assigned to top performers.

- A conducive working environment is created and maintained across the Business Resilience team where new ideas are heard, people are valued and opportunities are identified. As a rule of thumb, people should look forward to the next day at work and enjoy doing it.

- The process of finding talent for Business Resilience will be expedited, especially during high VUCA periods, because talented individuals who will remain loyal to the organization can be retrained in new Roles.

THE RIGHT PEOPLE APPOINTED IN MICROSOFT

Satya Nadella joined Microsoft in 1992 and transitioned through Roles to become its CEO and Chairman in 2014. He was given the opportunity to transform cloud services and products, a conducive environment for learning. His team launched Microsoft's Azure platform, which revolutionized cloud computing and the way it is used by digital and non-digital companies (Microsoft Media Relations, 2021). This appointment demonstrates the value of appointing the right people and the responsibility of the Business Resilience Owner in identifying those talented individuals who will contribute to the continued progress of the organization, delivering long-term resilience.

Leadership at the top is extremely important

Leadership at the top cascades down to every individual within the organization. Successful companies are built by leaders that rise above their personal gains and lead the organization to deliver what matters the most for their clients. The Business Resilience Owner, Progress Master and Initiative Leaders will ensure that they lead the development of Business Resilience with exemplary leadership and encourage this in their teams. The Business Resilience Owner ensures leadership is embedded at individual, team, department or division and organizational levels, and it is also encouraged in the partner network. Much of this happens during the recruitment process – for example, *the vodafone business future ready report 2020* (Vodafone, 2021) highlights the leadership challenges causing businesses to change the ways they recruit and nurture talent.

LEADERSHIP OF THE VENTILATOR CHALLENGE

The Ventilator Challenge (Ventilator Challenge UK, 2020), led by Dick Elsy, is an excellent example of leadership, where peak production exceeded 400 devices a day. Dick Elsy identified the partner organizations that had sufficient RESILIENCE Foundations and PACE Culture in place to be able to deliver at pace using their existing PROGRESS Cycles. It is the leadership provided that enabled this to be completed successfully. The shortest time taken to achieve 1,000 ventilators was three days during the Covid-19 pandemic. This included leadership at each level in each of the organizations involved so that they were prepared to pivot, as Adaptive Enterprises, to deliver ventilators instead of their BAU products. Dick Elsy recognized that leadership needed to be strong at all levels to deliver this progress at the pace required.

Culture of leadership is essential

Successful organizations have a culture of leadership that is characterized by complementing teams as opposed to command and control – attributing success to teams and owning failures, showing modesty and leading through standards rather than personal charisma. These leaders take whatever decisions are required for the success of their organization and refuse to settle for anything less (Collins, 2001). The Business Resilience Owner, Progress Master, Initiative Leader and other Roles in Business Resilience initiatives must ensure that this concept is embedded in their teams.

LEADERS AT ALL LEVELS

Welding Alloys Ltd UK (Welding Alloys Group UK, 2021) was founded in 1966 by Jan Stekly near Cambridge, UK. Under his leadership, the company identified innovation as the key to creating value for customers. They started as a welding wire consumable producer but soon realized that their customers wanted reduced downtime and outsourced maintenance services, which they fulfilled. The shift in focus from what they produced towards what the customers wanted was enabled by supporting the Initiative Leaders to lead initiatives by collaborating with customers, and by the Initiative Leaders taking the decisions required for the success of their organization.

Behaviours for effective Business Resilience Roles

The core Roles within Business Resilience teams operate and interact with behaviours that should be applied at all five levels of the organization for successful implementation of Business Resilience.

Turning a VUCA crisis into an opportunity

Business Resilience Owners should respond to any crisis by allocating resources so that opportunities brought by the VUCA events can be fully exploited and the wind of change coming towards an organization is used as a tailwind to survive and thrive.

AN OPPORTUNITY FOR NETFLIX

During 2020/21 Covid-19 national lockdowns, Netflix spotted an opportunity to increase subscribers across developed nations where high-speed internet was widely available. Netflix already had the digital infrastructure when they tested the waters with a few limited-episode Netflix series. As soon as their assumptions about the potential new subscribers were validated by the success of Netflix series, to build on this success they doubled (Dean, 2020) their UK production in November 2020, supported by an increase in the team based in the UK (Sweney, 2021). This led to 16 million new subscribers during the first quarter of 2020, resulting in more than 182 million subscribers worldwide, a revenue increase of more than 27 per cent compared with the same period in 2019 and profits during the first quarter of 2020 almost doubled compared with the first quarter of 2019 (BBC, 2020). This demonstrates how the Business Resilience Owner used the Evolving Vision element of the RESILIENCE Foundations to turn the crisis into an opportunity.

Prepare in the good times to progress during tough times

In the face of inevitable high VUCA scenarios, Business Resilience teams work even harder to develop or improve products and services that add value for their customers and organization. They don't wait for the Storm to pass or moan about tough situations. However, it cannot be decoupled from the fact that this strategy warrants preparing during good times, for instance by saving a percentage of reserves to be used during high VUCA periods.

PREPARATION REAPS REWARDS IN VUCA STORM

During the Covid-19 pandemic, customers of video conferencing platforms had privacy and security concerns. Microsoft's (MS) Teams had very low market penetration at the start of the pandemic. Microsoft's Evolving Vision prior to the pandemic included the need for an information security compliant video conferencing and collaborative working platform in the future. They recognized a demand from organizations that place high reliance on information security due to legislation, commercial or other needs. Microsoft had been preparing prior to the pandemic, so they were ready to accelerate this development when the crisis hit. Microsoft quickly completed securing 90 compliance certifications (Microsoft, 2021) for their platform, for cloud-hosted applications, including Teams. It included over 50 specific regions and countries and was followed by more than 35 compliance offerings specific to the needs of key industries. It consolidated their market positioning for information security-sensitive government and private entities. The preparation paid off, with many clients signing up to Teams. This resulted in recurring revenue and customer penetration during lockdowns and afterwards.

Developing and retaining Business Resilience teams

The Business Resilience teams need to be set up for success, and individuals need to be nurtured to ensure that these human assets are retained in the organization for a considerable time.

Selection of best practices and skills

Selection of the most appropriate best practice competences and skills for a value initiative will depend on the level at which it is commissioned, and the functional expertise required. The Business Resilience Owner, Progress Master(s) and Initiative Leader(s) can choose from relevant best practices. Many organizations will have established best practices for their areas of operations and, where this is not the case, the Progress Master or a Functional Lead should advise which are most appropriate to their operations.

Enabling and retaining Business Resilience teams through policy

Where possible organizations will utilize their existing people in Business Resilience. These individuals are already familiar with the organization and can be effective immediately. In some situations individuals may already be undertaking some of the Business Resilience responsibilities. A policy to build Business Resilience with in our existing talent pool should be used, where feasible.

Human resource policy will need to be reviewed to ensure the Business Resilience teams are appropriately recruited and developed, whether internal or external. This should cover which Roles are required, recruitment policy, training, support and learning lessons for continuous improvement. Organizations can consider hiring talent when others are firing as people become available who otherwise would not be. Another approach to consider is to hire talented individuals and then identify where best to deploy them. Highly capable people are able to take on any of the Business Resilience Roles.

Any lessons learned from Business Resilience initiatives will be reflected upon and, if appropriate, result in human resource policy updates.

Benefits, costs and risks

Benefits

Identifying and resourcing the Business Resilience Roles has several benefits. These include but are not limited to:

- Value initiatives will deliver products, services, processes or practices that should contribute to increasing Business Resilience.
- The Business Resilience Roles will understand each initiative's contribution to increasing the level of Business Resilience, which is assessed in the Good Alignment element of the PROGRESS Cycle. This becomes even more important during times of uncertainty and significantly improves the chances of any organization's success when faced with a tough external environment.

- The Business Resilience Roles will ensure the Principles, domains or elements of Business Resilience are embedded so that sustained progress is achieved, and the organization survives events which might otherwise cause them to fail.

- Business Resilience Roles will be available to exploit opportunities when there are high VUCA Storm conditions.

- Business Resilience Roles will influence the PACE Culture to underpin the RESILIENCE Foundations and support the PROGRESS Cycle to increase Business Resilience.

Costs

The costs will vary depending upon the size of an organization and the strategy implementation approach chosen. If existing resources are already being utilized for Business Resilience, costs will be very low. The main costs will be salaries and training. The costs will be in proportion to the size of the team. Any costs should be exceeded by the benefits that the expertise of the Business Resilience Roles bring. If in-house resources are utilized without the support of a Resilience Professional, the Roles will be cost-neutral.

Implementation risks

The main risks of implementing Business Resilience teams are listed below. The probability of all these risks happening is high when an organization starts adopting the Business Resilience Framework. Hence, the proximity of these risks will be short to medium term. Realization of these risks will have a high impact on the rollout of Business Resilience efforts, prevent the development of Business Resilience teams and hinder progress towards Business Resilience maturity. These risks will diminish the more the Business Resilience Framework is utilized:

- Selected team members won't have essential capabilities: mitigation is through learning from experience, selecting from in-house candidates and acting fast if a mistake has been made when appointing.

- Not understanding the Roles properly: mitigation is through training, shadowing Business Resilience Professionals and, over time, experience of implementing Business Resilience.

- Resistance to setting up Business Resilience teams: although a natural consequence of human bias towards change, it can be mitigated through examples where organizations that implemented Business Resilience fared better than the ones that didn't. For example, Morrisons supermarket going online with Amazon to grab the online shoppers market share.

- Under- or overestimating the size of the Business Resilience teams: organizations should always start with smaller teams, applying prioritization on the basis of 'must have', 'should have', 'could have' and 'won't have for now' (MoSCoW) on all initiatives and carefully assessing Rapids versus Lagoons for the scale of resources needed to deliver.

- Lack of process for setting up the teams: mitigation will be through adhering to in-house HR recruitment practices as the Business Resilience Framework doesn't recommend a one-size-fits-all approach.

Summary

The Business Resilience Framework and the Roles described in this chapter create winning teams that contribute to organizations' long-term success. The Roles will improve with each cycle, and lessons will be incorporated in Business Resilience processes, practices and initiatives. The objective is to have a repeatable, ever-evolving organizational structure where excellence gets rewarded and an environment of mutual accomplishments is established. The Roles will become established through enabling a PACE Culture that would not only support solid RESILIENCE Foundations but would also execute the PROGRESS Cycle to establish and improve Business Resilience.

The next step is to start the implementation of Business Resilience Roles, because organizations are never going to be the same and not taking action is not an option.

A famous quote from Abraham Lincoln says, 'Give me six hours to chop down a tree, and I will spend the first four sharpening the axe.' No organization can have unlimited resources, but it can strengthen considerably by appointing the right individuals and building on their competencies. Careful thought about who should be appointed into each role prior to the appointments will repay the organization.

QUESTIONS TO THINK ABOUT

- Are there any individuals in your organization who already have some Business Resilience responsibilities included in their Roles?

- Will a Business Resilience Professional add value to establish or improve Business Resilience in your organization?

- Which Business Resilience Roles should you establish in your organization next?

References

BBC (2020) Netflix gets 16 million new sign-ups thanks to lockdown, *BBC News Business*, 22 April, www.bbc.co.uk/news/business-52376022 (archived at https://perma.cc/4LFQ-2T3A)

BBC (2021) Egypt's Suez Canal blocked by huge container ship, *BBC News Middle East*, 24 March, www.bbc.co.uk/news/world-middle-east-56505413 (archived at https://perma.cc/7A3W-5TE6)

Collins, J (2001) *Good to Great: Why some companies make the leap... and others don't*, Harper Business, New York

Dean, C (2020) Netflix doubles its UK budget to $1billion following the success of its shows *The Crown* and *Sex Education*, *Daily Mail*, 25 November, www.dailymail.co.uk/tvshowbiz/article-8986403/Netflix-DOUBLES-UK-budget-1billion.html (archived at https://perma.cc/8H7Z-B62B)

Microsoft (2021) *Azure Compliance: Microsoft Azure*, 18 October, azure.microsoft.com/en-gb/overview/trusted-cloud/compliance (archived at https://perma.cc/2QET-6U5J)

Microsoft Media Relations (2021) *Microsoft News*, news.microsoft.com/exec/satya-nadella (archived at https://perma.cc/4AD3-425S)

Sweney, M (2021) Netflix paid £3.2m in tax on £940m of UK subscription revenue, *The Guardian*, 22 January, www.theguardian.com/media/2021/jan/22/netflix-paid-32m-in-tax-on-940m-of-uk-subscription-revenue (archived at https://perma.cc/6PL6-QVQW)

Ventilator Challenge UK (2020) *Ventilator Challenge UK*, 5 July, www.ventilatorchallengeuk.com (archived at https://perma.cc/GM7B-26YA)

Vodafone (2021) *The Vodafone Business Future Ready Report 2020*, www.vodafone.com/business/news-and-insights/white-paper/future-ready-report-2020 (archived at https://perma.cc/P6RG-KYGJ)

Welding Alloys Group UK (2021) *Welding Alloys Group UK*, 18 October, www.welding-alloys.com (archived at https://perma.cc/E2PW-X96T)

05

RESILIENCE Foundations

Purpose

The purpose of the RESILIENCE Foundations domain is to ensure the organization is robust and has the functionality to build Business Resilience, support the PACE Culture and deliver progress through the PROGRESS Cycle. It provides the building blocks on which a strong and resilient organization can be constructed.

Introduction

The purpose of this book and in particular this chapter is to discuss an approach that shows how organizations can survive and thrive by creating the tenacious resolve and strategic resilience to successfully work through business difficulties, problems and disruptions. The components that are needed by organizations to achieve this are presented overall in this book. Looking at the research, organizations at present rarely have an inbuilt strategy to deal with VUCA disruptions and often just deal with problems as they arise. Some organizations have a business continuity plan, but this only allows them just to weather the Storm to bounce back to a pre-storm level. They accept the harsh reality and try to understand the situation and then they create emergency programmes as an attempt to solve the problems as they arise. The main issue with this is that when there is a very drastic disruption, such as a recession, technology disruption or a pandemic, they are unprepared. This makes it very difficult to continually anticipate changes and improvise a solution quickly enough to keep pace and continue to receive business value. In the best-case scenario, they may just survive and bounce back close to their original level, but in many cases the businesses

FIGURE 5.1 RESILIENCE Foundations

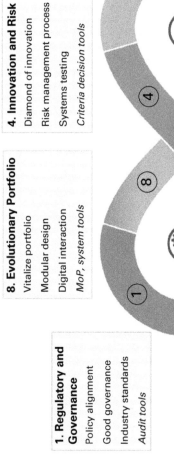

1. Regulatory and Governance
Policy alignment
Good governance
Industry standards
Audit tools

2. Evolving Vision
Appealing creative ideas
Modelling + quantification
Stakeholder engagement
MSP, agility and VUCA tools

3. Sustainable Operations
Open systems architecture
Lean production practice
Adaptability and modularity
TOGAF, digital Tx, tools

4. Innovation and Risk
Diamond of innovation
Risk management process
Systems testing
Criteria decision tools

5. Leading and Influencing
Inspirational leadership
Aligning to people's values
Brand values and positioning
SPL, champion/challenger tool

6. Enterprising Investment
Attracting investment
Attracting talent
Beyond budgets and control
Business case tools

7. Network Collaboration
Agile culture
Partner collaboration
Supply chain partners
Facilitation, ACE tools

8. Evolutionary Portfolio
Vitalize portfolio
Modular design
Digital interaction
MoP, system tools

collapse because they could not change and adapt fast enough. This book presents a solution – the Business Resilience Framework (see Chapter 3), which is a standard model that can be followed instead of ad hoc trial-and-error-based actions to deal with the problems and disruptions as they arise. The RESILIENCE Foundations domain can be seen as an infinity loop to achieve continuous improvement (Figure 5.1) in this framework. It provides firm RESILIENCE Foundations from which the PACE Culture highway leads to the PROGRESS Cycle to enable an organization to Progress @ Pace so they can survive and thrive, even during highly VUCA situations. Organizations need to view Business Resilience as a competitive advantage and proactively utilize the Progress @ Pace 8-4-8 Model. This chapter describes and discusses the RESILIENCE Foundations and provides a practical understanding of the elements needed to achieve this. RESILIENCE Foundations contain the eight elements that must be in place to support PACE Culture and progress. The reason for having this is to ensure the organization is robust, relevant to resilience and functionally complete.

Even organizations with a clear vision find it difficult to adapt and survive in an unpredictable world. RESILIENCE Foundations provide a robust risk-aware domain for doing business in good times and bad. Companies that use this domain exhibit certain traits as a result. They are well capitalized, with sustainable operations, staying close to customers, identifying future trends and investing through downturns to emerge leaner and stronger. Resilience is the cornerstone of the capacity to respond and make progress.

The eight elements of RESILIENCE Foundations work as follows:

1 Regulatory and Governance: the organization will clarify industry standards and ensure that their organizational policies are aligned to them, using auditable practice from which learning and improvement takes place.

2 Evolving Vision: a series of incrementally better organization design ideas where people collaborate within social and technological future environments to deliver benefits for all.

3 Sustainable operations: adaptable, digital and modular operational capability supporting lean practices with refined tools for the implementation of learning within networks.

4 Innovation and Risk: balancing the desire for portfolio innovation with resource availability from an enlightened value perspective on technological and financial risk assessment.

5 Leading and Influencing: understanding and inspiring others; creating belief in a future where organization brand values and positioning reflect the aspirations of the network.

6 Enterprising Investment: how to attract talent and investment into the organization by building believability in next steps and sharing the benefits of vision realization.

7 Network Collaboration: a spirit of collaboration and partnership, built upon application of an agile culture, where facilitation of stakeholders, testing and customer value predominate.

8 Evolutionary Portfolio: an abiding belief in market focus, digital by design and modularity combine to deliver lifecycle desirability with confidence to pivot due to VUCA conditions.

Each of the eight elements are explained in the next sections. After explaining these elements, an input/output diagram is presented showing the current situation of these RESILIENCE Foundation elements (RFE) in the organizations, followed by Business Resilience and initiative team (BRIT) workshops, which confirm how to respond to each element and suggest the pace and severity of the VUCA events they are dealing with. The result of the workshop allows organizations to respond appropriately to VUCA situations. A generic input/output diagram showing how they interact is shown in Figure 5.2.

As the organization evolves over time, they will amass a portfolio of scenarios from past VUCA disruptions and how they were dealt with so that these response scenarios can be easily and Rapidly deployed if they should occur in the future. It is also important for BRIT workshops to brainstorm various possible future scenarios of which they have no experience so it would be quicker to respond to these should they occur.

It is helpful to store these in the organization library, which could be a folder on a hard drive, printed files, etc.

VUCA DISRUPTIONS

Examples of these could include the VUCA disruption caused by countries adopting crypto currencies, supply chain disruptions due to Brexit, new UK trade deals with different countries of the world due to Brexit, new green economy policies that can impact an organization that might need to change their business processes. These and many other ideas can be brainstormed in the BRIT workshops. There may be occasions when a VUCA disruption occurs that the organization has not experienced in the past nor prepared for during BRIT workshops for brainstorming possible future events. These events that are not usual or normal and are difficult to predict have been referred to as unknown unknowns, or black swan events (Taleb, 2010).

FIGURE 5.2 Generic Business Resilience input/output diagram

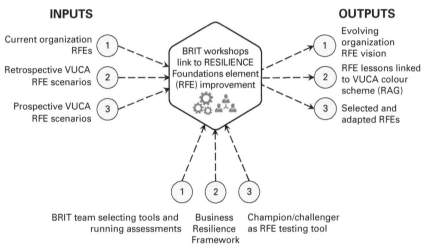

Element 1: Regulatory and Governance

Purpose

The purpose of the Regulatory and Governance element is to clarify industry standards, and to ensure that the organizational policies are aligned to them, using auditable practice from which learning and improvement takes place.

Description

Regulatory procedures and good governance policy alignment and compliance to industry and internal standards are very important organizational components that determine how successfully a resilience foundation can be established in an organization. It is extremely important a resilience foundation governance model is clearly identified. The regulatory procedures and governance set up the expectation of the organization, so that when the organization runs into trouble, it can fall back to clear procedures within the governance model that have been set up to deal effectively with disruption.

Also, it can be seen in many cases when this is not understood, considered and acted upon in the correct manner, it just becomes bureaucracy and can lead to a variety of problems in an organization. The UK government has set out a guide to good practice for corporate governance for central government departments (Cabinet Office, 2011). Also, the UK has a high-quality corporate governance code that sets out good practice for organizations in their governance structure; listed companies must comply with this code (Financial Reporting Council, 2016). It is good practice for organizations to design and build their specific governance structure taking into consideration the good practice guidelines set out by the Cabinet Office and the Financial Reporting Council.

For an organization to be resilient it must have a robust governance structure, which should include a mechanism to be adaptable during VUCA times. The policies that are designed and developed should enable organizational departments to develop risk-informed decision-making and include a detailed integrated risk management system. All stakeholders should work together to design and develop these policies, codes of practice and regulatory structures. The design and development should use evidence, based on science, in their political, social, educational and economic planning and then create an implementation and review process.

A champion/challenger model can be included here where someone acts as champion of the current state while anyone can challenge, but the current state remains unless the challenge is tested and accepted. They compare various strategies and, through experimentation and testing, make decisions to use the best one with the best results. Another alternative or addition to champion/challenger could be the process of 'red teaming' (Hoffman, 2017). Miessler (2021) gives an overview of red teams and blue teams, which are concepts in cyber security that can be adapted here to participate in BRIT workshops. Red teams in BRIT workshops will be focused on predicting and modelling solutions to future possible VUCA disruptions. Blue teams will be monitoring the current VUCA threat levels and responding to these with initiatives to take advantage of them and add value to the organization. This designing, planning, implementation and reviewing process, in BRIT workshops, should involve the organization Business Resilience and initiative teams and any relevant stakeholders, including champion/challengers and red and blue teams to identify and co-create a good, evidence-based, smart solution to respond to the VUCA disruptions as they arise. This will allow these organizations to adapt and evolve their governance model to help the organization to become resilient and to survive during these times, but also to enable them still to grow and make progress at the same time. The governance policies that are developed and evolved should continue to maintain the company's integrity, be transparent and have rigorous procedures to ensure financial, legal and political compliance.

GOVERNANCE REQUIREMENT

It is very interesting to note that plans for responding to a pandemic were set up by the UK government in 2005, but when the World Health Organization (WHO), on 11 March 2020, declared the novel coronavirus (Covid-19) outbreak a global pandemic (Cucinotta and Vanelli, 2020), the UK government could not consider or act upon it because these plans could not be found. The plans included building testing centres, good stockpiling of PPE, travel restrictions, testing people, isolation procedures, etc (Lovett, 2021). Since these plans were not available, the government was not fully prepared for the world pandemic and made many incorrect and late decisions, including not setting up testing procedures quickly enough, low PPE supplies, not implementing travel restrictions early enough, and many more. Could the Covid-19 pandemic have been managed more successfully if the UK government utilized these plans and put in regulations and policies earlier?

In an organization with good governance, the mechanism to ensure these plans were kept in a known location would be in place. These plans would have a system of review and updating, as appropriate, so that they could be used immediately should they be needed. It is also interesting to point out that the World Health Organization (2020) issued some guidance for countries worldwide to be prepared, be ready and respond appropriately to the Covid-19 pandemic.

FIGURE 5.3 Element 1: Regulatory and Governance input/output diagram

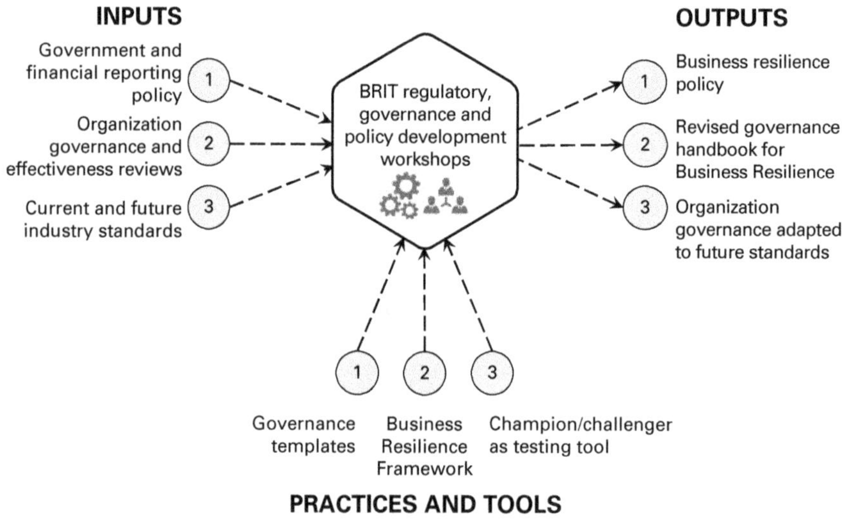

INPUTS

Government and financial reporting policy (1)

Organization governance and effectiveness reviews (2)

Current and future industry standards (3)

BRIT regulatory, governance and policy development workshops

OUTPUTS

(1) Business resilience policy

(2) Revised governance handbook for Business Resilience

(3) Organization governance adapted to future standards

(1) Governance templates

(2) Business Resilience Framework

(3) Champion/challenger as testing tool

PRACTICES AND TOOLS

Element 2: Evolving Vision

Purpose

The purpose of the Evolving Vision element is to have a series of incrementally better organization design ideas where people collaborate within social and technological future environments to deliver benefits for all.

Description

Creating a strategic vision in a world of changing VUCA conditions is a complex activity. A strategic vision involves knowing, understanding and modelling the current 'as is' environment and predicting, modelling and creating a strategic plan for a future 'to be' situation. The problem is that a future successful end state is very difficult to predict in a changing VUCA world. A resilient organization will put in a baseline strategic vision, and they will be prepared to adapt and evolve this vision as required. An incremental approach to the vision will enable the organization to adapt while maintaining direction and progress.

To enable the organization to keep changing and evolving the vision, it must be able to simulate several future scenarios efficiently and effectively. The organization will base this on their current understanding and experience of various past disruptions and thinking of hypothetical future disruptions, then designing hypothetical plans that allow the organization to quickly respond to these disruptions and Rapidly recover from any adverse effects of these disruptions. The organization will put in place a Business Resilience Owner who has the responsibility of creating a BRIT team of people that includes people as required from the organization, from external stakeholders, Resilience Professionals, subject-matter experts such as scientists, economists, politicians, strategists, etc. The BRIT is continuously monitoring the VUCA environment, using the VUCA Storm Scale (see Chapter 7), creating new ideas and ways of working, and simulating various hypothetical disruptions to design plans for the organization to respond. The BRIT can Rapidly deploy a new value initiative team as soon as a new real disruption hits the organization. As the BRIT has been designing plans to various hypothetical scenarios, if one of these takes place, the value initiative team can immediately start deploying this plan. If it is a situation that was not thought of, the BRIT will be in a good position with its experience to work with the appropriate people and, if required, also employ other, more specific subject-matter experts who will be more capable of coming up with ideas to respond to the disruption. The BRIT can create a simple colour scheme to communicate the VUCA score. BRIT workshops can be facilitated by the Progress Master or a professional facilitator. BRIT workshops can follow the facilitated workshop process iceberg methodology outlined in Mann (2021).

The BRIT strategy workshops can employ many existing strategic modelling tools to enable them to create and simulate these hypothetical strategic visions and plans. The Evolving Vision for the organization would be focused on adding value and could include thinking of different business models, pricing models, cost models, economic models, branding, ways of improving customer experience, ways of improving the customer base, improving the supply chain, etc. The BRIT can use various strategic techniques, such as business planning, capability analysis, competitor analysis, financial analysis, scenario planning, SWOT analysis, PESTLE analysis, balanced business scorecards, Porter's Five Forces and Porter's value stream analysis. A particularly useful tool in this context could be the Ansoff matrix (Ansoff, 1957) – also called the product/market expansion grid – which is a tool used by organizations to plan their growth strategies. It is not in the scope of this framework to describe all these approaches. The BRIT workshop facilitator can choose the most effective tool as and when required. There are 75 key management models described in Van den Berg and

Pietersma (2015), which can be used as reference material to choose the appropriate modelling tool. Appendix B also has established tools that can be used for Business Resilience.

EVOLVING VISION

Mullin (2020) discusses the evolving vison of Howell's Nyatex Adhesive and Chemical Co. The company normally makes automotive plastics and adhesives; however, at the start of the Covid-19 outbreak, they evolved their vision to manufacturing hand and surface sanitizer. The company was able to produce large quantities of sanitizers as they already had access to the suppliers and chemicals needed to make sanitizers, they were familiar with the alcohols and glycerine needed, and they had the chemical engineers who had the skillset. As the lockdowns eased, the company decided to stop producing sanitizers.

This demonstrates that by utilizing the Evolving Vision element they were able to evolve their business by producing a product that they had never made before the pandemic. The company prides itself in having an Evolving Vision and adjusting what it produces to meet industry requirements.

FIGURE 5.4 Element 2: Evolving Vision input/output diagram

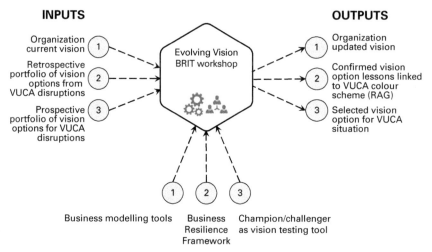

Element 3: Sustained Operations

Purpose

The purpose of the Sustained Operations element is to have adaptable, digital and modular operational capability supporting lean practices with refined tools for the implementation of learning within networks.

Description

A resilient organization needs to improve its business operational efficiency and sustain this even during a VUCA environment and be able to adapt and pivot their operations during disruptions. It has been suggested that resilient organizations use the lean operating model. Lean was first introduced by the Toyota Motor Corporation, and its Principles are described in Womack *et al* (2007). This lean model focuses on creating value for the customer, eliminating waste, using just-in-time production and continuous improvement. The lean model creates efficient, productive, optimized, stable and sustained organizational operations, which leads to improved revenue, profits and both employee and customer satisfaction. A Business Resilience Owner should anticipate variable VUCA conditions, working with the operational Initiative Leader and the Progress Master, so that business operations can be more resilient and can quickly adapt to VUCA disruptions. The organization remains lean and continues to progress. The main point is that when operations, business processes and workflows run smoothly, the organization can make progress and focus on adding more business value, becoming more efficient, improving order fulfilment, customer engagement and satisfaction, and identifying new ways of improving revenues and profit. Most of all, during VUCA disruptions organizations can focus on how to adapt and pivot the operations to sustain efficiency and lean operating.

To cope with the VUCA environment, organizations need to become an adaptive organization (Forrester Research, 2019) and proactively redesign their business during disruptions and constant business and technology changes. Forrester Research (2019) suggests that organizations can change their core business model to be flexible and dynamically adapt and diversify to a value-adding business model that utilizes the range of VUCA business environments. Organizations can exploit any new technologies and adapt the ways of working for the organization and employees to align with the new disruptions. It is interesting to note that the 2020/21 pandemic has accelerated the digital transformation, work-based practices and use of new technologies (Althoff, 2021). Video conferencing technology (such as MS Teams, Zoom, GoTo Meeting, WebEx, etc) has dramatically improved, and the number of users has dramatically increased. This has transformed the way people work and has proved that it is possible to make progress in adverse VUCA conditions. Business models may also have been adapted.

SUSTAINED OPERATIONS USING VIDEO CONFERENCING

There are many useful statistics presented by Keegan (2021) showing the dramatic increase in telecommuting because of the 2020 pandemic. 'The growth rate of video conferencing is going to be substantially affected by the Covid-19 pandemic with 2020 seeing an unprecedented amount more video conferencing usage than ever before. By 2022, it is expected that internet video traffic and worldwide IP video traffic will increase by 4x from 2017; 94% of businesses who use video conferencing state that the company benefits from greater productivity' (Keegan, 2021). Cloud-based services are now heavily used. Radoslav (2021) has also presented some interesting statistics; for example: '81% of all enterprises have a multi-cloud strategy already laid out or in the works. By 2022, it is expected that internet video traffic and worldwide IP video traffic will increase by 4x from 2017' (Radoslav, 2021). Business Resilience managers can organize BRIT workshops to continuously monitor and respond to operational disruptions.

FIGURE 5.5 Element 3: Sustained Operations input/output diagram

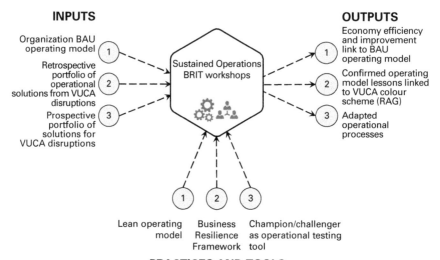

The BRIT team has the remit to secure progress during variable VUCA conditions.

Element 4: Innovation and Risk

Purpose

The purpose of the Innovation and Risk element is to balance the desire for portfolio innovation with resource availability from an enlightened value perspective on technological and financial risk assessment.

Description

A resilient organization constantly needs to be at the leading edge of innovation; however, this must be managed with care, taking into consideration how to improve business value, balanced with technology and risk assessment. When disruptions happen, organizations need to respond sometimes with innovative ideas to take advantage of the VUCA disruption. BRIT innovation workshops can be used to enable innovation and manage both the issues and risks associated with this.

There are many innovation-modelling approaches, and it is not in the scope of this framework to describe all these approaches. This section will refer to some existing approaches and the reader can research further into these or other approaches. The 'diffusion of innovation' is a model that shows the adoption of innovation bell curve (Rogers, 2003). The bell curve shows that there are a few early adopters of innovation, then over time there will be an increase of adopters of the innovation and finally, after a longer period, other people will start using the innovation and they are referred to as laggards. The 'diamond of innovation' (Shenhar and Dvir, 2007) shows four vectors with which to understand innovation: novelty shows how new and different it is from existing ideas; there is a need to understand the complexity of using the innovation; and also, the pace and immediate need of the innovation and the uncertainty of knowing if the innovation is worth the risk. A lot of research has been done with understanding the risk management process in the innovation cycle – for example Bowers and Khorakien (2014), who discuss integrating risk management in the innovation cycle.

When contemplating and developing innovation, good decision-making is required to manage the risk of adopting the innovation. BRIT workshops can be utilized to brainstorm and develop innovative ideas and practices, especially for competitive advantage and also to Rapidly come up with new ideas to respond to

VUCA disruptions. These Lagoon-type workshops could be run as business as usual with incremental innovation involving small changes, requiring little effort and cost, which could generate incremental value to the organization. In some cases, especially when there is a VUCA disruption, radical innovation may need to be created. In these situations, the BRIT workshops need to work in a Rapid style and invest heavily in resources to create successful innovations.

USING INNOVATION TO CREATE A VACCINE

Miller (2020) discusses in an article in the *Financial Times* the development of the mRNA vaccine. During the Covid-19 pandemic, many pharmaceutical companies commissioned vaccine development programmes, but traditional vaccine development methods required long development times to validate their efficacy and carried the side effects from live attenuated viruses, which could take time to onset. The German government rolled out an initiative under which they funded a German company, BioNTech, who decided to pursue a yet-to-be-realized vaccine technology that used mRNA aimed at expediting time to market with an efficacy of over 90 per cent. The initiative was led by experts in their field and partnered with Pfizer to develop, trial and roll out the first ever vaccine for Covid-19 on 9 November 2020. The risks were balanced through partnering between organizations with substantial experience in research and another in clinical trials.

FIGURE 5.6 Element 4: Innovation and Risk input/output diagram

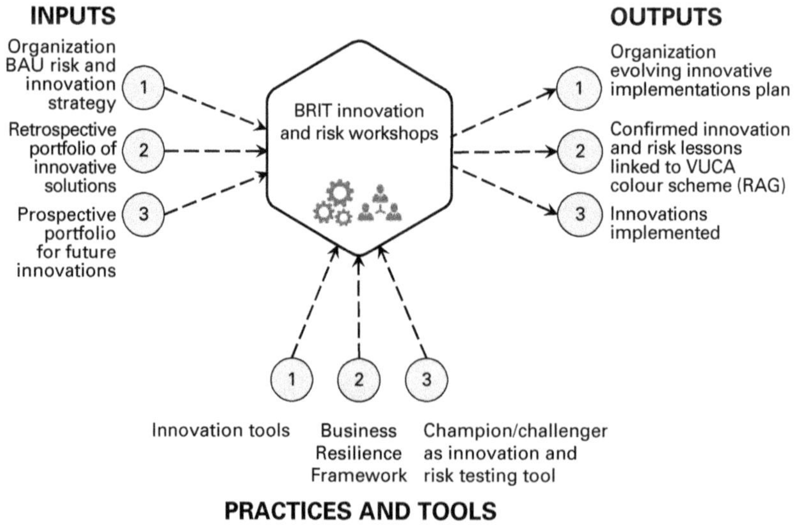

INPUTS

Organization BAU risk and innovation strategy (1)

Retrospective portfolio of (2) innovative solutions

Prospective (3) portfolio for future innovations

BRIT innovation and risk workshops

OUTPUTS

(1) Organization evolving innovative implementations plan

(2) Confirmed innovation and risk lessons linked to VUCA colour scheme (RAG)

(3) Innovations implemented

(1) (2) (3)

Innovation tools   Business Resilience Framework   Champion/challenger as innovation and risk testing tool

PRACTICES AND TOOLS

Considering the risks associated with innovation or VUCA disruptions should follow the organization's usual risk management processes and practices. If experience shows that there are areas of the risk management processes that are not as effective as preferred or needed, this should be updated using a value initiative in the PROGRESS Cycle.

Element 5: Leading and Influencing

Purpose

The purpose of the Leading and Influencing element is to understand and inspire others, creating belief in a future where organization brand values and positioning reflect the aspirations of the network.

Description

Leadership is suggested by Joiner and Josephs (2007) as the master competency needed by an organization. They suggest five levels of mastery to become a leader with agility. This approach to good leadership, along with others, is important for a RESILIENCE Foundation. A resilient organization needs resilient teams of people who are encouraged, inspired and influenced by a resilient and inspiring leader who has authority, respect, confidence, credibility, trust and integrity. When there is good leadership during business as usual and good times, teams will be resilient and cooperative, and willing to change and adapt during difficult, challenging and changing VUCA times. The teams will listen and trust their leadership and cooperate and collaborate with them to steer the organization to make progress and be successful during changing VUCA times. It is useful for good leaders, at all levels of the organization, to understand and apply, appropriately, a Business Resilience Framework as well as the Progress @ Pace 8-4-8 Model.

Good leaders understand their teams, bring out the best in them and promote a healthy organizational culture. They instil in their teams many good qualities that promote effectiveness, productivity, efficiency, sustainability, high performance, good results and job satisfaction. This all leads to an organization that is great and successful. The qualities they promote include: a sense of purpose, energy, passion and commitment; a sense of connection and belonging and alignment to the organization's Evolving Vision, mission and values; a sense of trust so they are empowered to make their own decisions within set boundaries; a sense of courage to be brave and take innovative action despite uncertainty and any fear of blame. These qualities enable the Purposeful Mindset element of the PACE Culture domain. It is not in the scope of this chapter to discuss all the qualities and competencies of a good leader here, but readers are encouraged to read further to discover other qualities and develop these competencies.

There are many ways to develop great leadership and influencing skills – and these competencies can be learned. This section will refer to some existing approaches to achieve this. Pink (2018) suggests that the traditional 'carrot and stick' or reward and punishment do not motivate people and concludes that the real motivating factors include: autonomy, mastery and purpose. Collins (2001) explains how organizations become great and successful. The author describes that these great organizations need leaders with characteristics that include humility, strong willpower and ambition to make the organization successful. They motivate and inspire their teams to increase their standards. Richard Branson, in Gallo (2011), suggests that inspirational leadership is the most important competency for successful organizations. Another leadership approach is the speed of trust, claimed by Covey (2008) as the number one leadership competency. The author states that 'Collaboration is the foundation of the standard of living we enjoy today. Trust is the glue.' Covey (2008) describes a deliberate process to create trust and explains that leaders should see the level of trust existing in the organization and increase this level of trust. They can speak about trust with a language that allows naming the underlying issues involved and talk about them to resolve them and behave in ways that build trust. It is important in an organization that trust is achieved from both leaders and their teams. The leader should trust the team to be transparent, engaged, productive and honestly working to the best of their potential. And, the team should trust the leader to provide the right environment, resources and personal safety.

Agile leaders

The Agile Business Consortium (ABC) has developed nine Principles and some guidance to develop agile culture and leadership (Agile Business Consortium, 2008). These Principles will also promote an agile organizational culture with great leadership and influencing skills. The ABC explains communication, commitment and collaboration are the key to good leadership, and each key can be achieved by following a principle. ABC Principles can be summarized as: lead by example; include deliberate thinking time; improve feedback; provide a purpose and inspire the team to align to the value of the organization and take inspired action; an agile leader should develop good emotional intelligence within themselves and the team; promotes leadership among the team; they have appropriate power and authority; and develop teams based on trust, respect and a productive and optimized working environment.

In RESILIENCE Foundations it is necessary to foster great leadership at all five levels of the organization and in all the Business Resilience Roles. This

---

LEADERSHIP

An IBM survey recently found that, out of 1,700 CEOs in 64 countries, CEOs mostly demanded three leadership traits: the ability to focus on customer needs, the ability to collaborate with colleagues and the ability to inspire (Zenger and Folkman, 2013).

In a business-resilient organization that delivers meals from restaurants, the leaders focused on the customer need to experience restaurant food during the pandemic, to expand their network and to develop 'dark kitchens' to enable new locations to be established without the overheads of having customer seating. A software algorithm to optimize delivery time from the 'dark kitchen' to the customer enabled the food to be fresh on arrival and reduced delivery times. The leaders at all levels of the organization were able to inspire their teams and customers to develop the new 'dark kitchens' so that the business increased during a time when restaurants were unable to welcome customers.

FIGURE 5.7 Element 5: Leading and Influencing input/output diagram

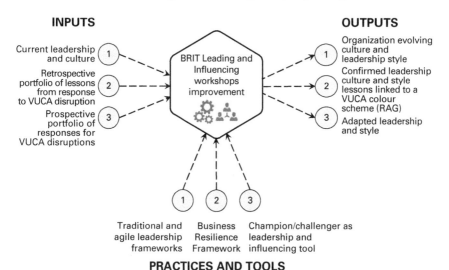

includes the Business Resilience Owner, who will lead Business Resilience for the organization, the Progress Master, who will work closely with the Initiative Leaders, who, in turn, will lead the value initiative teams. Functional leads have an equally important leadership responsibility to ensure all parts of the organization are embracing and developing Business Resilience. Leaders at all levels and across all areas of the organization will influence those working with them, including network partners. These opportunities to influence will also aid the embedding of Business Resilience elements and the PACE Culture cascading to all five levels of the organization.

Element 6: Enterprising Investment

Purpose

The purpose of the Enterprising Investment element is to identify how to attract talent and investment into the organization by building believability in next steps and sharing the benefits of vision realization.

Description

A resilient organization needs an effective and efficient process for attracting investments, talent, resources and assets in business-as-usual conditions so that when VUCA disruptions arise, it can Rapidly deploy new ways to survive and thrive when the business is challenged. They need to create an Evolving Vision and a talent base to dominate the market and have a successful business case creation and execution process. Resilient organizations need to be seen as a successful business with a believable Evolving Vision so that they can attract monetary investment as well as good talent to work in the organization to drive the organization forward.

External investment

Organizations attract external investment by communicating future value in a clear, exciting and trusted way. They clearly state and build convincing and effective business cases that show the return on investment, business spending proposals and a clear communication of continued and future business justification and value in terms of costs, risks and benefits. These business cases are presented in an exciting and trusted way to all the stakeholders, including shareholders, investors and network partners. These business cases should secure funding and ensure management buy-in, especially during VUCA disruptions when this funding is required quickly to deal with immediate challenges. The APMG Better Business Cases qualification (APMG, 2021) is based on the UK government best practice for developing successful business cases, which has been adopted by other major organizations and governments globally, such as the New Zealand government. This external investment builds strong foundations to face any VUCA disruption.

Internal investment

Talent management is a critical business discipline that must be managed effectively to ensure a clear alignment with business values and recruitment of talent that is suitable to achieve Business Resilience. This is so important that Nair (2018) has encouraged chief financial officers (CFOs) to work closely with the chief human resources officers (CHROs) so that they can both understand and respond to the entire business strategy together. It is suggested that human resource leaders can create data and people analytics to identify the talent that is needed which aligns with the business values of the organization. It is suggested by Nair (2018) that this can be done by identifying the top Roles that produce the most business value in an organization. This needs to be done during business as usual regularly, and especially during VUCA events when there is so much disruption. It is vital that organizational values for resilience are aligned to existing talent that is already in place. This is needed to support new investments, and if the organization and the people are not ready, it may result in the investment not achieving the expected business value and return on investment. Nair

---

ENTERPRISING INVESTMENT

A medium-sized consulting organization in the UK has attracted significant overseas investment that will be used to double their revenues by recruiting more consultants. This investment in talented consultants is aimed to increase the customer base by generating new opportunities and deliver more consulting assignments across the organization.

FIGURE 5.8 Element 6: Enterprising Investment input/output diagram

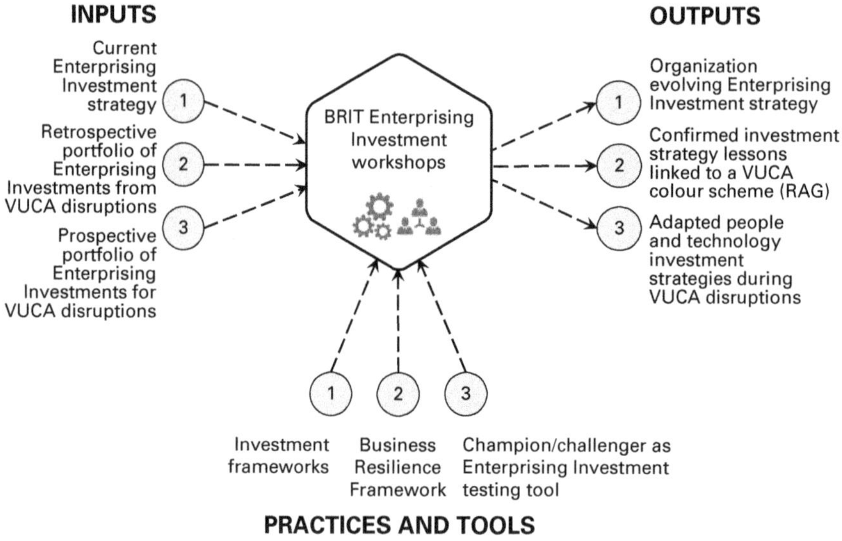

INPUTS

Current Enterprising Investment strategy ①

Retrospective portfolio of Enterprising Investments from VUCA disruptions ②

Prospective portfolio of Enterprising Investments for VUCA disruptions ③

BRIT Enterprising Investment workshops

OUTPUTS

① Organization evolving Enterprising Investment strategy

② Confirmed investment strategy lessons linked to a VUCA colour scheme (RAG)

③ Adapted people and technology investment strategies during VUCA disruptions

① Investment frameworks   ② Business Resilience Framework   ③ Champion/challenger as Enterprising Investment testing tool

PRACTICES AND TOOLS

suggests that data analytics should be carried out both from the human and organizational dimensions. People analytics are carried out to measure different talent variables to see whether they are equipped and their level of readiness, capability, passion, perseverance and resilience can be added to this list. Then the success of a team of people can be mapped to the investment into that business case. For example, it can be said that 'the team created a value of €100 million'. Enterprising Investment can involve investing in rainmakers who can add more value to the organization. Rainmakers are people who have exceptional skills in generating business value, such as leads, sales and profit for the organization.

Element 7: Network Collaboration

Purpose

The purpose of the Network Collaboration element is to engender a spirit of collaboration and partnership, built upon application of an adaptive

TYPES OF NETWORK COLLABORATION

Most importantly, organizations should give prior consideration to why a Network Collaboration strategy could improve Business Resilience and progress. Many models exist. Pop (2017) suggests four main types of business collaboration: alliances, portfolios, innovation networks and ecosystems.

Alliances

A key reason for collaboration to create alliances is to share or combine resources, enter new markets, or jointly develop or deliver products, services, processes or practices to increase competitiveness. Alliances will involve network partners.

Portfolios

Building portfolios involves establishing agreements with independent companies to share knowledge or patents to co-create but separately manage better products and services.

Innovation networks

A third type of collaboration is an innovation network, where firms share R&D goals related to products, services, processes or business models, and organizational wellbeing.

Ecosystems

More advanced forms of collaboration involve ecosystems, designed to create customer value and wellbeing collectively that cannot be achieved by the individual organization.

culture, where facilitation of stakeholders, testing and customer value predominates.

Description

A resilient organization needs good networking collaboration to consolidate its business success. Network Collaboration refers to sharing of ideas and information between different people and organizations to work together for a common interest. All organizations need to work with a spirit of collaboration and partnership with different customers, suppliers, stakeholders, government institutions, legal and financial institutions, business specialist interest groups, educational institutions and many other partners.

Types of collaboration

Pop (2017) discusses four main types of business collaboration: alliances, portfolios, innovation networks and ecosystems (see box on previous page). It is useful to take these types into consideration when trying to achieve effective Network Collaboration. Networking and collaboration lead to many benefits, such as gaining insights into different people, development models and experience, and keeping in touch with leading-edge businesses, technology and economic improvement trends, as well as accessing new business opportunities. Network Collaboration may be at different levels of closeness and coupling. Some organizations may be very important to partner with and are crucial for survival, and some partnerships may be just to keep in touch to share ideas, etc. Some partnerships lead to acquisition and mergers and some businesses may need to merge with other organizations to

---

NETWORK COLLABORATION ACROSS BOUNDARIES OF AN ORGANIZATION

Business Telegraph (2020) notes some interesting points about the Facebook merger with WhatsApp and Instagram, which has led to Facebook gaining many business benefits as a result in 2020: its user base has increased to 3.6 billion; the company's operating margins also managed to grow to 33 per cent; it has achieved $17.74 billion in revenue and $4.9 billion in net income for Q1 2020. Business Telegraph (2020) also notes that Mark Zuckerberg is still worried about the world economic decline due to Covid-19. He is taking a cautionary approach to stay resilient by not reopening certain workplaces during these stormy VUCA times.

---

improve their business success or sometimes just to survive. The PACE Culture supports clear and continuous communication and collaboration of all stakeholders throughout the organization and partner network.

COLLABORATION ACROSS BOUNDARIES

Network Collaboration applies equally within an organization as it does across organizational boundaries with partner organizations. It is often cited that issues in organizations arise when one part of the organization has not collaborated with another to clarify requirements or the impact of changes. Kramer and Pfitzer (2016) suggest that companies must team up effectively with different organizations in a spirit and practice of collaboration so that they can achieve economic success and social progress.

ADDRESSING SUPPLY CHAIN DISRUPTIONS WITH NETWORK COLLABORATION

Accenture has presented the following statistics in terms of supply chain disruptions (Accenture, 2021):

- 94 per cent of Fortune 1000 companies saw supply chain disruptions from Covid-19.

- 75 per cent of companies have had negative or strongly negative impacts on their businesses.

- 55 per cent of companies plan to downgrade their growth outlooks (or have already done so).

With Network Collaboration, suppliers enable organizations to survive by providing products and services despite the difficulties because they were kept informed and on board by their partners through regular communication, status updates and forecasts. This relied on collaboration within the organizations, as well as with their partners, so the internal requirements for what is urgent and what is less urgent can be identified with appropriate supply chain prioritization with the network partners. This enabled the network partners in the supply chain to plan based on firm purchase commitments that were honoured by their partners (as customers).

Organizations that work very closely with their supply chain are very successful. These organizations appear to have an ecosystem of collaborating networked partners.

NETWORKING IN THE SUPPLY CHAIN

One area where Network Collaboration is critical is in supply chain management. During the Covid-19 outbreak, starting in 2020, there was a substantial disruption to the supply chain due to many countries being in lockdown. Accenture (2021) states that future supply chain processes must be made resilient and responsible. They suggest many ideas on how to achieve this. A lot can be learned from how supply chain managers have demonstrated resilience by being flexible, innovative and determined to keep the supply chains operating during the Covid-19 VUCA disruption. Resilient organizations can use the Business Resilience Framework to stay resilient and flexible to improve their supply chain processes and be prepared for future disruptions (see box on previous page).

Kent and Rogers (2021) have presented a very useful comprehensive strategic partnering framework as a guide to a process of forming and maintaining a strategic partnership for national, government, local and any size partnership, from single partner to coalition. This is an example of one of the tools that can be used by the BRIT workshops.

In programme and project management, collaboration is promoted as a critical success factor for a successful outcome. Collaboration within teams accelerates learning, problem-solving and motivation. Enabling Teams through close collaboration with clear and continuous communication among project team members and with the business representative allows

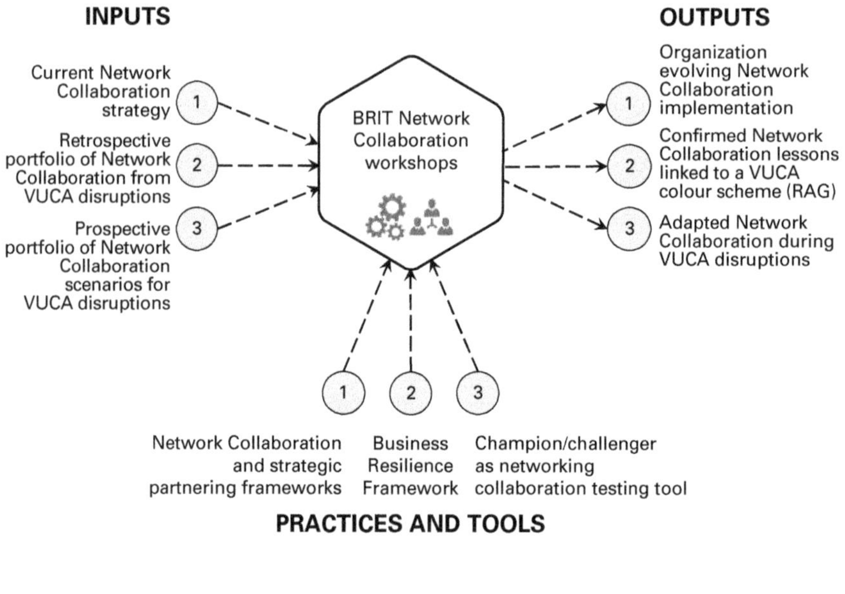

FIGURE 5.9 Element 7: Network Collaboration input/output diagram

for building solutions closer to customer values, requirements and expectations. Initiative team collaboration with the business allows for solutions that are developed that map the business benefits and fit into the Evolving Vision of the organization. Collaboration takes place in many formal and informal ways. Informally, all members can communicate with anyone as and when required. But there are many formal ways, such as reporting, during the different stages of development, during reviews and retrospectives and during various workshops. Collaboration during development allows for measuring the progress of the deliverables, which leads to delivering the project or programme on time. Team members become resilient, because they are motivated and empowered to work at their own productive pace, which allows the teams to work in a sustained way and not get burnt out. In projects sufficient contingency is built in, which allows for changes to the project as and when required. This means that when there is a VUCA disruption, there should be sufficient contingency to allow for the project to still be delivered on time, on budget, on quality and at least the 'must haves' will be delivered.

Element 8: Evolutionary Portfolio

Purpose

The purpose of the Evolutionary Portfolio element is to foster an abiding belief in market focus, digital by design and modularity combined to deliver lifecycle desirability with confidence to pivot due to VUCA conditions.

Description

A resilient and successful organization needs to keep changing, improving and keeping pace with shifting business processes and technology. Additionally, they need to transform themselves into a digital business. If organizations fail to do this, they risk being left behind, losing market share and eventually collapsing. Organizations must provide a digital platform due to changes in customer behaviour where there are customer expectations of engaging easily, quickly and effectively with the organization using digital technology and expecting their requirements to be met digitally. Donahue (2020) notes that 52 per cent of Fortune 500 companies have become obsolete due to their lack of keeping pace with the digital evolution. The UK government has proposed 'digital by default', which means all public services are delivered online or by some other digital means (Cabinet Office, 2010). It is important that all organizations follow this lead and carry out a digital transformation. Businesses are expected to have fast business processes, easy access to information and now more automation of processes.

Balancing the portfolio

A resilient organization needs to manage projects, programmes and portfolios efficiently and effectively so that they can create a prioritized, balanced and optimum portfolio, focusing on the organization's purpose, prioritized values, customer requirements, market focus and impact, and economic success criteria. The initiation of any value initiative in the portfolio must also take into consideration the correct timings, mapping to strategic objectives and good business cases which consider the optimization of risk, costs and benefits. This portfolio must be continuously revisited as the organization adapts, and especially during VUCA disruptions. This can be done by 'red teaming' (Hoffman, 2017), where red teams simulate threats and blue teams consider positive initiatives to take advantage of VUCA disruptions.

Portfolio implementation

Implementation of the portfolio will require BRIT workshops to bring about sustainable operations. There are many approaches to successfully developing, managing and implementing the items in projects, programmes and portfolios efficiently and effectively. It is not in the scope of this chapter to discuss in depth these approaches. Some examples include Managing Successful Programmes (MSP) (AXELOS, 2020) and Portfolio, Programme and Project Offices (P3O) (AXELOS and Roden, 2013).

As organizations become more complex, the organization portfolio becomes bloated and cluttered as more products, services, processes and practices (PSPP) are constantly added. This makes it difficult to scale the organization, make improvements, adapt and pivot during VUCA disruptions.

Modularization

An organization may create, from scratch, new PSPP items to the portfolio without considering work already completed that can be reused. This is very inefficient, ineffective, time-consuming and can create a lot of wasted money, time and resources. PSPPs must be developed in a way they can be reused when needed and can be customized as required. This has been common practice in many industries already, such as, for example, the car manufacturing industry, where parts are created that can be used by various models and products, such as car batteries, gearboxes, brakes, shock absorbers, etc. Similarly, in the electronic industry there are many electronic components that can be used by different products, such as computers with electronic chips, CPU chips, memory chips, etc. This componentization has been introduced successfully to the software products, such as interfaces, data, infrastructure, web services, programming libraries, etc.

It is very important for resilient organizations to use this approach consistently to develop reusable PSPP modules. This is referred to as modularization and it is this that can reduce complexity and allow customization in product development as required.

Modularization is key to Business Resilience and it enables the organization to make Progress @ Pace by building smaller components called modules as a part of complex systems. These modules can work indepen-

---

MODULARITY

The National Health Service 111 web-enabled service is modular by design (myhealthlondon, 2021). It has a text-sensitive intelligent front-end system that analyses the problem put forward by the user and, based on this, it presents a short list of conditions. The user selects a condition and further detailed questions are asked to triage to identify if it is an ambulance emergency, home treatment advice can be given or to contact the family doctor in due course. The modules can be further developed, added to or replaced as required. This has been developed with confidence that the users would use the digital applications for fast triage and reduce the burden on human resources to answer calls.

FIGURE 5.10 Element 8: Evolutionary Portfolio input/output diagram

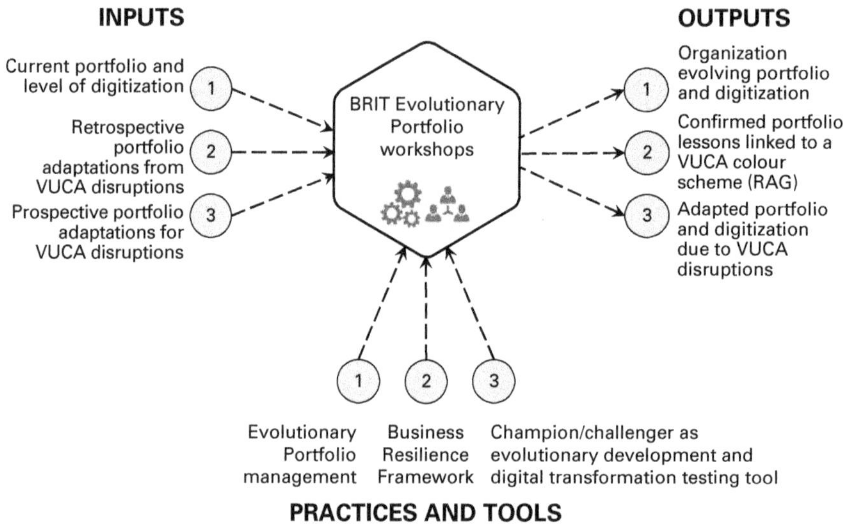

INPUTS

OUTPUTS

Current portfolio and level of digitization (1)

BRIT Evolutionary Portfolio workshops

(1) Organization evolving portfolio and digitization

Retrospective portfolio (2) adaptations from VUCA disruptions

(2) Confirmed portfolio lessons linked to a VUCA colour scheme (RAG)

Prospective portfolio (3) adaptations for VUCA disruptions

(3) Adapted portfolio and digitization due to VUCA disruptions

(1)   (2)   (3)

Evolutionary Portfolio management

Business Resilience Framework

Champion/challenger as evolutionary development and digital transformation testing tool

PRACTICES AND TOOLS

dently and can also function together as a whole. It is important to build the PSPP module strategically so that it is built as a value-adding module right from the start and can be reused and integrated without creating a new system from scratch. When there is a VUCA disruption, the organization can search for existing PSPP modules that match what is required, and these can be utilized and customized to solve the problem without starting from scratch. The searching and matching of modules is enhanced by creating a whole-organization accessible library that categorizes and documents the module details, interface, architecture, and where and how it can be utilized and adapted if required.

In modular design, organizations take resources and rearrange them to add more value. Although there is a higher investment in the initial design and creation of these modular components and the categorized library, the subsequent reuse of these components more than compensates the initial investment: the organization becomes more efficient and effective and reduces a lot of waste. Baldwin and Clark (2000), Lammers (2015) and Twin Cities Business Architecture Forum (2016) explain how business can be designed to be modular. These approaches to modularization can be used if required as a tool in the BRIT workshop.

Roles for the RESILIENCE Foundations domain

RESILIENCE Foundations provide the functional capability to the organization, and the Business Resilience Roles have clear responsibilities to support development of practices and processes that improve it. Responsibilities are:

Business Resilience Owner

- issues confirmation that RESILIENCE Foundations are 'fit for Business Resilience purpose';
- issues warnings where RESILIENCE Foundations cannot enable VUCA conditions to be met in the next PROGRESS Cycles;
- approval of implemented VUCA action plans in the Business Resilience library – eg adaptations that worked;
- approval of prospective VUCA action plans in the Business Resilience library – eg emergency action plans.

Progress Master

- run academy: analyse impact action plans to improve the domains and elements;
- propose innovative prospective action plans for domains and elements to owner;
- maintenance of implemented VUCA action plans in the Business Resilience library;
- maintenance of prospective VUCA action plans in the Business Resilience library.

Initiative Leader

- to test adaptations to the eight RESILIENCE Foundations elements with Resilience Profile;
- to conduct planned improvements using BRIT workshops.

The Business Resilience information about the domain and elements can be stored on internal websites and made available to all levels engaged in building resilience throughout the organization. A good way to actively share such information would be to have a Business Resilience organizational academy, led by the Initiative Leader or Progress Master.

Benefits, costs and risks

Benefits

There are many benefits to implementing the RESILIENCE Foundations domain. The biggest is that the organization has a resilient platform on which to operate. It links with the PACE Culture and enables the PROGRESS Cycles to operate more smoothly.

The benefits of RESILIENCE Foundations include but are not limited to:

- Using governance templates clarifies and improves alignments of initiatives
- Auditable practice enables learning and improvement to take place.
- Evolving Vision is created as incremental designs, facilitating ease of implementation.
- Stakeholder collaboration on social and technological future environments benefits all.
- Lean and modular operational best practices and tools allow plug-and-play sustainability.
- A balanced perspective on resourcing, Innovation and Risk improves portfolio efficiency.
- Facilitate and influence delivery of customer value through inspirational leadership.
- Create belief in the organization brand by aligning to stakeholder and customer values.
- Prioritize the value of talent over the cost of resources to create an enterprising workplace.
- Build a spirit of partnership through Network Collaboration.
- Realize the opportunity to pivot the portfolio through modular variant designs.
- The portfolio is purposefully designed for digital interaction.

Costs

The costs of implementing the RESILIENCE Foundations elements will depend on the baseline that is present in the organization prior to implementation and the choice of implementation approach (see Chapter 8) for the organization. Whichever approach is chosen and whatever the baseline position, the costs should always be balanced by the benefits of becoming more resilient. When planning the implementation, the choice of approach could be influenced by the level of adapting required and resources available. The main costs are likely to be the individuals to implement the RESILIENCE Foundations value initiatives.

Risks

The main risks are in common with introducing anything new. See the risks of implementing the Roles set out in Chapter 4. In addition:

- Staff may resist implementing the plans or new procedures that are identified for RESILIENCE Foundations, so reducing the benefits and requiring further explanations and management of the transition.
- Staff may not share the Evolving Vision for Business Resilience and so will need further explanations and sharing the purpose.
- Staff may not have the experience or expertise to identify how to implement one or more elements of the RESILIENCE Foundations domain, so requiring Resilience Professionals to be engaged.

QUESTIONS TO THINK ABOUT

- What are the types of governance templates that can assist in the alignment of initiatives to promote Business Resilience?
- What are the important leadership qualities needed by a resilient organization and how do these leaders work with the organization, effectively leading, inspiring and influencing the people in the organization to remain successful, resilient and motivated during extreme VUCA disruption?
- How does a resilient organization manage their modular portfolios purposely and pivot the portfolio as required during VUCA disruptions?

Summary

This chapter has explained the RESILIENCE Foundations infinity loop elements of the Business Resilience Framework. For an organization to be successful, these elements should form the foundations of their Business Resilience strategy. Each element has a corresponding input/output diagram that shows the organization's current situation in relation to each of the elements.

A portfolio of scenarios is stored in an organization library that details how each element was considered during various VUCA disruptions in the past. The library should also hold a portfolio of possible future VUCA disruption scenarios that have not happened yet, with ideas of how the organization can respond to those that may be predicted.

BRIT workshops provide an opportunity to input ideas and tools shown in the input/output diagrams. This enables the organization to develop Business Resilience and respond to new VUCA disruptions. The output of these BRIT workshops results in the organization successfully responding to various VUCA disruptions, at the pace and urgency needed depending on the severity of the VUCA event. All responses are then stored in the library of past responses to VUCA events. It is expected that the Business Resilience Owner will prioritize the initiatives, enabling the organization to optimize resilience from improvements to each of the elements. Organizations will implement initiatives according to resource availability and thereby deliver progress at a pace that is appropriate.

Putting in place the RESILIENCE Foundations enables the PACE Culture and PROGRESS Cycles to be built on these foundations, which results in an organization that enjoys Business Resilience and making progress in all conditions.

References

Accenture (2021) *Repurposed Supply Chains of the Future Must Have Resilience and Responsibility at Their Heart*, www.accenture.com/gb-en/insights/consulting/coronavirus-supply-chain-disruption (archived at https://perma.cc/4BZL-YWYL)

Agile Business Consortium (2008) *Culture and Leadership: The nine Principles of agile leadership*, www.agilebusiness.org/page/Resource_paper_ninePrinciples (archived at https://perma.cc/HWG2-BYKH)

Agile Business Consortium (2017) *Agile Project Management Handbook*, v2, Agile Business Consortium, UK

Althoff, J (2021) The way forward with digital transformation accelerated by a pandemic, *Harvard Business Review*, 11 January, hbr.org/sponsored/2021/01/the-way-forward-with-digital-transformation-accelerated-by-a-pandemic (archived at https://perma.cc/EL8N-U4KZ)

Ansoff, I (1957) Strategies for diversification, *Harvard Business Review*, Harvard University Graduate School of Business Administration, Boston

APMG (2021) *Better Business Cases*, APMG International, 19 October, apmg-international.com/product/better-business-cases (archived at https://perma.cc/AT5E-556N)

AXELOS (2020) *Managing Successful Programmes*, The Stationery Office, London

AXELOS and Roden, E (2013) *Portfolio, Programme, and Project Offices (P3O)*, The Stationery Office, London

Baldwin, C and Clark, K (2000) *Design Rules: The power of modularity*, MIT Press, Boston

Bowers, J and Khorakien, A (2014) Integrating risk management in the innovation project, *European Journal of Innovation Management*, January

Business Telegraph (2020), Facebook now has a combined monthly user base of over 3 billion, *The Tech Portal: Business Telegraph*, 2 May, www.businesstelegraph.co.uk/facebook-now-has-a-combined-monthly-user-base-of-over-3-billion-the-tech-portal (archived at https://perma.cc/Y568-EJZU)

Cabinet Office (2010) *Digital by Default Proposed for Government Services*, GOV.UK, 23 November, www.gov.uk/government/news/digital-by-default-proposed-for-government-services (archived at https://perma.cc/UHD2-T6CD)

Cabinet Office (2011) *Corporate Governance Code for Central Government Departments: Code of practice*, HM Treasury, 19 July, www.gov.uk/government/publications/corporate-governance-code-for-central-government-departments (archived at https://perma.cc/DDU8-M52Y)

Collins, J (2001) *Good to Great: Why some companies make the leap... and others don't*, Harper Business, New York

Covey, SR (2008) *Speed of Trust: The one thing that changes everything*, Simon & Schuster, New York

Cucinotta, D and Vanelli, M (2020) WHO declares Covid 19 a pandemic, *Acta Biomed*, pubmed.ncbi.nlm.nih.gov/32191675 (archived at https://perma.cc/226K-M7NJ)

Donahue, C (2020) How to keep pace with digital transformation and avoid becoming obsolete, *Forbes*, 12 February, www.forbes.com/sites/theyec/2020/02/12/how-to-keep-pace-with-digital-transformation-and-avoid-becoming-obsolete/?sh=6cd905744861 (archived at https://perma.cc/5S62-7Z59)

Financial Reporting Council (2016) *Corporate Governance and Stewardship*, Financial Reporting Council, www.frc.org.uk/directors/corporate-governance-and-stewardship (archived at https://perma.cc/43F5-VK39)

Forrester Research (2019) *The Adaptive Enterprise*, Forrester, go.forrester.com/adaptive-enterprise (archived at https://perma.cc/7UPG-PE99)

Gallo, C (2011) Richard Branson: The one skill leaders need to learn, *Forbes*, 29 July, www.forbes.com/sites/carminegallo/2011/06/29/richard-branson-the-one-skill-leaders-need-to-learn/?sh=1729f4327d6e (archived at https://perma.cc/X44X-39GW)

Hoffman, BG (2017) *Red Teaming: Transform your business by thinking like the enemy*, Piatkus, London

Joiner, B and Josephs, S (2007) *Leadership Agility: Five levels of mastery for anticipating and initiating change*, Wiley & Sons, Hoboken, NJ

Keegan, L (2021) Video conferencing statistics: All you need to know!, *SkillScouter*, 4 August, skillscouter.com/video-conferencing-statistics (archived at https://perma.cc/36HQ-UJYH)

Kent, L and Rogers, M (2021) *Strategic Partnering: A guide to the conceptual framework*, Disease Control and Prevention, www.cdc.gov/dhdsp/programs/spha/roadmap/docs/Strategic%20Partnering%20Conceptual%20Framework_ac.pdf (archived at https://perma.cc/9V9D-EGMH)

Kramer M and Pfitzer M (2016) The ecosystem of shared value, *Harvard Business Review*, October, hbr.org/2016/10/the-ecosystem-of-shared-value (archived at https://perma.cc/6T5J-S35S)

Lammers, T (2015) Modular product design: Reducing complexity, increasing efficacy, *Performance Journal*, 7 (1), pp 56–63

Lovett, S (2021) Revealed: Britain's lost blueprint for fighting a coronavirus outbreak – written 16 years ago, *Independent*, 4 August, www.independent.co.uk/news/health/Covid-plan-uk-government-sars-coronavirus-b1893726.html?utm_source=pocket-newtab-global-en-GB (archived at https://perma.cc/BD6E-CDJZ)

Mann, T (2021) *Facilitation: Develop your expertise*, RP Publishing House, UK

Miessler, D (2021) *The Difference Between Red, Blue, and Purple Teams*, 12 August, danielmiessler.com/study/red-blue-purple-teams (archived at https://perma.cc/3QGQ-KAV9)

Miller, J (2020) Inside the hunt for a Covid 19 vaccine: How BioNTech made the breakthrough, *Financial Times*, 13 November, www.ft.com/content/c4ca8496-a215-44b1-a7eb-f88568fc9de9 (archived at https://perma.cc/E8VG-64VB)

Mullin, A (2020) Howell Chemical Company switches to producing hand sanitizer, *MLive*, 9 June, www.mlive.com/news/ann-arbor/2020/06/howell-chemical-company-switches-to-producing-hand-sanitizer.html (archived at https://perma.cc/2G6S-2NQ9)

myhealthlondon (2021) *NHS 111*, NHS, myhealth.london.nhs.uk/nhs-111 (archived at https://perma.cc/ZD8U-EGCH)

Nair, L (2018) Talent management as a business discipline: A conversation with Unilever, *McKinsey & Company*, 9 March, www.mckinsey.com/business-functions/ organization/our-insights/talent-management-as-a-business-discipline-a-conversation-with-unilever-chro-leena-nair (archived at https://perma.cc/ 8JK8-3ESP)

Pink, DH (2018) *Drive: The surprising truth about what motivates us*, Canongate Books, London

Pop, O-M (2017) The four main types of business collaboration, *HYPE*, 18 July, blog.hypeinnovation.com/the-four-main-types-of-collaboration (archived at https://perma.cc/P2JT-S2RL)

Radoslav, C (2021) 37 heavenly cloud computing statistics for 2021, *techjury*, 2 October, techjury.net/blog/cloud-computing-statistics (archived at https://perma. cc/BLN2-C3YR)

Rogers, EM (2003) *Diffusion of Innovations*, 5th edn, Free Press, London

Shenhar, AJ and Dvir, D (2007) *Reinventing Project Management*, Harvard Business School Publishing, Boston

Taleb, NN (2010) *The Black Swan: The impact of the highly improbable*, Penguin Books, London

Twin Cities Business Architecture Forum (2016) *Modular Business Design*, tcbaf. org/wp-content/uploads/2016/10/TCBAF-Modular-Business-Design-FINAL.pdf (archived at https://perma.cc/AE9L-RXGP)

Van den Berg, G and Pietersma, P (2015) *Key Management Models: The 75+ models every manager needs to know*, Pearson Education Limited, London

Womack, JP *et al* (2007) *The Machine That Changed the World*, Simon & Schuster, London

World Health Organization (2020) *Critical Preparedness, Readiness, and Response Actions for Covid 19: Interim guidance*, World Health Organization, 7 March, apps.who.int/iris/handle/10665/331422 (archived at https://perma.cc/F2VP-PVQ6)

Zenger, J and Folkman, J (2013) What inspiring leaders do, *Harvard Business Review*, 20 June, hbr.org/2013/06/what-inspiring-leaders-do (archived at https:// perma.cc/RKA7-BJ5K)

06

A PACE Culture

Purpose

The purpose of the PACE Culture (Figure 6.1) is to enable the organization to optimize the capability of RESILIENCE Foundations and the PROGRESS Cycle in the development and delivery of processes, practices, products and services, required by the organization and its customers, in all conditions.

Using the PACE Culture will enhance the organization's functional capacity and development. PACE elements combine to create positive and collaborative working, adapting practices and processes so that customer value is optimized, whatever the economic or social conditions. This builds organizational strength, improves reputation and competitive advantage.

Introduction

The PACE Culture creates an environment to bring the best out of organizational teams, at every level; it is a practical way to ensure we drive best customer value in varying (VUCA) conditions, by opening minds to future opportunities and possibilities, adopting best practice skills, investing in appropriate tools and empowering our people to succeed.

Four PACE elements

The PACE domain comprises four people-centred elements, which are the Purposeful Mindset, application of tools, Capability and Skills plus Elevated Energy. These will improve application of RESILIENCE Foundations and

FIGURE 6.1 PACE Culture

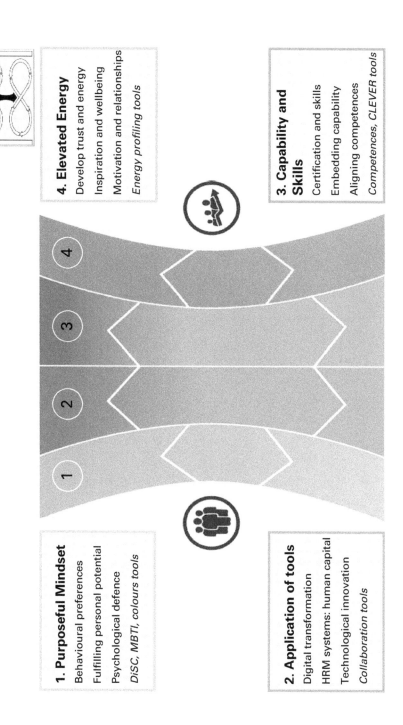

1. Purposeful Mindset
Behavioural preferences
Fulfilling personal potential
Psychological defence
DiSC, MBTI, colours tools

2. Application of tools
Digital transformation
HRM systems: human capital
Technological innovation
Collaboration tools

4. Elevated Energy
Develop trust and energy
Inspiration and wellbeing
Motivation and relationships
Energy profiling tools

3. Capability and Skills
Certification and skills
Embedding capability
Aligning competences
Competences, CLEVER tools

FIGURE 6.2 Progress @ Pace 8-4-8 Resilience Model

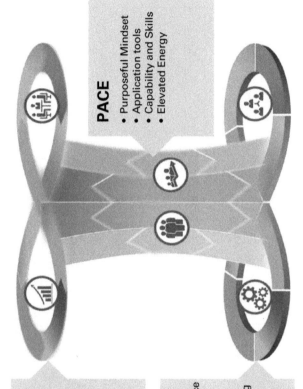

PACE
- Purposeful Mindset
- Application tools
- Capability and Skills
- Elevated Energy

PROGRESS
- Progress Definition
- Recognize Challenge
- Opportunity Assessment
- Good Alignment
- Rapids/lagoons
- Enabled teams
- Selection and Testing
- Success and Learning

RESILIENCE
- Regulatory and Governance
- Evolving Vision
- Sustainable operations
- Innovation and Risk
- Leadership and influencing
- Enterprising Investment
- Network Collaboration
- Evolutionary Portfolio

delivery of value initiatives in the PROGRESS Cycle. Individually, these four PACE elements form drivers, each contributing to the development of the organization culture that is required for Business Resilience throughout all five levels of the organization (individuals, teams, departments or divisions, the organization and its wider network partners). Importantly, the PACE Culture encourages a bilateral flow of understanding and learning between the RESILIENCE Foundations and PROGRESS Cycle, with teams motivated to make progress.

People drive organizations, but leaders inspire them. Business Resilience leaders need to inspire teams to provide the energy within an organization, engaging customers and providing value through its products, services and solutions. To sustain progress, organizations need even more energy to innovate and improve, while adapting to unpredictable and ever-changing conditions.

PACE – A culture for Resilience Professionals

The PACE elements shape an organization's culture. The culture permeates the entire Business Resilience Framework; it provides a highway connection between the foundations and progress domains shown in the Progress @ Pace Model (Figure 6.2), driving Business Resilience and progress as envisaged in the Evolving Vision of the organization and its partner network. PACE Culture is embedded in the people, and best processes and practices are provided to support them. The way PACE is implemented will characterize the organization, and the capacity of its people to obtain value from suppliers, develop solutions and deliver value to customers will critically depend on the bi-directional flow of activities, shared under varying VUCA (volatile, uncertain, complex, ambiguous) conditions. The PACE Culture should be implemented at all five levels of the organization to drive the realization of Business Resilience.

Investment in PACE

The PACE Culture encourages organizations to invest in behavioural, practical and innovative approaches, combining people skills, technological prowess, capabilities and team energy. As organizations move through cycles of VUCA conditions, the PACE Culture continues to build critical capability and confidence – to enable progress at pace to be achieved, maintained or improved and realize the organizational vision.

CONFIRMATION BIAS AND PACE

A challenge for all Resilience Professionals is to skilfully bring lifetime experiences and insights into present circumstances and conditions, to progress opportunities and overcome obstacles to success. A major obstacle to progress is unquestionably believing planning assumptions, selectively listening to or acting on information to support a confirmation bias, or simply dismissing learning opportunities from retrospectives with 'I knew that would happen'. The Resilience Professional should encourage BRIT teams to seek data from diverse sources prior to decision-making. This observation is discussed in relation to managing complexity (Green, 2017); and in a resilient organization, bias is actively addressed in each domain. Within the PACE Culture, consideration of bias is actively encouraged within each of the PACE elements.

PACE Culture emerges from the integration of individually valuable elements in an organizational context. Recognition of the importance of a mindset, skill-set and toolset is well known to management consultants, and research into organizational energy has developed a good following. PACE provides confidence across the five levels of organization that by investing in the four elements, it is possible to build a community of people committed to customer value and organizational success that contributes to Business Resilience.

Individual PACE elements can be implemented or improved on a modular basis, particularly where a Resilience Profile gap has been identified. While such activity will boost performance of an individual element, it is the combined impact of the four elements that will lead to a significant improvement in progress outcomes or Business Resilience because they work synergistically to provide more resilience when they interact than each one alone. For example, the Purposeful Mindset is enhanced by applying the right tools having the skills to use them which, in turn, elevates energy.

In this way the PACE domain provides the oxygen for inspirational leadership to succeed, learning from experience and embedding adaptive business behaviour across the organization.

The focus of PACE Culture on achieving the evolutionary vision is maintained by cross-checking Business Resilience Principles and involving Resilience Professional Roles. This ensures the right things are being done, by the right people, in the right priority. Resilience Professionals enhance PACE Culture by bringing insight from their understanding of the framework, delivering a fresh approach to Business Resilience implementation.

Importantly, there is no need for organizations to discard what is already known, hard-won and that evidence shows is working. PACE Culture offers organizations a distinctive dynamic culture in which teams develop a

Purposeful Mindset and the capability to improve both Business Resilience and progress simultaneously. As VUCA conditions change, teams adapt development and/or delivery, pivoting provision of portfolio products and services to meet the challenges. Acting on learning is a defining characteristic of the PACE Culture, resulting from the Elevated Energy within teams.

PACE Culture to drive sustained delivery

All PACE elements are needed to gain the most from building a PACE organization culture; it is expected that elements interweave to strengthen and improve each other, within the availability of the wider Business Resilience Framework, as demonstrated in Figure 6.3.

FIGURE 6.3   PACE Culture elements work together to deliver the culture for Business Resilience

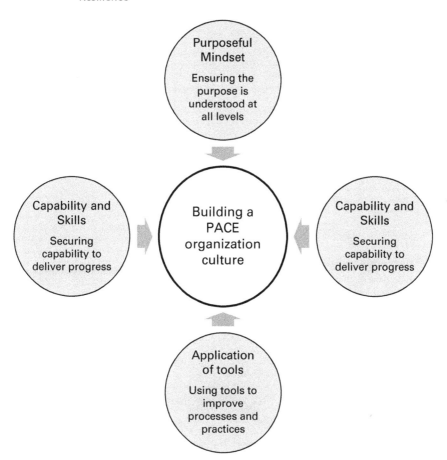

PACE is an evolving culture, increasing organizational capacity for dynamic drive of new ideas throughout the organization and facilitating the responsiveness that is key to VUCA environments.

PACE Culture in the Business Resilience Framework

PACE Culture is positioned at the centre of the Business Resilience Framework, as shown in Figure 6.4, because it provides the drive needed to bring other domains to life; in this sense it acts like the sun in the solar system. The PACE Culture enables professionals to identify better ways of achieving sustained progress in a changing environment, whatever the VUCA Storm Scale.

Integral to the Business Resilience Framework, investing in the four dimensions of PACE enables organizations to take advantage of challenging situations, delivering progress and improving customer value while supporting the creation of an Adaptive Enterprise. PACE Culture forms the basis of competitive advantage, linking RESILIENCE Foundations to the PROGRESS Cycle.

The PACE Culture continually strengthens RESILIENCE Foundations and the PROGRESS Cycle, while supporting the Business Resilience Principles and Roles (Figure 6.4). PACE contains the driving elements within this framework. Business Resilience is a good way of thinking about sustained progress, but its real value is in influencing responsive behaviour and delivering value in VUCA disruptions, at any point in a PROGRESS Cycle, to deliver products or services.

FIGURE 6.4 Business Resilience Framework

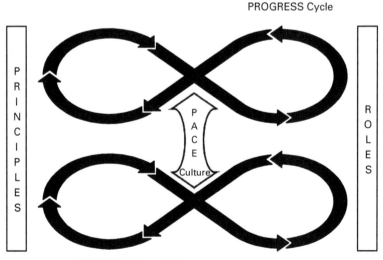

PROGRESS Cycle

RESILIENCE Foundations

In order for the Business Resilience Framework to be most effective, the organization must develop a satisfactory level of PACE Culture. To achieve a satisfactory level of PACE Culture, it is critical to build on prior experience and practice, with teams and partners honestly evaluating what is working and what must be adapted. A focus on next-level improvements is enhanced by the Elevated Energy of teams, resulting in skilful adaptation (supported by capability and tools); these improvements enhance or supplant PACE domain elements, best practices or tools. In this way the PACE Culture is connecting directly to the PROGRESS Cycle within the framework.

In adopting and adapting the PACE Culture, organizations collaborate with colleagues, customers, partners and professionals to harness the strength that comes from all five domains within the Business Resilience Framework. The PACE domain delivers a culture of team spirit, supporting continuing professional development of people in each domain of the framework.

Four elements of the PACE Culture domain

The development of a dynamic organization culture relies on investment in four PACE elements that are implemented through best practices with use of supporting tools, as appropriate. In order to attain a satisfactory insight into PACE Culture, approaches and examples of best practices that make a difference when innovating and improving organizational behaviour are set out within each PACE element.

These approaches and examples provide enhanced understanding of how customer value can be improved within the organization. The objective of enabling a PACE Culture to develop across the organization is to both increase Business Resilience and the capacity to make Progress @ Pace.

In considering each PACE element, indicative best practices and supporting tools are shown to illustrate how the element can be developed in the context of achieving a satisfactory culture to optimize the opportunity provided by RESILIENCE Foundations and drive progress.

Element 1: Purposeful Mindset

Understanding a Purposeful Mindset

The Purposeful Mindset element (Figure 6.5) utilizes the concept of a growth mindset that is adapted to include alignment with the organization's vision,

FIGURE 6.5 Purposeful Mindset

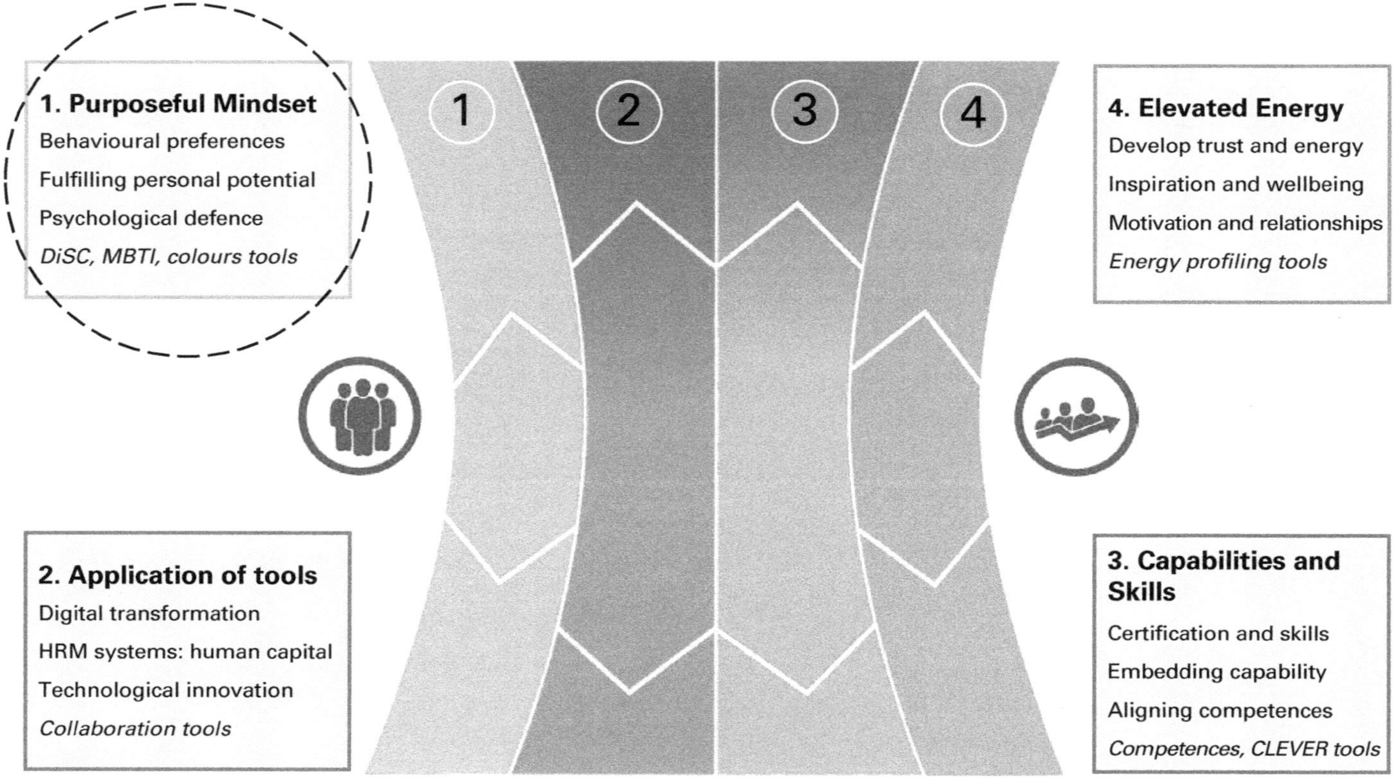

4. Elevated Energy
Develop trust and energy
Inspiration and wellbeing
Motivation and relationships
Energy profiling tools

3. Capabilities and Skills
Certification and skills
Embedding capability
Aligning competences
Competences, CLEVER tools

1. Purposeful Mindset
Behavioural preferences
Fulfilling personal potential
Psychological defence
DiSC, MBTI, colours tools

2. Application of tools
Digital transformation
HRM systems: human capital
Technological innovation
Collaboration tools

forming a Purposeful Mindset. This element is key to developing a PACE Culture. PACE Culture uses Purposeful Mindset to drive adaptability and innovation, enabling organizations to embrace VUCA disruptions.

Carol Dweck (2008) identified a growth mindset as one that believes talents are developed (through hard work, good strategies and input from others). More is achieved with a growth mindset than with a fixed mindset (belief that talents are innate gifts) because these people worry less about looking smart and they put more effort into learning.

When entire organizations embrace a growth mindset, staff report feeling far more empowered and committed, with greater support for collaboration and innovation. In turn, more Business Resilience is realized. In contrast, people in primarily fixed-mindset companies report more of only one thing: cheating and deception among staff, presumably to gain an advantage of one sort or another.

In Business Resilience, the organization shares its emerging vision (an element of RESILIENCE Foundations) with stakeholders and teams engaged in development and delivery at all levels, to ensure they share an insight into a possible future for the organization. And within a PACE Culture, organizations engage and encourage their people to see themselves making a difference within this future environment. Purposeful Mindset is the first PACE element.

It has been recognized for many years that mindset is a critical factor in the success of individuals, teams and organizations. When great hurdles have been overcome, Purposeful Mindset of the individual or team will frequently be quoted as making the difference in many great sporting achievements, research breakthroughs and military victories. This mentality applies to all organizations, where individuals and teams aspire to reach next-level achievement. Believability in Progress @ Pace is a vital element of PACE Culture; without it, organizations will be unable to keep their best people or they will simply not fulfil their potential, so neither progress nor Business Resilience will be delivered. In Business Resilience, a Purposeful Mindset helps individuals maintain focus on customer value, enthusing collaborative working in a spirit of 'one dream, one team' to achieve progress goals, succeed in delivering value and in turn embed the PACE Culture.

Approaches to developing a Purposeful Mindset

Organizations need to consider how best to invest in developing Purposeful Mindsets. The journey of most professionals will include negative feelings following untoward outcomes in the past; but what enabled or helped them to recover, re-evaluate and retry? In her book *Mindset: The new psychology of success* Carol Dweck (2008) argues that a growth mindset – the belief that abilities can be developed and the desire to embrace learning, challenges and setbacks as sources of growth – creates the drive and resilience that influence success in virtually every area of life.

Organizations can enhance Purposeful Mindset by creating opportunities for individuals or teams to strengthen self-belief through purposeful experiences, insights into purposeful achievements of others or exploring best practice learning programmes. An example would be that an initiative team finds a better way to achieve an outcome, and others can learn from this in a 'lunch and learn' session or utilize a specialist training programme. The combination of these approaches encourages early realization of the Purposeful Mindset element of PACE Culture, whatever the organizational level or industry.

ILLUSTRATING THE JOURNEY TO THE NEXT LEVEL

Working from the gaps between the current and target Resilience Profiles (Chapter 10) for Purposeful Mindset, the Business Resilience Owner will be responsible for defining value initiatives to develop a Purposeful Mindset. This investment will also reflect the Evolving Vision in RESILIENCE Foundations and the Progress Definition within the PROGRESS Cycle.

William Marston's work as an American psychologist in the 1920s underpins the DiSC model; his tool classifies people's behaviour into four types (dominance, influence, steadiness and conscientiousness) by looking at their preferences on two scales linked to standardized data (Marston, 1928). These scales are:

- task versus people;
- fast-paced versus moderate-paced.

In developing a programme, diversity of thinking is supported by a recognition of these four preferences, as each adds a different dimension to Purposeful Mindset.

It is vitally important for the Business Resilience Owner to recognize when investing in Purposeful Mindsets that individual mindsets vary all the time and people may fall back into a fixed mindset at times of stress and challenge. Internal politics also play a significant role in Purposeful Mindset behaviour, such as sharing of information and ideas, collaborating, innovating, seeking feedback, or admitting errors, and should be determinedly encouraged. Behavioural types must be taken into consideration when implementing and monitoring development programmes.

A RULES-BOUND ORGANIZATION

In a rules-bound organization, individuals or teams were willing to complete repeated tasks, but had little inclination towards the challenge of Innovation and Risk posed by new work. The organization wanted to improve this situation by investing in Purposeful Mindset, but recognized that staff whose preference was for steadiness and conscientiousness might find this more challenging.

A programme was developed encouraging staff in the organization, stakeholders and partners to participate in work-related challenges and learning opportunities. This enabled participants to recognize that, if there is too much challenge, it is not always necessary to succeed alone – collaboration can be both more rewarding and effective, and can include different personality types and behavioural preferences. This practical approach led to greater individual awareness, development and growth of a Purposeful Mindset across established and loyal members of the workforce.

Benefits were captured in the retrospectives (review of the process and team interactions): learning points included that fear of failure reinforces a fixed mindset, whereas learning from failure reinforces a growth mindset, which, combined with the vision, leads to participation in innovation and purposeful action.

Within the development programme, a Progress Backlog was used to capture 'ideas for improvement', to encourage sharing and engage in developing proposals. This supported a more purposeful approach to iterative development and a willingness to be responsive to test data or feedback, enabling the PROGRESS Cycle to deliver improved outcomes at pace.

Martin Seligman from the University of Pennsylvania believes anyone can learn how to become more optimistic, improving their emotional health (Seligman, 1998). His ideas are not only compelling, but, as importantly, there are practical models and tools that enable individuals and organization to improve Purposeful Mindsets.

Purposeful Mindset is built upon behavioural preferences, realizing potential and self-belief – positive individual traits that, when combined in an organizational setting, build positive experiences and outcomes. This situation enables customer value to be delivered, with positive feedback reinforcing a Purposeful Mindset towards the Evolving Vision of sustained progress at pace.

In developing the ABCDE (adversity, belief, consequence, disputation, energization) and PERMA (positive emotion, engagement, relationships, meaning, achievement) models, Seligman embraces the concepts of learned optimism and self-belief that assist individuals and teams as they develop Purposeful Mindsets and resilience.

Best practices and supporting tools

There are many best practices that can be used in the development of a Purposeful Mindset (Figure 6.5). The best practices and supporting tools indicate how to make progress in developing a Purposeful Mindset in organizational settings. Other practices and tools may also be used, as each organization will identify the best tools that are most appropriate to their industry or situation.

Purposeful Mindset could be developed by linking best practices and tools, as shown in Table 6.1.

The tools listed below may be of assistance in developing a Purposeful Mindset, as although these are not directly linked to Business Resilience, they are relevant to understanding individuals and their potential contribution:

- personality types – MBTI (Myers & Briggs Foundation, 2021);
- behavioural preferences – DiSC (Discprofile.com, 2021);
- fulfilling personal potential – quiz (Study.com, 2016);
- psychological defence – ABCDE model (Seligman, 1998).

TABLE 6.1 Linking best practices and tools to develop a Purposeful Mindset

PACE element or practice	Purposeful Mindset	Behavioural preferences	Personal or team potential	Psychological defence
Goal or ambition for PACE element	Contribute to the Progress Definition	Work interactively with others on ideas, testing and feedback	Embracing diversity of thinking and collaborate	Face challenges bravely as individuals or team
Insights colour discovery tool	Red/blue	Blue/green	Green/yellow	Yellow/blue
Mindset tools	Growth mindset	DiSC	MBTI	ABCDE model

Many organizations use or have used these indicators or similar tools to help people understand themselves, their relative strengths and weaknesses, and how to work well with others. As a Resilience Professional, it is worth recognizing that individuals and teams can 'remodel their minds', leading to higher organizational performance. Five key points are:

- Know your own mind, relative strengths and weaknesses, and own your attitude.

- Be open-minded to the value that other personality types bring to the organization.

- Recognize the value of learning in pursuit of challenges and goals.

- Persistence is as important as intelligence, and opportunities will emerge from innovation.

- Resilience Professionals should recognize that if a challenge is 'not yet' overcome, persistence, learning and testing will lead to improvement and a better outcome.

FIGURE 6.6 Purposeful Mindset tools and links to RESILIENCE Foundations and PROGRESS Cycle

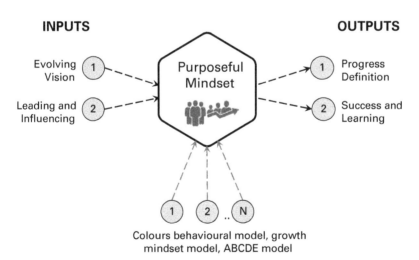

Element 2: Application of tools

FIGURE 6.7 Application of tools

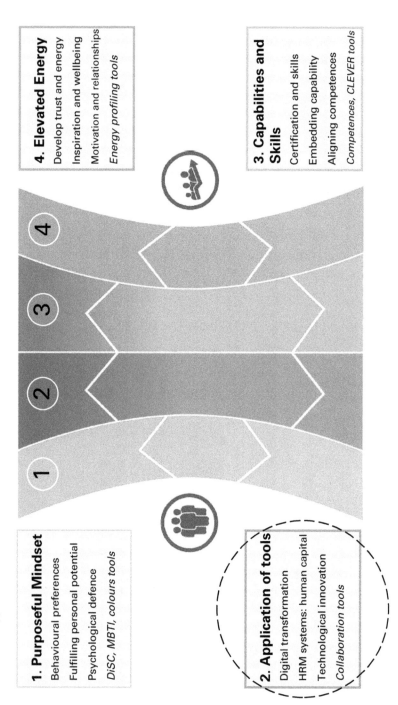

4. Elevated Energy
Develop trust and energy
Inspiration and wellbeing
Motivation and relationships
Energy profiling tools

3. Capabilities and Skills
Certification and skills
Embedding capability
Aligning competences
Competences, CLEVER tools

1. Purposeful Mindset
Behavioural preferences
Fulfilling personal potential
Psychological defence
DiSC, MBTI, colours tools

2. Application of tools
Digital transformation
HRM systems: human capital
Technological innovation
Collaboration tools

Understanding application of tools

Machine learning and artificial intelligence tools hold out the prospect of learning from experience with increasing efficiency; but it is human capital that remains the most adaptable tool – at least for now! So, organizations looking to sustain success will need to invest in driving value from human capital by the application of tools (Figure 6.7).

Tools must be enablers of better performance, providing a route for teams to build, adapt and innovate working solutions, taking advantage of opportunities to overcome challenge. Tools must support this approach, sharing new insights across the five levels of organization, whenever possible. In this way, tool selection and training, and application of tools, should support the rollout of a PACE Culture.

Digital transformation, development of human systems and technological innovation characterize many organizations; each of these work streams rely on tools for innovative products and services to build the thriving organizations of today. Making these tools work together is what provides the seamless services valued by customers and is a key focus of an organization's development and delivery teams.

In many organizations tools are available to support processes and practices, which may not be used nor be fully utilized, thus missing many benefits from the added functionality, responsiveness or time available to innovate. It is not enough to have tools available; they also need to be applied.

Approaches and examples

The tools required will vary depending on the organization and its objectives. While some tools will be needed in many organizations, some are very specific to the industry or, indeed, individual company. For example, most organizations need a tool to ensure they are paying their staff accurately, while a global logistics company will also need to have tools to manage where goods are at any point in time, deliver the goods and route the items, among a wide range of other tools.

The application of tools needs to be closely linked to the capabilities and skills to use them. A tool can be available, but without the appropriate capabilities and skills, it may not be able to be used.

INTENSIVE CARE UNIT

An intensive care unit (ICU) of a hospital had a kidney dialysis machine that required specialist nurses to operate it. When the dialysis nurses were not available (nights and weekends), this tool could not be used. The newly appointed ICU sister assessed the impact on care and identified that a tool that did not require use of specialist nurses could be applied at all times and would improve the outcomes for more patients, at lower costs. This tool (hemofiltration) was introduced and the ICU nurses were trained, immediately improving the care of critically ill patients.

David Rogers (2016) argues that digital transformation does not rely on upgrading technology tools but is reliant on changes to strategic thinking to make the difference and enable success.

Ensuring the appropriate application of tools is achieved by supporting staff understanding and confidence to apply the tools. Some approaches that could be used are e-learning, coaching and face-to-face training; it is most helpful that off-the-shelf solutions are often available with self-learning and help options built into the tool. It is worth remembering the old adage: 'a fool with a tool, is still a fool'. Many off-the-shelf products can be used immediately and, with appropriate training and support, will improve performance.

There is also an opportunity for teams to collaborate, sharing experience and elevating the effective application of tools quickly. A practical way to do this is by establishing self-help teams or communities of good practice. In this way, tools experience can be shared and can expand the appropriate application of tools. This is of particular value where tools are subject to regular updating.

Iain Henderson (2019) states that human resource management needs to link to strategy and development. He is clear about the need to apply appropriate models and tools for organizational culture and change, performance management and talent management for the organization to succeed. For progress to be made at speed, the right application of tools is necessary to enable each team member to deliver their part with the most effectiveness and efficiency.

Illustrating the journey

As the tools required are specific to an organization, an audit of the tools required and the tools that are currently in place should be undertaken to assess which are available (including whether they are being utilized) and the gap that exists. The Resilience Profile can be used to establish this baseline. Then an assessment can be made of the tools that would improve the organization's operations or development by being available or utilized. Technology accelerators can add considerable pace to progressing Business Resilience. A systematic progress way to improve operational performance of the business is called business process re-engineering, a range of techniques for teams to implement Rapid improvements discussed by Giles Johnston (2017).

WORKING VIRTUALLY

A technical team working virtually from different country locations was in the discovery phase of developing a complex system. Virtual meetings enabled stakeholder perspectives to be captured prior to creating a workable increment. In a retrospective, one of the team suggested that instead of one team member capturing observations as minutes, they should simply activate the 'dictate' function in Word (Office 365 version) during collaboration calls and edit the content. To maximize the value of the application of this tool, meetings adopted a structure to align directly to follow-on actions. This application of an existing tool enabled all participants to contribute equally to the meeting and saved time preparing the minutes. Inevitably, many improvements to this tool application will be made, but its value and wide-ranging applicability is clear and the organization benefitted from sharing it across teams.

Best practices and supporting tools

In building the RESILIENCE Foundations, a focus on Sustained Operations and Enterprising Investment in tools enables innovation in development and delivery. It is also necessary to consider how organizations apply tools across all five levels at pace to enable them to overcome challenges and realize an opportunity.

In linking the application of tools with capabilities and skills (Figure 6.8), there is a CLEVER list of critical capabilities that aid Business Resilience:

- Clarity of Evolving Vision;
- Living the customer experience;
- Energize and enhance our people;
- Value drives portfolio innovation;
- Engagement in products and services;
- Resilient team culture and processes.

For each of these capabilities there are tools (Table 6.2) that can be applied to support them and enhance their effectiveness.

TABLE 6.2 Tools to support and enhance the effectiveness of capabilities

Capabilities	Tools
Clarity of Evolving Vision	Audio visual software; communication tools
Living the customer experience	Focus groups + personas; customer journeys
Energize and enhance our people	MBTI; colours profiling; continuing professional development
Value drives portfolio innovation	Value profiling; net present value; Pareto
Engagement in products and services	Stakeholder mapping and workshops
Resilient team culture and processes	Agile culture matrix

FIGURE 6.8 Application of tools and links to RESILIENCE Foundations and PROGRESS Cycle

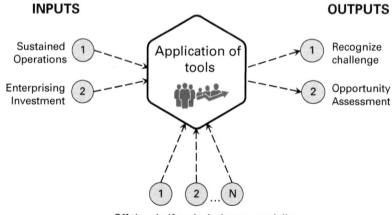

PRACTICES AND TOOLS

Element 3: Capability and Skills

FIGURE 6.9 Capability and Skills

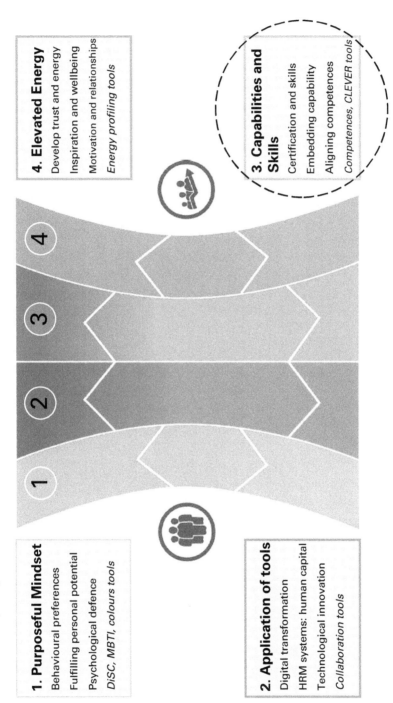

4. Elevated Energy
Develop trust and energy
Inspiration and wellbeing
Motivation and relationships
Energy profiling tools

3. Capabilities and Skills
Certification and skills
Embedding capability
Aligning competences
Competences, CLEVER tools

1. Purposeful Mindset
Behavioural preferences
Fulfilling personal potential
Psychological defence
DiSC, MBTI, colours tools

2. Application of tools
Digital transformation
HRM systems: human capital
Technological innovation
Collaboration tools

Understanding Capability and Skills

A significant strength of the PACE Culture is building on best practices, good experience and lessons learned. Capabilities and skills are needed to support the selected strategy implementation approach chosen, integrating what works well into the capabilities and skills (Figure 6.9).

The Capability and Skills element recognizes individuals and teams contribute to future sustainability and are central to progress and enhancing Business Resilience itself (Figure 6.10).

Progress Masters recognize that capabilities and skills enable teams to understand customer needs and enhance the emotional or rational appeals of products and services. Processes and practices rely on more functional appeals. These different requirements must be reflected in core and specialist capabilities and skills. As Business Resilience relies on development and delivery of value improvement, organizations must continually improve capabilities and skills. It is important that individuals believe they can develop the appropriate capabilities and skills and understand their contribution to the Evolving Vision and Progress Definition through a Purposeful Mindset and application of tools.

Approaches and examples

The skills required will be unique to each organization and will be defined in BRIT workshops as appropriate to the situation. Acquisition of new skills will continue to be required with realization of the Evolving Vision, whereas existing skills may no longer be required. Organizations will adapt to this changing requirement by optimizing core and specialist capabilities and skills with flexible resource management. Ensuring the quantum of skills is both sufficient to meet BAU (business as usual) and VUCA disruptions is the responsibility of the Business Resilience Owner.

WORKING OVER THE LIFECYCLE

A nuclear energy plant will need to have a range of skills at different times during its construction, energy generation and decommissioning. Business Resilience depends not only on the Business Resilience Roles having the skills but also the specialist teams who will deliver the Rapids and Lagoons initiatives. Some skills will need to be recruited, such as nuclear scientists, with sufficient and relevant experience, some skills can be developed on the job, such as administration, and others can be a combination, such as project management. Skills acquisition is evolutionary, driven by the stage of development or lifecycle operations of the facility.

FIGURE 6.10   Capability and Skills tools and links to RESILIENCE Foundations and
              PROGRESS Cycle

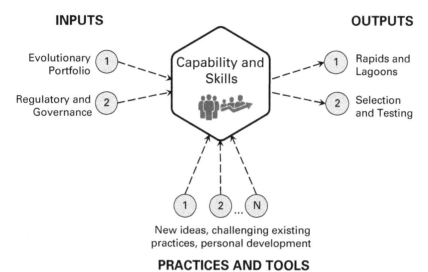

Constance Helfat and her team identified in the book *Dynamic Capabilities*
(Helfat *et al*, 2007) that to survive and progress through volatile conditions,
organizations need to develop the 'dynamic capabilities' to create, spread
and adapt the ways they operate. Thus, the capabilities and skills needed
should be regularly reviewed and the target Resilience Profile updated.

For the majority of people, skillsets are built from an early age, developed
through certifications and refined through implementation in business,
trades and professions. Continuous working and learning is a feature of
protected-time work periods (sometimes called sprints or gold periods),
when tight teams focus on issues and develop solutions together; this is
recognized as an essential practice leading to practical and professional
development, whatever the industry or organization level. Thus, the
protected-time process supports evolutionary development and the capacity
to respond to VUCA disruptions, at pace.

In Business Resilience, connectivity of individuals and teams through the
PACE Culture means that Purposeful Mindset and application of tools
supports Capability and Skills, are enabling 'dynamic capabilities', generating
energy and boosting productivity.

Illustrating the journey

In the Capability and Skills element, people are valued and recognized for investing to provide dynamic capabilities. Skills are more valued in extreme VUCA situations, where the ability of people to deploy underutilized capabilities, adapt organizations and deliver more value is both important and necessary to sustain delivery or make progress.

Whatever the range of skills needed, the Resilience Profile will provide a baseline. The organization may have a system of skills audit that can be used. It is likely that the assessment of the whole organization will hide variations across different areas. There may be sufficient capabilities in software development but insufficient in marketing of the products that will mean the organization cannot achieve its objectives, despite development of good products. For this reason, capabilities and skills in departments or divisions could be weighted, identifying those that could prevent the Progress Definition being delivered. Value initiatives to address these should be added to the Progress Backlog.

Specialist skills assessments may be needed, with some frameworks readily available. An example is the Association for Project Management Competence Framework (Association for Project Management, 2017), which is used to assess the project management competences of staff by corporates in diverse industries, from oil and gas to defence engineering. This can provide an input to the Resilience Profile.

Through identification of gaps to the target level, the Resilience Profile will input to the development of a Capability and Skills learning programme. There are many certifications or assessments available that can be combined with any bespoke learning required. The goal is to embed capability and align competences. In shifting existing capabilities and skills into a new, more resilient environment, it will be important for the Progress Master to check alignment to the Resilience Profile and confirm the target can be met by a programme developed.

Jo Owen (2013), in *How to Coach*, identifies that great managers do more than manage. They coach the whole team to get better at what they do, improving productivity, motivation and expertise. Coaching is a very effective approach to improving capability and is specific to the organization and skills for the Roles.

The combination of approaches to develop Capability and Skills will be prioritized and authorized by the Business Resilience Owner (advised by the learning and development Functional Lead) and supported by the Progress Master.

Best practices and supporting tools

Best practices and tools for capabilities and skills may be quite extensive in many organizations and should be categorized, eg as core or specialist, and subject to audit. The tools to develop capabilities and skills can be advised by learning and development specialists and should consider learning approaches that include but are not limited to:

- qualifications and certifications;
- e-learning with check to ensure understanding;
- development programmes, including apprenticeships;
- workshops;
- coaching.

A CLEVER checklist of critical capabilities that are key to Business Resilience links to the skills that are needed for the capabilities:

- Clarity of Evolving Vision;
- Living the customer experience;
- Energize and enhance our people;
- Value drives portfolio innovation;
- Engagement in products and services;
- Resilient team culture and processes.

The skills that underpin execution of these capabilities are shown in Table 6.3.

TABLE 6.3 Skills underpinning the execution of capabilities

Capabilities	Skills (and experience)
Clarity of Evolving Vision	Leadership and visioning
Living the customer experience	Market research; customer-centricity
Energize and enhance our people	Coaching teams
Value drives portfolio innovation	Value studies
Engagement in products and services	Stakeholder management
Resilient team culture and processes	Self-managed work teams; modular design

The CLEVER checklist can be used to check skills are strongly aligned to the Evolving Vision and Progress Definition and will utilize tools as shown in the previous element. This is the starting point for a Capability and Skills audit, identifying what should be added, deleted or adapted to ensure this element of the PACE Culture remains fit for purpose, using the champion/challenger model.

Element 4: Elevated Energy

Understanding Elevated Energy

The energy in the organization needs to be captured and directed constructively to enable progress at pace. Organizational energy is the force that an organization uses to purposefully put things in motion. Elevated Energy (Figure 6.11) is the extent to which a company, department or team has extended its capacity and capability to compete and succeed, whatever the VUCA conditions. Individually and collectively, organizations rely on mobilizing emotional, cognitive and behavioural potential to meet a Progress Definition, achieve business goals and attain the next level of its Evolving Vision.

A classic response to VUCA disruptions is provided by the OECD (2021) guidance issued in light of the Covid-19 pandemic. In short, it comprises a series of de-risking strategies for organizations. While respecting the intention of this work, the dominant mindset clearly veers more towards stress-testing than innovation. There is undoubtedly a place for risk management and certainty in challenging times. Nonetheless, this shows the challenge posed to Resilience Professionals when seeking to raise elevating energy in VUCA disruptions; it will certainly be required to achieve sustained progress and, without it, innovation and customer value may prove insufficient to maintain Business Resilience.

The impact of PACE Culture is observed in the organizational energy levels enjoyed by employees and teams within the organization, as well as the products and services, practices and processes reflected in its portfolio. Elevated Energy is what makes an organization an attractive and enjoyable place to work; it is an environment where people want to work, to invest their time and enjoy the reflected benefits of success. Without it, Business Resilience would not be possible and the organization would not deliver its promise of 'sustained progress delivered at pace'.

FIGURE 6.11 Elevated Energy

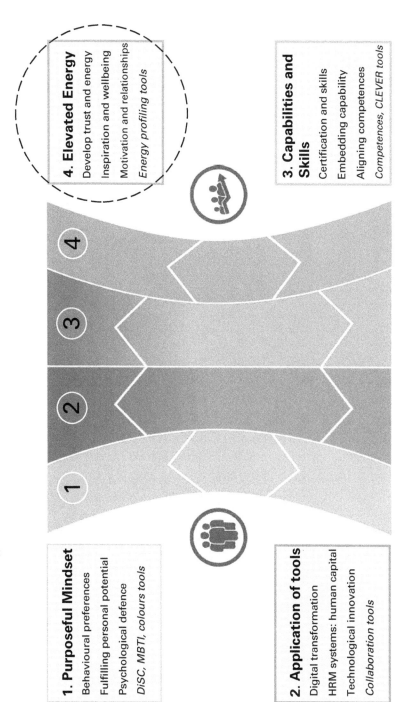

1. Purposeful Mindset
Behavioural preferences
Fulfilling personal potential
Psychological defence
DiSC, MBTI, colours tools

2. Application of tools
Digital transformation
HRM systems: human capital
Technological innovation
Collaboration tools

3. Capabilities and Skills
Certification and skills
Embedding capability
Aligning competences
Competences, CLEVER tools

4. Elevated Energy
Develop trust and energy
Inspiration and wellbeing
Motivation and relationships
Energy profiling tools

PACE Culture builds upon the behavioural understanding of scholars, such as Professor Carl Gustav Jung, who espoused concepts of individualism and energy drives associated with introversion and extroversion in the early 1900s. This work provides the rationale and value for investing in diverse personalities and productivity of teams. Many management models and tools used in organizations today are based upon these observations and beliefs.

Elevated Energy is an essential element of PACE and is required at all levels; the approach equips organizations with the confidence and vigilance to invest in the Evolving Vision and people resources to realize the next Progress Definition. Building high-performance teams is a feature of the PACE Culture, powering organizations to feel optimistic about the future, face challenging scenarios and VUCA environments, to deliver improvements and realize business opportunities.

Approaches and examples

To make sustained progress in a changing world, organizations need the energy to innovate and, by working with network partners, manage risk. Teams need to be enabled and propositions aligned to the Evolving Vision and Progress Definition.

The work of Bruch and Vogel (2011) is an accessible approach to understanding energy in organizations. It evolves from dynamic interactions and is based upon cognitive and emotional belief that drives behaviour. Two dimensions – intensity and alignment of energy to company goals – result in four types of behaviour: productive, comfortable, resigned and corrosive. These categories are observable concepts that could enable Resilience Professionals to monitor the PACE Culture.

Reflecting on best practices and tools used in commercial and technological systems provides an insight into what energizes organizations, or human systems. Understanding the extent to which team performance benefits from Elevated Energy is the responsibility of the Business Resilience Owner. It is also of great value to Progress Masters and Initiative Leaders in delivering their work within Business Resilience and initiative teams (BRITs).

Richard Branson (Schawbel, 2014) has been quoted as saying 'the most important leadership skill is the ability to inspire'. Initiative leaders will most certainly be committed to inspirational leadership, ie the ability to infuse energy, passion, commitment and connection to an organization's goals and strategies. In organizations, leaders need to go beyond 'one dream, one team', a beloved mantra by those coaching competitive sport; organizations rely upon trusted partnerships, confirmed by partnership agreements, in order to build the energy and enthusiasm needed to sustain performance and growth to manage in all VUCA conditions.

ENERGY THROUGH A PARTNERSHIP AGREEMENT

Developing trust and energy between organizations is typically formalized through contracts and agreements, enabling the respective parties to make progress in all areas, with redress through financial penalties. Partner agreements and contracts have proven benefits. When changes in VUCA environments occur, agreements provide time for each party to realign their commitments and make progress. Where contracts are ineffective, organizational energy is consumed.

Inspired employees are more than twice as productive as satisfied employees, according to a survey conducted by Bain Research (Garton and Mankins, 2015). In Business Resilience, PACE Culture encourages inspirational practices. It is as vitally important in delivery of professional services as it is in business development, where BRITs provide energetic development to business units and deliver value solutions.

LEADERS INSPIRE PRODUCTIVE ENERGY

The need for organizational energy is evident in Laura Empson's (2017) work on leading professionals, where complex, rational and emotional challenges of leading professional organizations requires the building of complex power relationships among colleagues to deliver work at pace. It also suggests adaptive strategies are needed to sustain progress by individuals and organizations.

Illustrating the journey to the next level

Perry Timms (2020), in considering wellbeing at work, examines the energized workplace: he reflects that in organizations where productivity is stalling, employee wellbeing is at an all-time low and stress at an all-time high. UK mental health disability is estimated to cost up to £100 billion each year (The Prince's Responsible Business Network, 2020). A new culture is Rapidly becoming essential for organizational success.

Embracing digital technology and systems is a much-heralded approach for improving organizational performance. Making the transition to digital is energy-sapping, as is operating new technologies, so it is vital organizations estimate the Elevated Energy level required prior to implementing it.

FACILITATING A PEER-TO-PEER DIGITAL NETWORK TO REDUCE WASTED ENERGY

In digital systems and protocols, eg blockchain, it is possible for an untrusted party to be given permission to access a trading system in a peer-to-peer (P2P) networks. A model called proof of work (PoW) provides blockchain security in trust-less P2P environments, but it comes at the expense of wasting huge amounts of energy. Bahri and Girdzijauskas (2018) put forward a proof of trust (PoT) waiver model to reduce the wasted energy. Starting from the assumption that trust is inherent to any collaborating system (as peers can form opinion about each other through time based on the transactions they share or the behaviour they observe in the network), they consider the use of a PoT waiver to minimize the amount of energy spent on PoW as more trusted peers appear in the network. That is, install a mindset of 'the more trusted you are, the less energy you are required to expend'.

In the case of digital systems, logical thinking demonstrates the value of learning from managed trust relationships in peer-to-peer networks. So commercial and technical partnerships, like intra-organizational relationships, demand energy if they are to be resilient. In highly regulated organizations, such as professional practices, conduct may be established by protocols. However, in lightly regulated organizations, intra-organizational relationships are seldom subject to strict regulation; this lack of governance can lead to energy-sapping behaviour. So, it is good practice to maintain governance protocols that enhance trust while minimizing wasted energy.

Elevating energy is the antidote to working on products and processes of low value to customers, resulting in low recognition and self-worth. In this way Elevated Energy not only impacts the wellbeing of individual employees, but it also positively impacts business outcomes, as organizations provide the opportunity for staff to reach their full potential.

Best practices and supporting tools

In selecting best practices and tools that are effective, the underlying drivers of Elevated Energy directly influence business benefits. Trust and shared purpose are central to building Elevated Energy. Care must be taken to ensure new tools, processes and practices create net positive energy and avoid wasting energy. This situation can arise from many causes in the organization, eg ineffective procurement practices that result in wasted effort, such as laptops that cannot interface with networks or that break down.

All environments benefit from practices and tools to deliver progress while building organizational energy, encouraging collaboration and effective communication between people, when working in partnerships, completing transactions or initiatives. The key to elevating energy is to utilize just a few tools that are simple to learn, support realization of the Progress Definition and fit into the Evolving Vision, where everyone can participate in adopting generic approaches to make progress easier and team collaboration more resilient. Progress Masters may have experience of generic tools such as Asana, Basecamp, Mural or Trello.

Central to Business Resilience is the Progress @ Pace 8-4-8 Model. This provides an environment to complete work and is supported by the Resilience Profile, which includes a subjective scale to assess organizational energy and monitor improvements.

FIGURE 6.12 Elevated Energy tools and links to RESILIENCE Foundations and PROGRESS Cycle

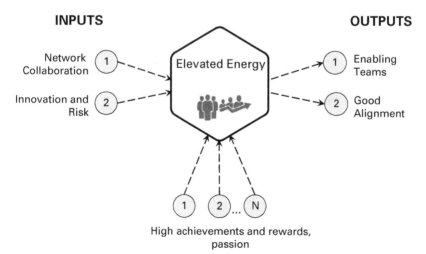

INPUTS

OUTPUTS

Network Collaboration ①

Innovation and Risk ②

Elevated Energy

① Enabling Teams

② Good Alignment

① ② ... Ⓝ

High achievements and rewards, passion

PRACTICES AND TOOLS

Developing Elevated Energy includes the need for best practices and related tools, although organizations may substitute practices and tools that they have found to be effective.

Tools and best practices that can assist organizational energy, trust, inspiration and wellbeing, motivation and relationships are shown in Figure 6.12.

Realizing an organizational PACE Culture

PACE element initiatives will be developed in the context of closing the gap between the current and target Resilience Profile levels. Value initiatives to improve one or more of the PACE Culture elements are placed on the Progress Backlog, and so the Progress Backlog is the starting place to review initiatives for each PROGRESS Cycle; this is where organization needs are captured, prioritized and ranked for the next cycle.

Progress to a PACE Culture

A progress status board, or Kanban board (Figure 6.13), is an effective visual tool for capturing PACE value initiatives. Regularly maintained, this is familiar to many teams and may be used to provide tracking to make progress. The PACE Culture elements may require learning modules, assessments and the communication, rollout and deployment across the five levels of the organization.

FIGURE 6.13 A progress status board showing value initiatives allocated to initiative teams

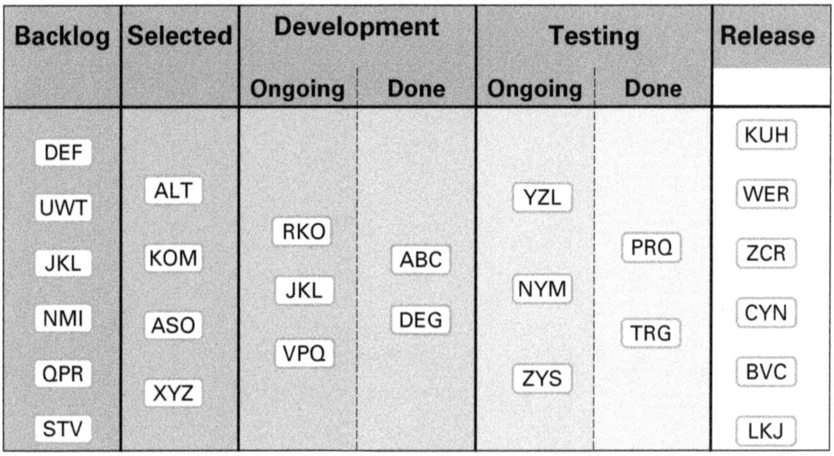

Backlog	Selected	Development		Testing		Release
		Ongoing	Done	Ongoing	Done	
DEF						KUH
UWT	ALT			YZL		WER
JKL	KOM	RKO	ABC		PRQ	ZCR
		JKL		NYM		
NMI	ASO		DEG		TRG	CYN
QPR		VPQ		ZYS		BVC
STV	XYZ					LKJ

Adapting the PACE Culture

Different parts of an organization may have unique cultures and require the Business Resilience Framework to be applied differently, including the PACE Culture. Implementing the PACE Culture can be done as a stand-alone domain, or as part of a wider Business Resilience Framework implementation. Observation of successful professional practice identifies four elements that are important in building an effective culture; these are captured in the PACE elements, which, combined, provide a powerful culture, releasing energy for developing and delivering progress. Blending PACE elements drives the culture and progress and is why it is the central domain within the Business Resilience Framework and the Progress @ PACE 8-4-8 Model.

Tools for PACE

Checklists structured around the PACE elements are a practical way to realize organizational PACE Culture. By identifying practice gaps, or good practices, teams will be able to strengthen PACE elements impacting the PACE Culture and encourage dynamic innovation. Actions will then be able to be prioritized to close the gaps in future PROGRESS Cycles, encouraging insights and lessons to be shared at learning events. Practical learning experience gained on the job or through peer-to-peer reviews can be shared, in addition to studying Business Resilience learning modules. The Business Resilience Owner and Progress Master will identify the best combination for the organization.

An audit of investing in the PACE Culture should be able to report that the character and dominant behaviour of the organization has influenced sustained progress delivered at pace. An organization's Resilience Profile reflects investment in all five domains of the framework, with dynamic capacity coming mainly from its people and culture.

Maintaining motivation for a PACE Culture

Inspirational leadership releases natural, biological energy, which flows from being part of a team engaged in a purposeful journey – a team that is totally motivated to realize a shared goal. The role of leaders in setting the PACE Culture is to clarify goals, while enabling and empowering teams to do it. So, by clarifying purpose and supporting capability with skills and tools, inspirational leaders are energizing direction and delivery. Thus, individuals and teams enjoy 'autonomy, mastery and purpose', which are the three elements suggested by Dan Pink (2009) to create motivation.

The result is outstanding innovation, because value initiatives are aligned to a common purpose valued by the organization and its customers. It is this common purpose that drives products and services on the 'good to great value journeys'; teams deliver together because they have the positive energy to never give up.

The Business Resilience Framework is most compelling when the value and resilience impact on new products and services, processes and practices is clear; when individuals or teams are provided with sufficient autonomy; and when organizational investment in functional tools and staff capabilities is visible. With the sense of true purpose, it energizes the whole organization.

In a PACE Culture staff share a common desire to enable the organization to flourish in ever-changing conditions. Political and technology environments are driving ever faster and more profound changes in the socio-economic landscape. As legal frameworks often lag behind, gaps appear, providing opportunities for resilient organizations. These dynamics provide an excellent opportunity for organizations with a strong PACE Culture to deploy strong adaptive capability.

The PROGRESS Cycle reinforces the PACE Culture; by keeping stakeholders and teams engaged in decisions to develop and deliver improved practices and processes, they also benefit from motivational feedback in Success and Learning. This elevates energy across the organization, increasing motivation for improvement, building the PACE Culture for Business Resilience and ensuring competitive advantage in VUCA disruptions.

Roles for the PACE Culture domain

The Business Resilience Owner and teams should provide leadership to those who might have preferred selection of another vision, approach or initiative as well as supporters, demonstrating generosity and a commitment to learn together from the implementation experience. They should review regularly, and, if necessary, pivot towards another strategy if VUCA disruptions require it. In implementing the Progress Definition, there is always a risk that a chosen Progress Definition may need to be adapted. By adopting a gracious approach towards all stakeholders, Elevated Energy for the preferred Progress Definition will emerge and be preserved. As is so often the case in life, experience is the thing that you receive just after you need it! And at that point, it is important to have support to pivot to an alternative.

Summary responsibilities for PACE

Business Resilience Owner – is responsible for implementing the PACE Culture in the organization. They will delegate to the appropriate people to ensure it is implemented at all five levels of the organization. The Business Resilience Owner will be supported by Functional Leads and specialists in the organization, such as human resources or technical leads for the use of tools, in addition to the Progress Master. The Business Resilience Owner will work with the senior management team to ensure that the PACE Culture is understood and there is board-level support to implement and maintain this culture.

Progress Master – is responsible for advising the Business Resilience Owner on the PACE Culture elements of the Business Resilience Framework. They will also support the Functional Leads, as required, when implementing the PACE Culture elements. The Progress Master can provide insight by undertaking the Resilience Profile of the PACE Culture elements, advising on value initiatives to improve PACE Culture elements and tracking progress as improvement is made.

Initiative Leader – is responsible for delivering the value initiatives that they are allocated to implement or improve the PACE Culture. The Initiative Leader will be identified to deliver the value initiatives, using the PROGRESS Cycle, following the initial Business Resilience implementation. The Initiative Leaders will work with the Progress Master to ensure the Initiatives deliver the benefits to contribute to the PACE Culture of the Progress Definition.

Resilience Professional – is responsible for developing the PACE Culture to support the Evolving Vision of Business Resilience. The Resilience Professional will already be mindful of the PACE Culture and will be able to align their working practices to the Resilience Profile, contributing appropriately to development and improvement in PACE Culture, when undertaking any of the three key resilience Roles, or supporting their introduction.

Benefits, costs and risks

It is the collective, coordinated effort of the organization and its partnership network that will deliver Business Resilience and achieve the Evolving Vision.

A great way of enhancing PACE Culture is to define benefits and demonstrate a more resilient organization. Elements can be enhanced by adding or supplanting them with proven and effective practices and processes, enabling a target Resilience Profile element score to be achieved in a low-risk, low-cost manner. Benefits, costs and risks will ultimately be accounted for in the PROGRESS Cycle, as a precursor to initiative development and release.

PACE element developments can be piloted at any level, with rollout of effective initiatives to all levels subject to cost–benefit analysis. Deployment of PACE improvements should be rolled out to all levels, where customer value and increased organizational responsiveness is cost- and risk-effective.

Benefits

Benefits of a PACE Culture include:

- More is achieved collectively in teams than by individuals.
- Embracing diverse thinking creates innovation.
- Organizational purpose is strengthened through self-belief.
- Clarity of the customer value proposition is enhanced.
- Partners are engaged in driving progress.
- A culture matrix balanced scorecard creates a baseline for the PACE Culture to go forward.
- There is clarity of skills that exist and those needed to deliver the Progress Definition and Evolving Vision.
- There is delineation of skills that are core and specialist ones to be acquired for limited use.
- Practical insights for improvements in engagement and wellbeing are identified.
- The scope to improve productive energy in the organization is identified.
- What will improve motivation of staff and network partners is identified.

Costs

Costs of investing in a PACE Culture will vary depending on requirements and the chosen Business Resilience (PUR) implementation strategy. Some PACE enhancements may be done at equivalent cost to current practices; some might be done at little or no cost to the organization – for example, supporting staff to believe they can meet challenges could be done by adapting on-the-job training to include PACE retrospectives, or participation in an academy or development programme.

Costs involved in developing and delivering formal training, coaching or personal development will vary considerably.

Risks

Inevitably, risks are associated with introducing a PACE Culture in the organization. These include:

- Possible resistance to the development of PACE Culture, its delivery and maintenance by staff who do not welcome innovations, reducing effectiveness;
- lack of availability of Resilience Professionals to implement or advise on PACE Culture, delaying implementation;
- lack of or ineffective PACE or Business Resilience programmes;
- a VUCA disruption leading to an 'all hands on deck' mentality to overcome operational imperatives, impacting development or delivery of PACE improvements.

Balancing benefits, costs and risks

In a PACE organization, purposeful teams thrive by working in collaboration to drive learning opportunities from failure, adapt and innovate new approaches. Finding a potential solution to a new challenge, or overcoming a belief that because an individual or organization has not done something before, it cannot be done or delivered, is a true joy of purposeful, collaborative working.

The Business Resilience Owner is responsible for authorizing resources to build and maintain PACE, focusing on the Progress Definition and the Evolving Vision. A customer value-driven approach, ensuring improvements are repaid through better capabilities and skills, and utilization of tools, is required. This will result in Elevated Energy and can be tracked using Business Resilience profiling.

In developing a PACE Culture, each element makes a major contribution to powering teamwork through the eight steps of the PROGRESS Cycle, building on the functional capability residing within RESILIENCE Foundations. Making the case for next-level PACE elements within a Business Resilience culture must balance benefits against the costs and risks of taking action or not; costs and risks can be difficult to assess without the benefit of a Resilience Professional and experience of business impacts over the short and medium term. For this reason, the Business Resilience Owner will want to provide a robust business case to business leaders and receive support from stakeholders to proceed, whatever the VUCA conditions.

Summary

The PACE Culture domain demonstrates the importance of investing in stakeholders, staff and network partners. By investing in PACE Culture, the organization will be prepared to make progress and strengthen Business Resilience, addressing VUCA disruptions as opportunities. The ability to support, develop and authorize variants to products, services, processes and practices provides the organization with an opportunity to pivot, which is critical to making progress at pace.

The four elements of PACE provide a culture in which individuals are encouraged to innovate and improve the portfolio, optimize functional capability found in RESILIENCE Foundations and velocity through the PROGRESS Cycle. The PACE Culture elements operate in a bi-directional flow, connecting RESILIENCE Foundations to the PROGRESS Cycle and vice versa. This provides a virtuous circle of learning, resilience testing and improvement.

PACE Culture delivers portfolio value by taking advantage of VUCA disruptions where other competitors cannot. It is at the very heart of the Business Resilience Framework, enhancing confidence and courage to take on challenges, turning them into opportunities and driving improvement. Resilience Roles and BRITs are central to improving the PACE Culture as well as initiatives throughout the organization.

QUESTIONS TO THINK ABOUT

- How can PACE Culture elements assist in aligning professional and organizational interests to provide mutual benefits?
- What more do organizations want from capable, skilled professionals than excellent products, services, processes and practices?
- What more do professionals want from organizations that have already adopted a Purposeful Mindset and built capabilities and skills to apply tools effectively in their organization culture?

References

Association for Project Management (2017) *What is the APM Competence Framework?*, www.apm.org.uk/resources/find-a-resource/competence-framework (archived at https://perma.cc/443Z-VXEP)

Bahri, L and Girdzijauskas, S (2018) When trust saves energy: A reference framework for Proof of Trust (PoT) blockchains, In *Companion Proceedings of the Web Conference 2018 (WWW '18)*, International World Wide Web Conferences Steering Committee, Republic and Canton of Geneva, doi.org/10.1145/3184558.3191553 (archived at https://perma.cc/E5FK-YPL8)

Bruch, H and Vogel, B (2011) *Fully Charged: How great leaders boost their organization's energy and ignite high performance*, Harvard Business School Press, Boston

Discprofile.com (2021) *How DiSC® Works*, www.discprofile.com/what-is-disc/How-DiSC-Works (archived at https://perma.cc/D2AY-3HNQ)

Dweck, C (2008) *Mindset: The new psychology of success*, Random House, New York

Empson, L (2017) *Leading Professionals: Power, politics, and prima donnas*, Oxford University Press, Oxford

Garton, E and Mankins, M (2015) Engaging your employees is good, but don't stop there, *Harvard Business Review*, 9 December, https://hbr.org/2015/12/engaging-your-employees-is-good-but-dont-stop-there (archived at https://perma.cc/4KXP-AWCR)

Green, P (2017) *This Cognitive Bias Kills our Ability to Thrive in Complexity*, 20 March, agileforall.com/this-cognitive-bias-kills-our-ability-to-address-complexity (archived at https://perma.cc/99TR-GRHB)

Helfat, CE *et al* (2007) *Dynamic Capabilities: Understanding strategic change in organizations*, Blackwell Publishing, Malden

Henderson, I (2019) *Human Resource Management System for MBA and Business Masters*, Chartered Institute of Personnel and Development/Kogan Page, London

Johnston, G (2017) *Business Process Re-engineering: A simple process improvement approach to improve business performance*, Smartspeed Consulting Ltd, USA

Marston, WM (1928) *Emotions of Normal People*, Routledge, London

Myers & Briggs Foundation (2021) *MBTI® Basics*, www.myersbriggs.org/my-mbti-personality-type/mbti-basics (archived at https://perma.cc/S24F-S8YC)

Organization for Economic Co-operation and Development (2021) *Keys to Resilient Supply Chains: Policy tools for preparedness and responsiveness*, www.oecd.org/trade/resilient-supply-chains (archived at https://perma.cc/MUA2-J6DF)

Owen, J (2013) *How to Coach*, Pearson Business, London

Pink, D. (2009) *Drive: The surprising truth about what motivates us*, Riverhead Books, New York

Rogers, D (2016) *The Digital Transformation Playbook: Rethink your business for the digital age*, Columbia University Press, New York

Schawbel, D (2014) Richard Branson's three most important leadership Principles, *Forbes*, 23 September, www.forbes.com/sites/danschawbel/2014/09/23/richard-branson-his-3-most-important-leadership-Principles/?sh=6e46a0353d50 (archived at https://perma.cc/XJ4E-J8UW)

Seligman, M (1998) *Learned Optimism*, Pocket Books, New York

Study.com (2016) *Fixed vs. Growth Mindset – Quiz & Worksheet*, study.com/academy/practice/quiz-worksheet-fixed-growth-mindsets.html (archived at https://perma.cc/4VZF-QVKF)

The Prince's Responsible Business Network (2020) *Employee Wellbeing Measurement and Metrics*, Business in the Community

Timms, P (2020) *The Energized Workplace: Designing organizations where people flourish*, Kogan Page, London

07

PROGRESS Cycle

Purpose

The purpose of the PROGRESS Cycle is to enable an organization to move to a qualitatively better state as a result of progress consistent with the Business Resilience Principles (Figure 7.1). The PROGRESS Cycle has eight elements, which are triggered by its internal needs or an external event. These elements could be seen as elements to deliver progress for Business Resilience.

The progress is purposeful and deliberate, as organizations actively realize meaningful improvements to their position, whether the internal and external conditions are favourable or not. The cyclical nature of the PROGRESS Cycle, created by the infinity loop, enables a continuous stream of positive improvements commensurate with the challenges and opportunities presented by the organizational context combined with the external environment, to facilitate sustained progress.

Introduction

The PROGRESS Cycle is a domain of the Progress @ Pace 8-4-8 Model, which is at the heart of the Business Resilience Framework. The PROGRESS Cycle links through the PACE Culture domain to the RESILIENCE Foundations and is supported by the Principles and Roles domains within the Business Resilience Framework.

FIGURE 7.1 PROGRESS Cycle

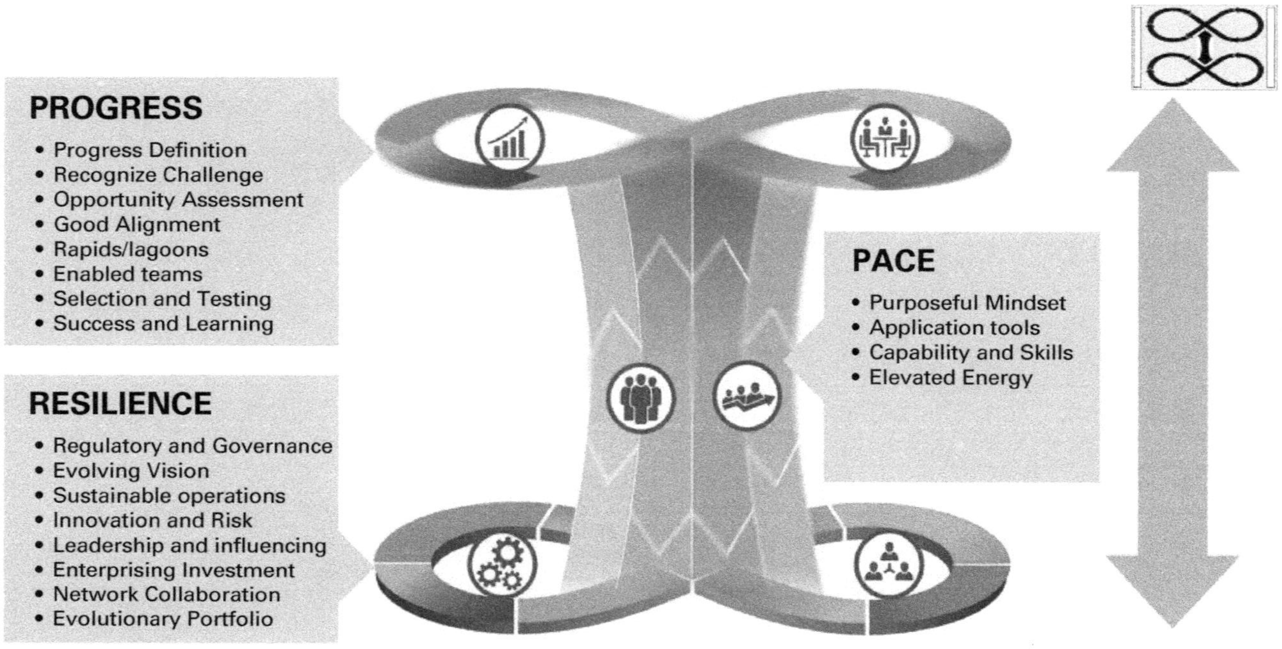

PACE

- Purposeful Mindset
- Application tools
- Capability and Skills
- Elevated Energy

PROGRESS

- Progress Definition
- Recognize Challenge
- Opportunity Assessment
- Good Alignment
- Rapids/lagoons
- Enabled teams
- Selection and Testing
- Success and Learning

RESILIENCE

- Regulatory and Governance
- Evolving Vision
- Sustainable operations
- Innovation and Risk
- Leadership and influencing
- Enterprising Investment
- Network Collaboration
- Evolutionary Portfolio

Element 1: Progress Definition

Description

Progress Definition lays the foundation for the whole cycle and, indeed, to the very idea and definition of progress for an organization.

Like any other significant undertaking in the life of an organization, no significant improvement to the current state can be achieved with certainty before there is a clear understanding of what exactly constitutes the improvement. Importantly, the idea of progress must permeate every level of organizational activity, from the top (eg new market or product line expansion, significant internal restructuring, etc) to the bottom (eg team-level decisions on production process reorganization, specific product improvements, etc). Any level of improvement contributing towards the desired state of the organization must be treated as part of the concerted effort towards progress.

The extant literature offers various approaches to measuring progress, but as the term generally implies some advancement or improvement, the model and measures differ for every specific context. In the context of Business Resilience, the following key aspects should be considered:

- *better organizational efficiency* – this can be achieved through better internal processes (for example, strategy, financial planning, communication, team organization, operation, client interaction, etc) and practices (eg balanced scorecards, lean manufacturing, time-boxing, team-building, feedback);

- *more efficient outputs* – achieved through the balanced portfolio of products and services that are better aligned with the organizational capabilities and deliver greater customer value.

Together, these two aspects contribute to a state where the organization is both capable of utilizing its resources to a greater effect and enabling it to produce outputs that provide it a competitive advantage over its competition. Ultimately, this should result in an increased capacity to operate successfully in environments where other organizations would underperform or fail altogether, ie Business Resilience.

Therefore, organizational progress is defined as an organization achieving an improved state with a higher level of organizational efficiency and/or higher-quality outputs. The organizational efficiency is represented by processes and practices and judged on their optimality, whereas outputs are represented by products and services and judged on their contribution to customer value (Figure 7.2).

FIGURE 7.2 Organizational progress (example)

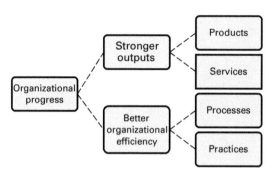

Organizational activities that contribute to better organizational efficiency and more efficient outputs are ultimately delivering value, either to the organization itself or to its customers; therefore, they are referred to as value initiatives. While the distinction between a product and a service may be understood, it is important to provide a definition for process and practice in the context of Business Resilience. Process is defined as a mechanistic or procedural type of activity (Cambridge Dictionary Online, 2021a), while practice is more skill-based (Cambridge Dictionary Online, 2021b).

Managing value initiatives of all types is a key activity in the PROGRESS Cycle, which can be accomplished in various ways depending on the organizational setup, preferred or mandated management paradigm, and specific operation and project management practice in place. As circumstances of individual organizations vary, there can be no strict requirement as to the use of a specific management method. Yet, given that organizations nowadays must operate in an environment with high levels of volatility, uncertainty, complexity and ambiguity (VUCA), it is recommended that a consideration be given to some use of agile and lean-based portfolio, programme, project and product delivery approaches to enable and facilitate flexible delivery embracing and capitalizing on change.

It is important to note that the definition of progress would change over time for any given organization. For instance, if today's definition of progress is the expansion into a new market or the design of a breakthrough new product, tomorrow it may be minimizing losses and surviving in the abruptly changing marketplace, only to go back to the global expansion plans a year later. Progress Definition, therefore, must accommodate such variability and provide the means for flexible re-assessment and tracking of what constitutes improvement for the organization at any point in time, whatever the circumstances are.

Activities

A1.1 PROGRESS DEFINITION AND GAP ASSESSMENT

While organizations continuously react to the need to change prompted by internal circumstances or external pressures, their reactions are not necessarily deliberate or disciplined and thus do not ensure progress. To address this, an organization needs to both define progress in terms of value initiatives and establish a system of measures so that the progress made could be tracked, assessed and communicated to key stakeholders.

Progress Definition is the measurable improvement of organizational efficiency or outputs resulting from selected value initiatives, which contribute to stronger Business Resilience. Realization of the Progress Definition is confirmed by measuring key elements of the Business Resilience Framework (see Chapter 3). These should result in better organization products, services, processes and practices. The measures used to determine progress must be specific to the organization, type of business or industry and tailored to the specific context.

Progress would be achieved through an improved market share (+5 per cent) within the next year. It should be achieved by the following value initiatives:

- a marketing campaign utilizing a new customer communication platform;

- release of an enhanced service to customers in the 25–35-year-old target segment.

The Resilience Profile (see Chapter 10) is used to diagnose and baseline the resilience level of the organization before the value initiatives are implemented, and subsequently assess the improvement in Business Resilience achieved upon their completion, thereby establishing how the implementation of the value initiatives have contributed to progress in this iteration of the PROGRESS Cycle. The Resilience Profile is updated at the start of each cycle. A VUCA event may also trigger a new PROGRESS Cycle due to the urgency of newly identified requirements.

Every PROGRESS Cycle starts with the identification of the Progress Definition and current resilience level of the organization. By utilizing the measures of progress (specific to the organization, type of business or industry, and tailored to the specific context), a structured and measured view of

FIGURE 7.3 Gap to progress position input/output diagram

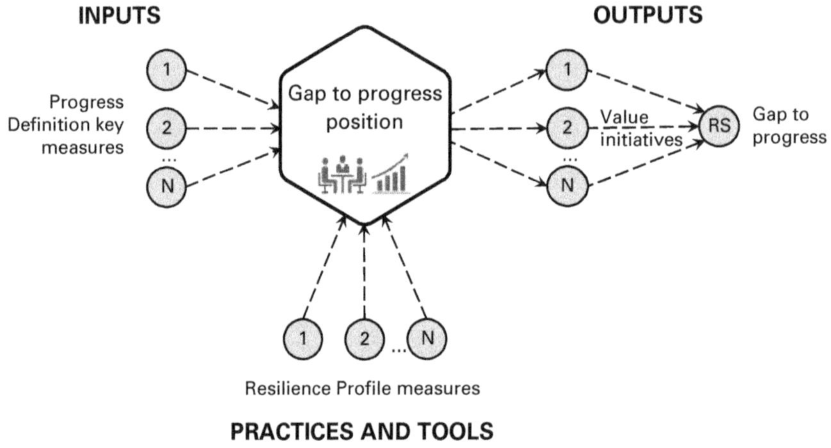

PRACTICES AND TOOLS

progress is produced, which will enable highlighting of specific types of value initiatives to implement and goes beyond creating a vision. Progress made at the end of the cycle could be acknowledged by a summary, such as 'we now have X per cent more capability to create value through Y'.

Inputs and outputs   Progress Definition measures are inputs to this activity, while gap to progress is the output (Figure 7.3). The Resilience Profile is used initially to baseline the resilience level of the organization at the beginning of the first PROGRESS Cycle and then subsequently used to both assess the Business Resilience progress made and update the Progress Definition for the next cycle.

A1.2 VALUE INITIATIVES

Any progress for the organization must be viewed through the prism of value initiatives that are focused on better organizational efficiency or stronger outputs. It is therefore essential that such initiatives are clearly identified and understood. Depending on both internal and external factors, an organization's needs may vary from a brief review of the existing detailed Progress Definition to a robust and comprehensive analysis. Hence, the spectrum of methods that could be employed is quite broad and utilizes tools of organizational strategy and operations (see Appendix B for examples).

ANALYSIS TO CREATE THE PROGRESS DEFINITION

Utilizing the SWOT/TOWS model (referenced in Appendix B), one could arrive at a conclusion to 'stop all R&D projects in the internal combustion engine development division or divest the division entirely in response to the mass migration of other car manufacturers away from the fossil-fuel-based engines', as was the case with Jaguar cars.

Once identified and understood, the value initiatives must be captured in a way that is both straightforward to communicate to stakeholders and conducive to flexible change of the implementation priorities. These are captured in a backlog – a indexed list of 'things to do' that prescribes execution of the items top to bottom but also allows changing the items' position in the list relative to the other items, as well as the inclusion or exclusion of items based on the evolving understanding of what is currently relevant and important. This is the Progress Backlog.

PROGRESS BACKLOG PRIORITIZATION

For instance, the development of a new line of products may be delayed or cancelled altogether if the new market analysis suggested there is no longer a demand for it or that there were new factors constraining the promotion and distribution. Consequently, these initiatives will be either moved down the Progress Backlog or removed from it altogether. Conversely, if the new market situation demands a Rapid introduction of a new or updated service or product, an item for this value initiative may be created and placed right at the top of the backlog to accommodate the situation.

The number of value initiatives for a large organization will typically include items for strengthening both the organization efficiency and outputs and may be significant. Depending on the scale and composition of the Progress Backlog, it may be sensible to split it into several complementary streams, ie one for outputs and another for efficiency-oriented initiatives, or indeed have separate streams for products, services, processes and practices (PSPPs). These are the PSPP backlogs that should be prioritized in accordance with the current understanding of which of the value initiatives must be implemented first and which later (see Chapter 9 for methods and tools).

Once the value initiatives in the PSPP backlogs have been prioritized, a decision must be made on which of the top value initiatives are going to be considered for implementation in a short- to mid-term perspective. Clarity of objectives and pragmatism must guide this exercise:

- *Clarity of objectives* – as benefits of any value initiative may constitute an improvement of a specific kind (eg financial return, market position, brand recognition, improved communication and collaboration within teams, etc) or several, it is important to decide which combination of benefits constitutes the best possible value for the organization at this time. The decision may use a scoring or ranking model (eg a ranking model used in popular project portfolio management methods (AXELOS, 2011)) or emerge from a debate within the organization along the line of 'what does progress mean for us?'

- *Pragmatism* – as organizations operate with limited resources, the job of decision-makers defining progress is to determine which specific initiatives of those considered high priority and high value are to be focused on and actioned, while recognizing that often only a limited number could be worked on within the existing constraints.

Inputs and outputs   As value initiatives are identified, the Progress Backlog gradually emerges in the first cycle or is updated in all the subsequent cycles. Items in the backlog will belong to any of the four PSPP (products, services, processes and practices) categories and at this point are added to the Progress Backlog on a first-come, first-served basis. Once the addition of items is deemed complete and depending on how expansive it is, the Progress Backlog is split into two to four complementary PSPP streams. Figure 7.4 shows the split into the efficiency-focused and outputs-focused initiatives. Initiatives in those PSPP streams are then prioritized and assessed for urgency within the current constraints (Figure 7.5).

A1.3 ROADMAP TO PROGRESS

Once the Progress Backlog and the highest priority value initiatives have been identified, an outline plan or roadmap for execution must be created. Depending on the preferred planning methodology, the roadmap may take the shape of a programme or project schedule or a business plan. Examples

FIGURE 7.4 Value initiatives, Progress Backlog and PSPP backlogs

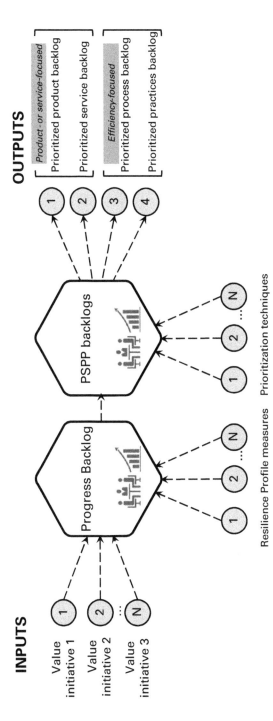

FIGURE 7.5 Select prioritized PSPP backlogs

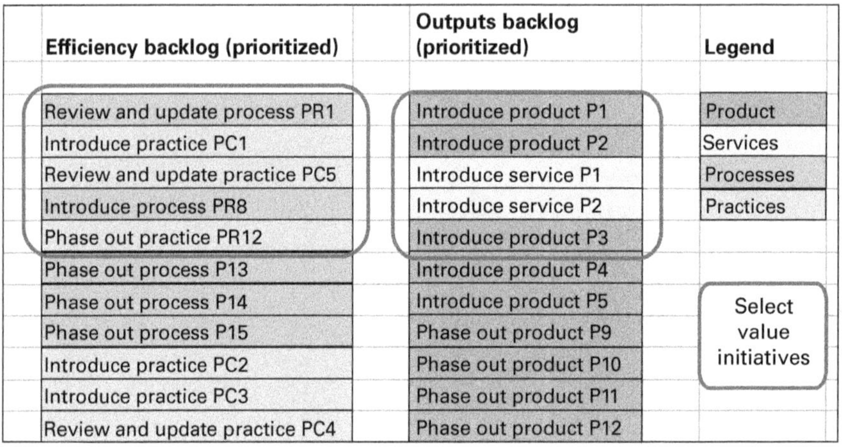

Efficiency backlog (prioritized)	Outputs backlog (prioritized)	Legend
Review and update process PR1	Introduce product P1	Product
Introduce practice PC1	Introduce product P2	Services
Review and update practice PC5	Introduce service P1	Processes
Introduce process PR8	Introduce service P2	Practices
Phase out practice PR12	Introduce product P3	
Phase out process P13	Introduce product P4	
Phase out process P14	Introduce product P5	Select
Phase out process P15	Phase out product P9	value
Introduce practice PC2	Phase out product P10	initiatives
Introduce practice PC3	Phase out product P11	
Review and update practice PC4	Phase out product P12	

of such a schedule may include a generic flowchart, Gantt or network diagram, or any other suitable tool (see Figure 7.6).

The progress roadmap presents the longitudinal view of progress for the current cycle. The roadmap can be used to establish the actual progress achieved at the end of the cycle in terms of specific PSPP initiatives completed or still under way. The review of progress at this point may yield additional value over the straightforward account of which individual initiatives have been realized so far. Namely, by looking at the updated PSPP backlogs at the end of the cycle, it would be possible to ascertain the progress and future needs on the level of organizational outputs and efficiency.

PROGRESS

'We would like to improve certain processes, upskill certain categories of staff, introduce changes or improvements to some of our services, rebalance the product portfolio, or respond to a certain crisis in one of those categories, to be more attractive to our users. If we are more attractive to users, we will also be more resilient.'

FIGURE 7.6 Progress roadmap example

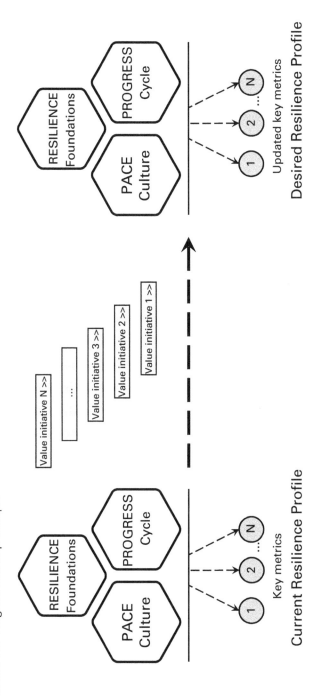

Inputs and outputs   Building a roadmap to progress in the current cycle would make use of prioritized PSPP backlogs and result in an outline sequence of the selected value initiatives. The roadmap may be structured for short-, medium- or long-term perspectives depending on what value initiatives are being considered, and the level of detail may vary according to the needs of the organization. For instance, it may include high-level requirements such as introducing a range of new products and replacing several working practices with their improved versions or cover specific activities realizing various individual aspects of those initiatives (similar to rolling-wave planning).

Summary

The Progress Definition element:

- establishes measures used to assess the level of resilience for the organization;
- measures the current level of resilience and elicits the future desired one;
- identifies the gap between the two above states and builds a roadmap with selected high-priority value initiatives considered for implementation in the current cycle.

This element lays a solid foundation and sets the direction for all the subsequent activities of the PROGRESS Cycle.

Element 2: Recognize Challenge

Description

Once progress is defined for the current organizational situation, it is important to understand the factors that might challenge the progress. The following questions must be asked:

- 'What is our current capacity load?' The organization still has to resource and implement a given value initiative as opposed to just willing it to happen (eg 'If we are inundated with urgent client orders or firefighting with all hands on deck, are we still realistically able to handle this initiative?').

- 'How sensitive is our external environment?' To acknowledge that a less predictable environment (eg the volatility, uncertainty, ambiguity and complexity) would, in most cases, be less conducive to the implementation of value initiatives.

- 'How adaptable are we?' To acknowledge that the presence of skills, knowledge, processes and practices allowing the organization to flexibly change would mean a higher chance of making meaningful progress.

- 'How urgently is the response needed?' The urgency for any given value initiative would reflect both the severity of consequences if no action was taken and be indicative of the potential risks associated with that action.

Providing clear answers to these questions assesses the level of challenge the organization is facing to implement the proposed value initiatives in the current internal and external context. See Chapter 9 for further details.

CHALLENGE IDENTIFIED

On 23 May 2021, Belarus forcibly and illegally landed a Ryanair flight passing over its territory (Wood, 2021). Within days, the EU closed its airspace for carriers operating out of Belarus and introduced broad economic sanctions against the country (Emmott *et al*, 2021). This put an already struggling national air carrier, Belavia, on the brink of collapse and prompted massive restructuring of the airline (Stolyarov and Balmforth, 2021).

Activities

A2.1 CAPACITY LOADING

Assessing the capacity for the organization establishes whether progress can be reliably delivered through the implementation of the value initiatives planned. This is an internal assessment that applies at two levels – the team and the organization as a whole.

Many organizations, manufacturing or service-based, will have a split between production (or business-as-usual) and development (innovation) initiatives that are both part of scheduled workstreams. While the methods for measuring capacity load may vary based on industry practice and organizational specifics, ultimately, they will come down to some kind of resource (workforce or equipment) utilization or productivity rate expressed as a ratio of committed load versus total capacity.

Ranking the available capacity will depend on the internal standards of capacity loading and an agreed ranking. The capacity could use the formula below in terms of hours or other agreed units (see Chapter 9 for further details).

$$\text{Available capacity} = \text{Total capacity} - \text{Current load} \qquad (7.1)$$

AGREED RANKING

For a specific healthcare organization, available bed capacity in the summer is usually around 20 per cent, while in the winter it is reduced to 5 per cent. So, in the winter the available Capacity Scale would be adjusted accordingly, and may look like this:

Available capacity rank 1: 0–2.99 per cent (very low available capacity);

Available capacity rank 2: 3–3.99 per cent (low available capacity);

Available capacity rank 3: 4–5.99 per cent (medium available capacity);

Available capacity rank 4: 6–7.99 per cent (high available capacity);

Available capacity rank 5: 8–10 per cent (very high available capacity).

Inputs and outputs   Total capacity and current commitments at the team or organization level are inputs to this assessment (Figure 7.7). In a basic example, these would be expressed as total available hours and currently committed hours per individual team member, the team or the organization. The output would be available capacity.

A2.2 VUCA SENSITIVITY

Alongside assessing the available capacity of the organization, it is vitally important to understand how sensitive the external environment is and the implications of this for meaningful progress. Although various approaches to assess sensitivity exist, Business Resilience uses factors impacting the unpredictability of the external environment, the VUCA Storm Scale. The VUCA Storm Scale measures the sensitivity of the external environment and reflects the 'strength of the Storm that needs to be navigated'.

FIGURE 7.7 Capacity loading input/output diagram

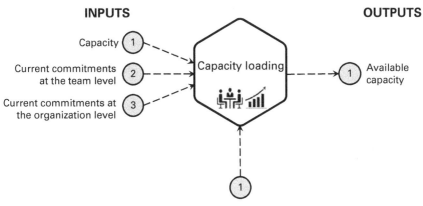

Available capacity calculation

PRACTICES AND TOOLS

The VUCA Storm is measured along four dimensions – volatility, uncertainty, complexity and ambiguity – and expressed in a single cumulative score, the VUCA Storm Score. Expressed as a grade or rank (eg 1 – lowest, 5 – highest), the score reflects the degree to which the sensitive and unpredictable external environment would challenge the realization of high-priority value initiatives (see details in Chapter 9). For instance:

VUCA Storm Score 1: (very low or Calm);

VUCA Storm Score 2: (low or Breeze);

VUCA Storm Score 3: (medium or Gale);

VUCA Storm Score 4: (high or Storm);

VUCA Storm Score 5: (very high or Hurricane).

Inputs and outputs   Inputs are the data from the external environment analysis, and the output is the VUCA Storm Score (Figure 7.8).

A2.3 ADAPTIVE ENTERPRISE (AE) CAPABILITY

Adaptive organizations are highly flexible and can change or adjust in almost real time by altering routines and practices in response to environmental changes (Moitra and Ganesh, 2005). Practically, this determines the amount of effort and resources required to execute organizational progress

FIGURE 7.8 VUCA sensitivity input/output diagram

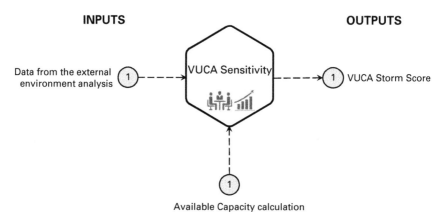

PRACTICES AND TOOLS

and is an important factor in assessing and recognizing the challenge to value initiatives' implementation. This capability for the organization is assessed using the Adaptive Enterprise Scale based on the aspects presented in Table 7.1. There is a natural overlap between the Adaptive Enterprise aspect and elements of the Business Resilience Framework and this recognizes the contribution of organizational adaptability to Business Resilience.

TABLE 7.1 Adaptive Enterprise aspects

Adaptive Enterprise aspect	Characterized by
1. Customer value	Customer relevance at the heart of everything an organization does
2. Inspirational leadership	Visionary and inspired standards
3. Energized collaboration	Delegated authority and ownership
4. Adaptive modular processes	Sufficiency for the purpose combined with reconfigurability
5. Engaged 5-level Progress @ Pace network	Network of empowered teams and open environment
6. Innovation practices and processes	Product, process and distribution services
7. One dream, one team	Shared purpose and self-organizing, with role mobility
8. Growth mindset	Openness to learning new things and continuous positive evolution

The assessment produces a cumulative Adaptive Enterprise Score expressed as a figure in a specific range (eg 1–40) or rank (eg 1 – lowest, 5 – highest). This score would reflect the degree to which the organization is capable of adjusting to the changing realities of its internal structure and processes, as well as the external environment (see details in Chapter 9). For instance:

Adaptive Enterprise Score 1: (very low adaptability);

Adaptive Enterprise Score 2: (low adaptability);

Adaptive Enterprise Score 3: (medium adaptability);

Adaptive Enterprise Score 4: (high adaptability);

Adaptive Enterprise Score 5: (very high adaptability).

Inputs and outputs   Inputs are the data from analysing the above Adaptive Enterprise aspects, whereas the output is the Adaptive Enterprise Score or rank (Figure 7.9).

A2.4 URGENCY (OF THE CHALLENGE)

Urgency is the final factor to recognize the challenge, which combines with the organization's capability to adapt and capacity to implement chosen value initiatives in a VUCA environment. Assessing the urgency is based on the organization's understanding of its internal needs and the demands of the environment (including customers). It would be reasonable to assume

FIGURE 7.9 Adaptive Enterprise (AE) capability input/output diagram

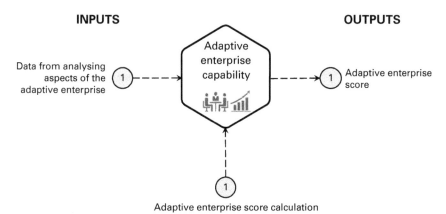

that, in most cases, implementing progress in a tighter timeframe carries more risk than doing similar work at a more relaxed pace.

URGENCY

A global pandemic made the need to switch to homeworking immediate, whereas the 2008 financial crisis created a need to implement new rules for the global financial system, with some being brought in within a year and some spanning a decade. This demonstrates that the different types of crisis required different levels of urgency of response.

Urgency can be categorized in different ways for different organizations. The Business Resilience Framework uses five categories that represent gradually increasing urgency levels. Here every individual urgency class is associated with a rank (1 – least urgent, 5 – most urgent) or Urgency Score, which makes it straightforward to use in calculating the overall Challenge Score. The assessment is based on judgement but has clear criteria and can be categorized (see the details in Chapter 9). The scores would be:

Urgency Score 1: (very low or Back-burner);

Urgency Score 2: (low or Usual);

Urgency Score 3: (medium or Speedy);

Urgency Score 4: (high or Time-critical);

Urgency Score 5: (very high or Blitz).

Inputs and outputs   As the urgency assessment is based on the mix of priorities dictated by the internal organization's needs and the external environment, the inputs are linked to those used in assessing the capacity, VUCA sensitivity and AE capability (activities A2.1, A2.2 and A2.3). The output of the assessment would be the Urgency Score (Figure 7.10).

CALCULATING THE CHALLENGE SCORE

The final part of the Resilience Challenge element is to calculate the Challenge Score representing an overall level of the challenge to progress that the organization is facing. The VUCA Storm Score, Adaptive Enterprise

FIGURE 7.10 Urgency of the challenge input/output diagram

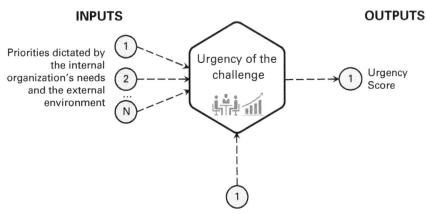

PRACTICES AND TOOLS

Score, Urgency Score and Available Capacity Score are combined in the following formula (see the calculation details in Chapter 9):

$$Cs = \frac{VSs * Us}{AEs * ACs} \tag{7.2}$$

where,

Cs = Challenge Score;

VSs = VUCA Storm Score;

Us = Urgency Score;

AEs = Adaptive Enterprise Score;

ACs = Available Capacity Score.

The resulting cumulative Challenge Score is expressed as a score (eg 1–25) or rank (eg 1 – least challenging, 5 – most challenging). For instance:

Challenge Score 1: 0–5 (very low opportunity);

Challenge Score 2: 6–10 (low opportunity);

Challenge Score 3: 11–15 (medium opportunity);

Challenge Score 4: 16–20 (high opportunity);

Challenge Score 5: 21–25 (very high opportunity).

Further information is in Chapter 9.

FIGURE 7.11 Challenge Score input/output diagram

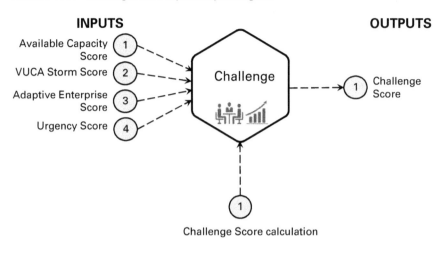

PRACTICES AND TOOLS

Summary

The Recognize Challenge element weighs up the balance between the sensitivity and unpredictability of the external environment combined with the urgency of the progress needed and the adaptability of the organization, combined with its available capacity to implement the progress. The Challenge Score gives decision-makers a single measure indicating how challenging it would be to realize the current proposed cycle of progress.

Element 3: Opportunity Assessment

Description

After identifying the value initiatives and the level of challenge to implement them, it is important to understand the level of opportunity this progress presents, specifically in terms of benefits, value and how sure the organization is that it will be able to deliver.

The benefits sought will dictate the approach to valuing the value initiatives, and some will be easier to measure than others. It may be due to the fact that if a benefit is financial in nature, it can be valued in financial terms (eg return on investment, cost–benefit analysis), whereas other types may be less quantifiable. Also, when it comes to value, the difference between the benefit and value is the perception of the stakeholder, so adequately assessing the value requires the involvement of key stakeholders and is based on the value for most of them (if not all). It is important to remember that there are up to five stakeholder levels in the organization structure to be considered. Note that the network level includes the partners (see Chapter 4).

OPPORTUNITY

Implementing an initiative could produce a monetary sum. The benefit of that, however, may only go to a limited number of key partners. In this case, the organization may struggle to agree this as an opportunity that all key stakeholders support. This can impact the level of opportunity perceived, as the impact on the relationship with stakeholders may cause a stakeholder to reduce their working with the organization and, in turn, reduce the monetary benefit.

Activities

A3.1 BENEFITS ASSESSMENT

Assessing the benefits will depend on their nature and may involve financial and non-financial measures. The definition of benefits plays a pivotal role, and many organizations will have benefits categorizations in place. Some examples of measures (and goals for them) that could be used are presented in Table 7.2.

TABLE 7.2 Examples of measures to assess benefits

Category	KPI	Goal to achieve benefit
Customer	Satisfaction: Complaints	Under 1%
Productivity, cost and quality	Value added (orders per production employee)	1.5
	Orders per day	+35
	First pass approval %	99%
Delivery	On-time/in full	1%
	Lead time (weeks)	1 week
	Backlog (weeks)	3 weeks
People	Loss time	< 0.5 hour per person
	Housekeeping	100%
	Loss time from injuries	0

FIGURE 7.12 Benefits assessment input/output diagram

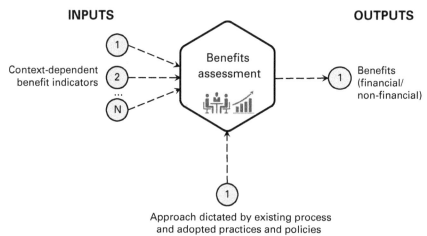

Approaches to measuring such benefits will be largely determined by the existing process and adopted practices of the organization.

Inputs and outputs   Agreed organizational benefit indicators will serve as inputs to this activity, whereas the financial or non-financial value of benefits forecast is the output (Figure 7.12).

A3.2 VALUE TO PARTNERS

As satisfaction with the outputs of a given initiative is often subjective, it is essential that any measurement is based on an agreement between the key stakeholders. Here, the input of specific stakeholders may be adjusted based on their role, contribution and stake in the outputs being assessed and can be expressed as a willingness to pay, stated or revealed preferences (Jenner, 2012), or similar terms. To facilitate an agreement, conventional practices of surveys and facilitated discussions can be employed. The result can be expressed in financial and/or non-financial terms that, in turn, should be weighed against the total amount of resources spent to achieve the outputs.

The following formula adapted from the management of value (MoV) guidance by AXELOS (2010) will aid the assessment:

$$Value = \frac{\begin{array}{c}\textit{Satisfaction of stakeholder needs}\\ \textit{financial and non-financial}\end{array}}{\begin{array}{c}\textit{Total use of resources}\\ \textit{money, people, time, energy and materials}\end{array}} \qquad (7.3)$$

where,

Satisfaction of need = defined as a balance between stakeholder views;

Total use of resources = defined as the use of total resources of all types.

Inputs and outputs Satisfaction of stakeholder needs and total use of resources are inputs to the calculation, with the output being value expressed either as a ratio or percentage (Figure 7.13).

A3.3 DELIVERY CONFIDENCE

The final part of the Opportunity Assessment is assurance that the value initiative has a high chance of being delivered by the organization as planned. This should take account of the key risk factors affecting the delivery, such as the effort needed, timescale and the demonstrable capability of the team to

FIGURE 7.13 Value to partners input/output diagram

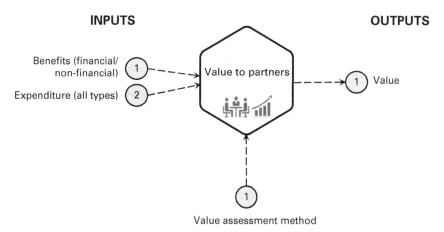

deliver. This assessment should be linked directly to the current available capacity of the team (or organization as a whole) (see A2.1 Capacity loading). DICE is a popular framework by Boston Consulting Group (Sirkin *et al*, 2005), which offers a statistical analysis-based method for this assessment. The formula to calculate DICE is:

$$Ds = D + (2 \ x \ I) + (2 \ x \ C1) + C2 + E \qquad (7.4)$$

where,

Ds = Delivery Confidence Score;

D = project duration (to deliver a value initiative);

I = team performance integrity (with specific emphasis on the ability of the Initiative Leader);

C = commitment, ie levels of support, composed of two factors:

- o C1 = visible backing from the sponsor and senior executives for the change;

- o C2 = support from those who are impacted by the change;

E = effort above and beyond business as usual required for the project.

See Chapter 9 for details.

Other delivery confidence assessments can be used, particularly if an organization already has a preferred way of calculating the delivery confidence. Whichever method is used, the single score provides confidence (based on historical performance and the current project plan) that the project can be delivered successfully or may face issues.

Inputs and outputs   The inputs are the project duration (to deliver the value initiative), initiative delivery team's integrity, organizational commitment and effort required, and the output is the single score reflecting the confidence in the successful delivery of the planned project outcomes (Figure 7.14).

CALCULATING THE OPPORTUNITY SCORE

Having assessed the benefits and value of the chosen initiative, along with the confidence of delivering it, the Opportunity Score provides a single indicator to apply in decision-making. The organization and network partners can look at it collectively and come to a view on whether to proceed with the prospective value initiative, analyse it further or discard it. The calculation involves weightings

FIGURE 7.14 Delivery confidence input/output diagram

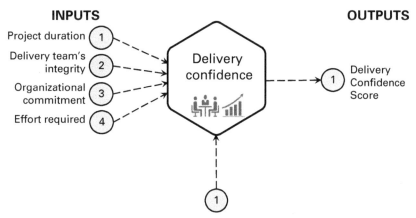

INPUTS

Project duration ①

Delivery team's integrity ②

Organizational commitment ③

Effort required ④

Delivery confidence

OUTPUTS

① Delivery Confidence Score

① Delivery confidence calculation

PRACTICES AND TOOLS

applied to the benefits, value and confidence elements based on the organization's context (Figure 7.15). The weightings are developed from stakeholder opinion and as such are subjective values (see Chapter 9). The following formula to calculate the Opportunity Score is used for illustration purposes:

$$Os = Benefits \times Wb + Value \times Wv + Confidence \times Wc \qquad (7.5)$$

where,

Os = Opportunity Score;

Benefits = ranked (1–5);

Wb = weighting applied to benefits;

Value = ranked (1–5);

Wv = weighting applied to value;

Confidence = ranked (1–5);

Wc = weighting applied to confidence.

The resulting cumulative Opportunity Score is expressed as a score (eg 1–25) or rank (eg 1 – least opportunity, 5 – most opportunity). For instance:

Opportunity Score 1: 0–5 (very low challenge);

Opportunity Score 2: 6–10 (low challenge);

Opportunity Score 3: 11–15 (medium challenge);

Opportunity Score 4: 16–20 (high challenge);

Opportunity Score 5: 21–25 (very high challenge).

Further information is in Chapter 9.

OPPORTUNITY SCORE WEIGHTINGS VARY FROM EACH ORGANIZATION'S PERSPECTIVE

A commercial organization specializing in management consulting and training sought to partner with a business school to develop and deliver a range of commercial short courses. The organization had a proven capability to produce the outputs (hence the high weighting applied to confidence) and considered the initiative's projected benefits and overall value to be quite high. However, while not disputing the capability, the business school questioned the overall benefits and value of the undertaking from their perspective. As a result, the weightings applied by the business school to value and benefits were quite low, thereby rendering the initiative's Opportunity Score low and the initiative did not proceed.

Summary

The Opportunity Assessment provides a measured, balanced evaluation of benefits projected from implementing chosen value initiatives, value attained

FIGURE 7.15 Opportunity Score input/output diagram

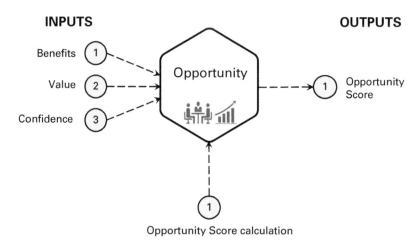

from benefits realization, and the level of confidence to deliver. In doing so, it provides Resilience Professionals with the information to decide on whether the proposed value initiative(s) implementation is practically viable for the organization.

Element 4: Good Alignment

Description

Having defined progress and assessed the challenge and the opportunity it brings, there is a need to confirm that the selected value initiatives align well with the objectives of its partnership network and Resilience Profile of the organization, to deliver the Progress Definition. This is to answer the question, 'Is there a Good Alignment of what is intended to be done with the Progress Definition or Evolving Vision and the relationship with partners in the future?'

Activities

A4.1 ALIGNMENT WITH RESILIENCE PROFILE

When assessing alignment with the Resilience Profile, the following question is answered:

Does the current Resilience Profile enable the value initiatives to be delivered?

Defining progress and recognizing the challenge and opportunity gives an understanding of which value initiatives may need to be implemented to realize progress. Assessing the alignment of those initiatives with the current Resilience Profile gives the confidence that they can be implemented in practice or flags the reasons why they could not (eg perhaps some essential skills or RESILIENCE Foundations are too low or missing in the organization). The alignment to the Resilience Profile allows the portfolio to be assessed as well as individual value initiatives.

Inputs and outputs   High-priority value initiatives from the PSPP backlogs and elements of the organization's Resilience Profile are used as inputs in this activity, whereas the decision about whether they are realizable by the organization is the output (Figure 7.16).

FIGURE 7.16 Alignment with Resilience Profile input/output diagram

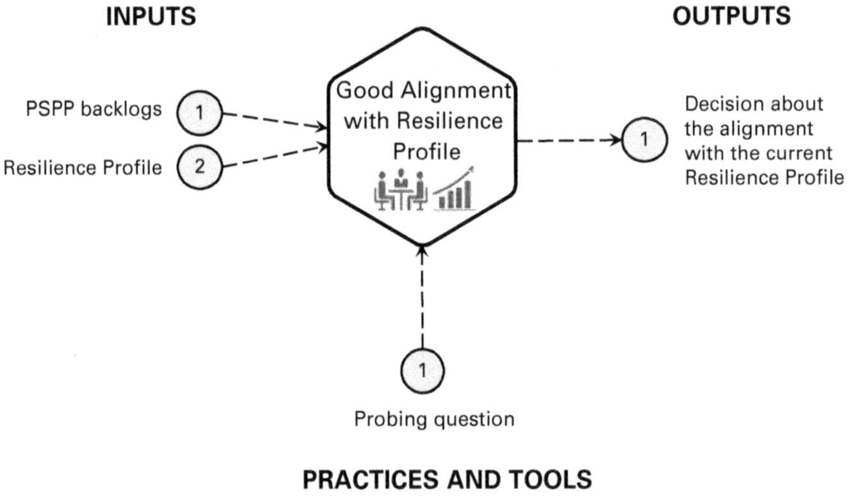

A4.2 ALIGNMENT WITH PARTNER NETWORK

Partner networks, especially for larger organizations, can be quite diverse, with many parties who have different objectives and needs. The fact that these parties are in the organization's orbit presumes a certain broad alignment of objectives; however, it does not automatically mean a close fit between the benefits of one organization's current value initiative(s) and a partner's. It is therefore important to know the effect the implementation of the proposed set of value initiatives would have on the network partners. Ideally, the benefits and value accrued by the partner network and the organization would be aligned. Methods for assessing benefits and value described in the Opportunity Assessment of the cycle can now be applied to the entire partner network.

MULTIPLE FACTORS ARE TAKEN INTO ACCOUNT FOR ALIGNMENT

Fresh rationalization of the product line may be good for us in saving costs and optimizing production and marketing, but at the same time, it may alienate a significant part of our loyal customer base, end contracts with long-standing suppliers and resellers, and affect staff in selected divisions or the entire company. We should reassess how to minimize these negative impacts and still achieve the Progress Definition.

Inputs and outputs The organization and partner Progress Definitions will be used as inputs, whereas identification of how closely these are aligned to each other is the output (Figure 7.17).

A4.3 OVERALL CONTRIBUTION TO PROGRESS

Delivery of progress for the organization, the objectives and benefits beyond those of immediate value initiatives should also be considered. That is, while timely delivery of high-quality outputs in budget is a standard measure of success for the majority of small-scale initiatives, wider measures must also be considered, including the realization of the Evolving Vision. This is

FIGURE 7.17 Alignment with partner network input/output diagram

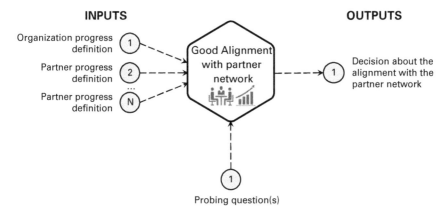

FIGURE 7.18 Resilience Value model

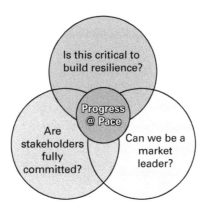

through strategic objectives and long-term resilience (eg improvement of practices and processes, higher motivation of staff, better position in the market, better flexibility of the business), and less tangible success factors (eg 'We are successful because we are passionate about what we do'), in addition to narratives of success and failure (eg 'We have prevailed against all odds! We have done it now, and we can do it again!'). To assess such contribution, one must define the broader benefits. A useful aid to assess contribution to progress is the authors' own resilience value model, in Figure 7.18. This uses criticality to resilience, stakeholder commitment and belief in being a market leader. Regardless of the model chosen, it must be able to be mapped against the Resilience Profile and Progress Definition to enable proper assessment.

Milestone: Decision Gate 1

Assessing the overall contribution of value initiatives to an organization's progress and the associated risk to delivery is the final stage before commitment to development. At this point, the Progress Backlog (and respective PSPP backlogs) have been created, the challenge and opportunity assessed, and the delivery of progress for the organization and its partner network confirmed.

The proposals must be assessed against the following questions:

- Is it affordable? (cost)
- Can it be delivered at pace? (time)
- Will there be a significant contribution to the Progress Definition? (effectiveness)

Decision Gate 1 takes all the information from the elements undertaken to decide to proceed to development, delay or reject the value initiative(s). The decision considers whether the Progress Definition can be delivered with the proposed value initiative(s), given the level of challenge to delivery, size of opportunity and confidence in delivery. The information can be presented as a business case, business justification or other standard that the organization uses.

Following a decision to proceed to development (or not), priorities of value initiatives in the Progress Backlog can be updated, ie decide whether the priority level of each of them must be upgraded, downgraded or remain unchanged. Ultimately, the exercise serves as a gate that approves only the value initiatives considered viable for implementation in the current PROGRESS Cycle.

FIGURE 7.19 Overall contribution to progress input/output diagram

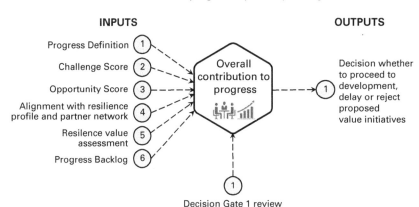

INPUTS

Progress Definition (1)

Challenge Score (2)

Opportunity Score (3)

Alignment with resilience profile and partner network (4)

Resilence value assessment (5)

Progress Backlog (6)

Overall contribution to progress

OUTPUTS

(1) Decision whether to proceed to development, delay or reject proposed value initiatives

(1) Decision Gate 1 review

PRACTICES AND TOOLS

Inputs and outputs   Inputs to this activity include value initiatives from the Progress Backlog and the broader benefits for the organization, while the value initiatives considered viable for implementation in the current PROGRESS Cycle are the output (Figure 7.19).

Summary

Good Alignment and Decision Gate 1 is the final assessment for value initiatives to proceed to implementation planning and subsequent release into production. Assessing the alignment with the existing capability of the organization, projected benefits to the partner network and overall contribution to the Progress Definition leads to a decision gate. This gate is where value initiatives from the Progress Backlog are reprioritized and qualified to either be released into development or remain on the Progress Backlog until the next PROGRESS Cycle.

Element 5: Rapids and Lagoons

Description

Once the progress (or PSPP) backlog has been updated at the Decision Gate 1, approved value initiatives are passed to development. It is important at this point to distinguish between two types of value initiatives, ie the ones that require Rapid implementation and the ones that require longer periods of development or are of lower priority and can be executed at a slower pace in the background. Just like a river flowing through a mixed landscape navigates Rapids and slower lagoons, organizations navigate through unstable and fast-changing environments as well as having more stable environments. Thus, depending on their type, value initiatives are allocated to backlogs for development referred to as either Rapids or lagoons. Rapids and Lagoons backlogs are used by Implementation Teams to prioritize, track and monitor delivery.

Activities

A5.1 BACKLOG MANAGEMENT
Value initiatives released through Decision Gate 1 and classed as requiring Rapid or slower Lagoon execution are fed into consolidated Rapids and Lagoons backlogs, which add to any existing initiatives already on the back-logs. Both these backlogs are then prioritized in the same manner as the Progress Backlog in the earlier elements of the cycle. Initiative Leaders are now confirmed and may provide useful input to prioritization. After the prioritiza-tion is completed, the backlogs can be handed over to initiative teams.

Inputs and outputs   Value initiatives approved at Decision Gate 1 are inputs to this activity, and consolidated Rapids and Lagoons backlogs are the output (Figure 7.20).

FIGURE 7.20 Backlog management input/output diagram

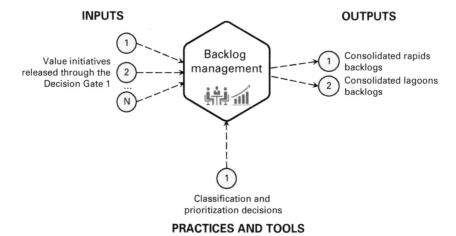

A5.2 RAPIDS/LAGOONS PROGRESS MONITORING

Once the consolidated Rapids and Lagoons backlogs have been handed over to Implementation Teams, progress charts need to be set up as a means of organizing and tracking the delivery. Progress charts will have a basic set of statuses, eg 'to do', 'in progress' and 'done' can be used; however, the exact configuration of those progress charts will be determined by the processes used by the organization. Once set up, the Rapids and Lagoons progress charts are continuously updated and can persist through several PROGRESS Cycles as new value initiatives of work across teams, focus on continuous delivery, and are a straightforward way to track and document the implementation of value initiatives.

Inputs and outputs   Consolidated Rapids and Lagoons backlogs will be used as inputs, whereas Rapids and Lagoons dashboards will be the output (Figure 7.21).

A5.3 IMPLEMENTATION OF ITEMS IN THE RAPIDS/LAGOONS CONSOLIDATED BACKLOGS

Organizations can employ a range of methodologies to implement value initiatives. They include delivering the initiatives as standalone programmes, projects or a continuous stream of improvements to existing products. Waterfall, agile or mixed approaches may be used for programmes and projects dependent on organizational practices or preferences. Examples

FIGURE 7.21 Rapids/lagoons dashboard input/output diagram

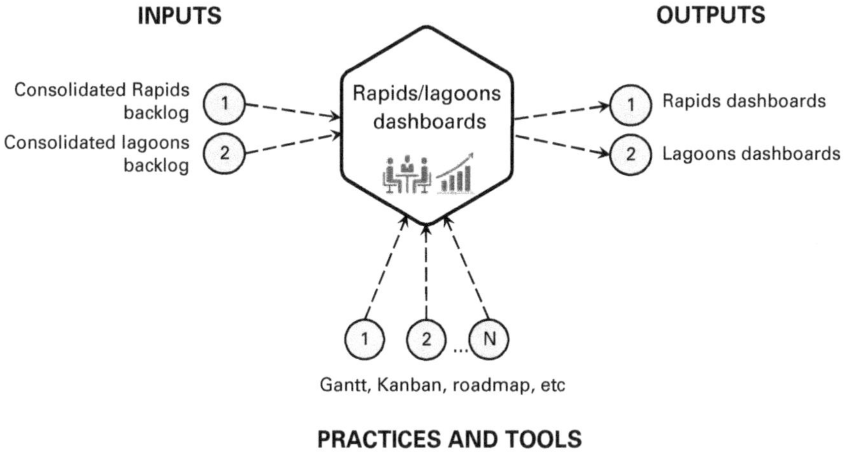

include PMBoK (Project Management Institute, 2017), PRINCE2 (AXELOS, 2017), Managing Successful Programmes (Sowden and Cabinet Office, 2020), PRINCE2 Agile (AXELOS, 2015), AgilePM (Agile Business Consortium, 2014a), AgilePgM (Agile Business Consortium, 2014b), AgileDS (Agile Business Consortium, 2018a), Scrum (Scrum.org, 2021), Scrum@ Scale (Sutherland and Scrum Inc., 2021), Disciplined Agile Delivery (IBM Corporation, 2011), LeSS (Larman and Vodde, 2021), and the like.

Inputs and outputs Consolidated Rapids and Lagoons backlogs will be inputs, and the implementation of selected value initiatives and updated Rapids and Lagoons progress charts are the output (Figure 7.22).

Summary

Rapids and Lagoons is all about planning the execution of the value initiatives released through Decision Gate 1. Organizing the initiatives into consolidated and prioritized backlogs representing complementary streams of work for urgent (Rapid) and slower-paced (lagoon) execution enables appropriate focus for teams and the organization. It also allows balancing of the implementation of progress with business-as-usual activities. The implementation of Rapids and Lagoons makes it possible for organizations

FIGURE 7.22 Implementation input/output diagram

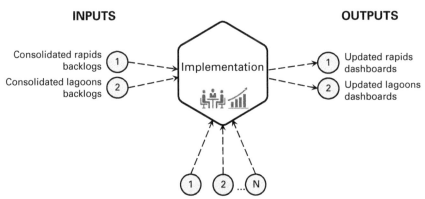

PMBoK, PRINCE2/MSP, PRINCE2 Agile, AgilePM/AgilePgM/AgilePfM, AgileDS, Scrum, Scrum@Scale, Disciplined Agile Delivery (DAD), LeSS, and work delivery status data

PRACTICES AND TOOLS

to realize progress with maximum utilization of the existing skills and resources, while the use of progress charts enables work visibility across teams, the entire organization and partner network if appropriate.

Element 6: Enabling Teams

Description

To ensure the selected value initiatives are implemented efficiently, the organization must enable its teams by creating a working environment conducive to productive work. This is achieved by appropriate regulation and governance combined with the PACE Culture elements of Purposeful Mindset, Elevated Energy, embedded Capability and Skills, and application of collaboration tools (see Chapter 6). As a result, everybody should work in enabled teams that actively collaborate.

Activities

A6.1 SELF-MANAGED TEAMS

Team organization is one of the key aspects of effective work, and the approach to set up the teams must be decided. Each set-up – functional, matrix, projectized or hybrid – has benefits and limitations, but whichever is chosen, a decision about the level of self-management is needed. The balance between the managed and self-managed is initially dictated by the prevailing organizational model but may be adjusted. Agile culture Principles (Agile Business Consortium, 2017), agreed values as well as corporate governance can be useful for the adjustment towards greater autonomy, innovation and motivation within teams. The team will agree their ways of working to utilize strengths and manage delivery of the value initiative most effectively.

Inputs and outputs The existing organizational model and current team set-up will be inputs, and decisions about the level of team autonomy and ways of working are the output (Figure 7.23).

A6.2 COLLABORATION METHODS

To enable progress, collaboration must be active in teams across the organization, but also across the entire partner network. This collaboration will be shaped by key factors, such as the type of partner organization, their

FIGURE 7.23 Self-managed teams input/output diagram

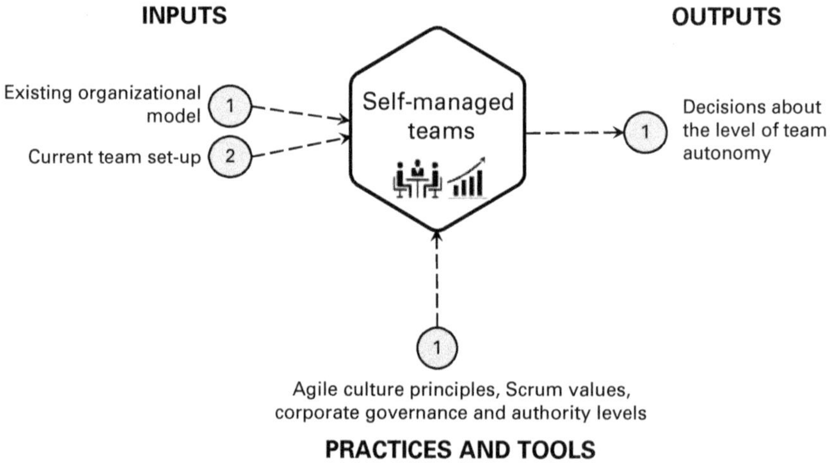

INPUTS

Existing organizational model (1)

Current team set-up (2)

Self-managed teams

(1)

OUTPUTS

Decisions about the level of team autonomy

(1)

Agile culture principles, Scrum values, corporate governance and authority levels

PRACTICES AND TOOLS

relationship with the organization, and the preferred or mandated way of operating. It is important to clearly define the degree of collaboration that is optimal and also practically possible. Tools to facilitate the collaboration may include nurturing a Purposeful Mindset, as well as the supporting skills, tools and systems. Accelerating Collaboration Everywhere (Assentire, 2021), Agile Culture Matrix (Agile Business Consortium, 2018a) and similar tools can be instrumental in achieving this objective.

Inputs and outputs   The existing partner network operating models and current team set-up will be inputs, and decisions about the degree of collaboration within teams, across the organization and the partner network are the output (Figure 7.24).

A6.3 FACILITATION METHODS

Developing teams with the required degree of autonomy and capability for effective collaboration requires focused facilitation. The depth and scale of facilitation would depend on factors such as the availability of appropriate tools, organizational provision of facilitation and general awareness and receptiveness of the audience to the facilitation process. Process Iceberg Model (Mann, 2021) and similar tools can be instrumental in achieving this objective.

Inputs and outputs   The existing team set-up will be used as the input, while the increased effectiveness of collaboration will be the output (Figure 7.25).

FIGURE 7.24   Collaboration methods input/output diagram

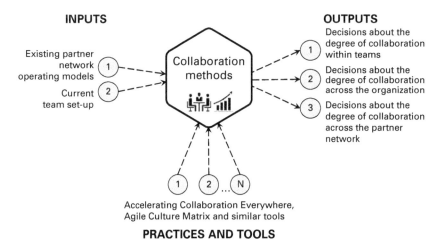

FIGURE 7.25   Facilitation methods input/output diagram

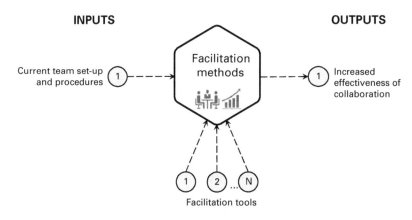

Summary

Teams capable of delivering value initiatives efficiently feature high levels of autonomy and motivation and collaborate effectively both within the organization and across its partner network. The role of the organization is to put the governance and PACE Culture elements in place that would enable and facilitate that autonomy and collaboration while ensuring robust systems to ensure accountability.

Element 7: Selection and Testing

Description

As value initiatives are implemented by delivery teams, they must be quality tested (eg checked against the definition of 'done') and subsequently marked as ready for release into production or use. At this point, the outputs must go through two assessments – market and user acceptance testing (UAT). The market assessment is required to confirm that the output delivers progress as planned, and the UAT is needed to confirm there is still a user demand. Both assessments are needed to take into account changes that may have occurred between the Progress Definition and the end of enabled teams. This ensures that however fast-paced the environment is, the outputs released into live use/production are relevant both to the organization and end user.

Activities

A7.1 QUALITY TESTS AND REVIEWS

The approach to testing the value initiative outputs is determined by the nature of those outputs and the preferred organizational practice. Notable types of testing include but are not limited to:

- functional/non-functional/performance;
- unit/integration/regression/end-to-end.

Reviews can be formal or informal and occur both during and at the end of delivery as well as various interim points.

Inputs and outputs   Deliverables from the implementation of value initiatives are inputs in this activity, whereas the decision of whether they qualify to be released into production/live use will be the output (Figure 7.26).

A7.2 MARKET ASSESSMENT AND USER ACCEPTANCE TESTING

After the outputs have been tested to perform in line with their original design, it is necessary to confirm they are still in demand. Focus groups and pilot testing are particularly useful methods for market and user acceptance testing. Focus groups can be an effective way to test products and services, whereas pilot testing can be useful to evaluate processes and practices.

FIGURE 7.26 Quality tests and reviews input/output diagram

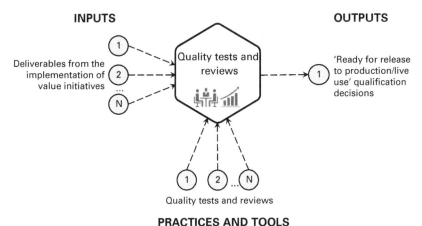

PRACTICES AND TOOLS

MARKET AND USER ACCEPTANCE TESTING

Focus groups can be used to identify demand and expectations for a new
health diagnostic service, while pilot testing could be used to test a new
customer service procedure within the health organization.

Both market assessment and user acceptance testing could be employed to
perform a limited pre-launch evaluation of the proposed value initiative.
Any opportunities or issues would be addressed in the value initiative
proposal.

THE VALUE INITIATIVE OF LAUNCHING LUXURY SKIING HOLIDAYS
IN A NEW DESTINATION

Market assessment – survey to assess the new destination profile and
standards versus the current luxury skiing holidays for potential market
demand.

User acceptance – pilot holidays offered to prospective new and returning
customers; survey the in-holiday experience and the post-holiday
satisfaction. Build the insights from the user assessment, including the
likelihood of recommendation, into the proposal.

FIGURE 7.27 Market assessment and user acceptance testing input/output diagram

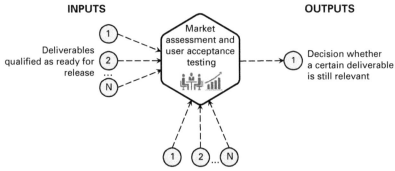

PRACTICES AND TOOLS

Inputs and outputs   Deliverables qualified as ready for release are inputs in this activity, and the output is the decision that a certain deliverable is still relevant to users in the current market (Figure 7.27).

A7.3 IMPACT ON THE PROGRESS DEFINITION

The final part of Selection and Testing is to acknowledge the progress made through this cycle by linking back to the Progress Definition at the start of the PROGRESS Cycle. The impact would be assessed using the measures identified in the Progress Definition. For practicality, a scoring system reflecting the extent to which the outputs produced meet the expectations set at the beginning of this cycle should be used. As a result, one should be able to acknowledge the progress made in the current cycle, such as 'at the end of this year we have X per cent more capability to create Y per cent more value in this area'.

Inputs and outputs   Measures for the success criteria of the value initiatives outputs implemented in the current cycle and the Progress Definition are inputs, while the measured improvement toward progress is the output (Figure 7.28).

Summary

Selection and Testing ensures that the value initiatives outputs implemented in this cycle comply with their design specification, success criteria, perform as expected, and are relevant in today's market. Their overall contribution to progress is benchmarked against the original measures in the Progress Definition.

FIGURE 7.28 Impact on the Progress Definition input/output diagram

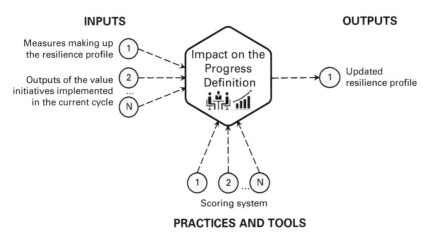

Element 8: Success and Learning

Description

Before the qualifying outputs are released into production or live use, a review of the organization's portfolio and operation will take place and may be adjusted, if necessary, to avoid duplication or inadvertent damage to the company's other products, services, or processes and practices. Sustained progress is difficult to achieve unless the learning process is organized and efficient. Reviews are also an opportunity to revise organizational practices and decision-making processes. Last, it is important to acknowledge success and celebrate when the cycle is completed, and the job is well done. This may relate to individual initiatives or the whole PROGRESS Cycle backlog.

REVIEWING THE PORTFOLIO

It is necessary to stop production and sales of a mobile phone when its replacement sales begin, or to modify, phase out or abandon an existing process or working practices when a new one is introduced that is more effective.

Activities

A8.1 PORTFOLIO REVIEW AND RELEASE

When released into production or live use, the new outputs may replace or substitute existing products and services or trigger the need to adjust the organization's operational processes and practices. To make room for the new outputs and avoid costly redundancy and inconsistencies, the portfolio may have to be adjusted. The organization can use its normal portfolio review method to achieve this. Ultimately, the release must be relevant to the company's situation today, and its portfolio should duly reflect this.

Milestone: Decision Gate 2

The assessments and testing in Opportunity Assessment, Good Alignment, and Selection and Testing ensure that only the outputs that truly represent value and progress for the organization at this time are released into production or live use. The portfolio adjustment, in turn, makes sure that any risks or unintended negative side effects the release may have on the existing product, service or operations are mitigated. In such a way, portfolio adjustment immediately before the release works as a second and final gate for the value initiative to go live. Thus, Decision Gate 2 is the decision about which outputs will be released, based on the impact on the overall portfolio.

DECISION TO GO LIVE OR NOT

Introduction of a new way of tracking projects may clash with an existing HR practice or financial planning routine and lead to unnecessary duplication of effort and waste of valuable resources. Thus, Decision Gate 2 would identify that the clash would need to be resolved prior to release to live use. This would be done by adding a value initiative to the appropriate backlog for reprioritization against the other value initiatives proposed. If the clash is very minor, it may be amended quickly as a simple small change.

Inputs and outputs   Ready-to-go live deliverables from the value initiatives, the organization's portfolio and existing practice are inputs in this activity, and the adjusted portfolio, practice and released value initiatives are the outputs (Figure 7.29).

FIGURE 7.29 Portfolio review and release input/output diagram

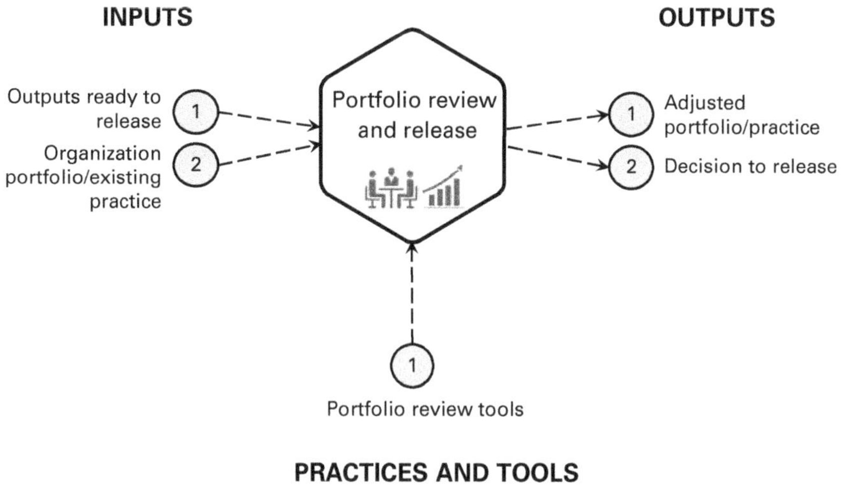

INPUTS

OUTPUTS

Outputs ready to release (1)

Organization portfolio/existing practice (2)

Portfolio review and release

(1) Adjusted portfolio/practice

(2) Decision to release

(1)

Portfolio review tools

PRACTICES AND TOOLS

A8.2 LEARN FROM EXPERIENCE

To ensure sustained progress, lessons must be learned and embedded in the organization with every iteration of the PROGRESS Cycle. It is recommended to be done throughout the cycle using both formal and informal channels. Organizations are free to choose the way it is accomplished and will be constrained primarily by their method, availability of resources and training. Organizational learning is a field too broad to be covered in any level of detail here, but it is important to consider the impact of learning from the PROGRESS Cycle on elements of the PACE Culture and RESILIENCE Foundations. In that respect, the learning is underpinned by Purposeful Mindset and selected application of tools and skills. In turn this supports Evolving Vision, Evolutionary Portfolio and Network Collaboration. The lessons must be embedded in the organization for the learning to be complete. This learning may also identify backlog items for future PROGRESS Cycles.

SHARING LEARNING

Adoption of a cutting-edge knowledge management technology and teamwork practice may result in an increased level of shared learning. This improves communication and collaboration within teams across the organization, as well as improved motivation and innovation. This, subsequently, impacts on the organization's capability to evolve its vision and portfolio that will contribute to improved Business Resilience.

FIGURE 7.30 Learn from experience input/output diagram

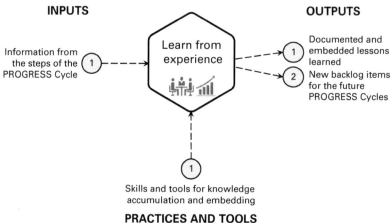

Inputs and outputs   Information from the elements of the PROGRESS Cycle are inputs to this activity, the outputs are documented, embedded lessons learned and (potentially) new backlog items for future PROGRESS Cycles (Figure 7.30).

A8.3 CELEBRATE SUCCESS

The last – but not least – element of the PROGRESS Cycle acknowledges the completion of work and recognizes success. There is a strong connection between taking stock of what was achieved, giving and receiving praise, and positive reinforcement of the practices that made the achievement possible. Even if a value initiative is stopped prior to release, there are likely to be areas of success to celebrate, and this should be used as an opportunity to reinvigorate the team. Related elements of the PACE Culture include Purposeful Mindset, application of tools, Capability and Skills, and Elevated Energy. Essentially, when after a long and possibly difficult cycle, the team and organization as a whole celebrate the achievement, it provides a necessary boost to confidence, reinvigorates staff and prevents possible burnout. Celebrating success can also include network partners, as well as sending a positive message to the partner network.

CELEBRATING SUCCESS INCLUDES NETWORK PARTNERS

A public sector organization was required to submit a competitive bid for delivery of services, which were being provided in-house at the time. After winning the tender against commercial competition, the Business Resilience Owner (CEO) took the bid team out for a meal to celebrate their success. This reinforced the Purposeful Mindset and Elevated Energy for the implementation of the new ways of working set out in the bid. Improved Business Resilience was achieved due to the team having worked with the unions as network partners for the bid and celebrating the success with them as well.

Inputs and outputs The achievements of individuals and teams are the inputs, while Elevated Energy of the staff and organization are the outputs (Figure 7.31).

Summary

To ensure the release of outputs from the value initiatives does not interfere with the current business as usual, the portfolio, processes or practices may need to be adjusted. Once this is done, it is safe to release the outputs into production or live use and realize the benefits of the progress that has been made. Lessons must be learned and embedded in the organization to make progress sustainable. Celebrating the successful completion of the cycle is important as it helps build the energy level required for the next PROGRESS Cycle and continued improvement to Business Resilience.

FIGURE 7.31 Celebrate success input/output diagram

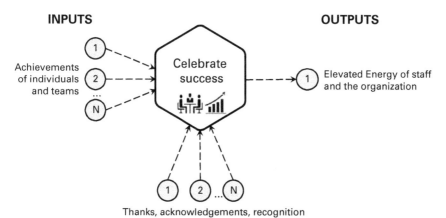

Roles for the PROGRESS Cycle domain

Progress Definition to Decision Gate 1

Business Resilience Owner – will own the Progress Definition at the organizational level and provide input of the organizational constraints, direction and vision, and other details required in the assessment. They agree the challenge, opportunity and Alignment Scores with stakeholder input where appropriate, inform senior management of the score, and mobilize the support for data collection where needed. They make the decision at Gate 1.

Progress Master – will support the Business Resilience Owner to utilize the Resilience Profile tool, create and update Progress Backlog and PSPP backlogs, and produce the progress roadmap. They advise the Business Resilience Owner on the use of the scores and appropriate rankings, undertake the data collection, and perform the challenge, opportunity and Alignment Score calculations.

Resilience Professional – will support the Business Resilience Owner and Progress Master to use the tools appropriately, interpret the results and advise on the processes. They may be engaged as the Business Resilience Owner or Progress Master, if the organization does not have suitable individuals to fill these Roles, or for initial implementation.

Rapids and Lagoons to Decision Gate 2

Business Resilience Owner – liaises with initiatives' sponsor (or act as a sponsor, if appropriate), provides input to consolidated Rapids and Lagoons backlog prioritization updates, and receives work delivery status updates. They approve the contribution to the Progress Definition, Decision Gate 2 and the adjustment of the portfolio, agree the items to go on the backlog for future cycles, approve lessons to be embedded, recognize success and authorize celebrations.

Progress Master – advises Business Resilience Owner on the use of consolidated Rapids and Lagoons backlogs, appointment of the Initiative Leaders, and implementation methods. They also support and advise Initiative Leaders on facilitation, collaboration and self-management and act as a facilitator where needed, including market and user acceptance testing and impact on the Progress Definition. They provide information for Decision Gate 2, identify items to add to the Progress Backlog for future cycles, identify lessons to improve the Business Resilience Framework or recommend adapting, identify achievements and recommend celebrations of success.

Initiative Leader – will be responsible for the value initiative delivery, liaise with the Progress Master on the delivery methods and provide status updates. They provide input to prioritization of backlogs and are responsible for developing a self-managed team, which actively collaborates. They arrange quality testing and reviews, market and user acceptance testing, and input to the impact on the Progress Definition. They indicate items to add to the backlog for future cycles, highlight lessons to improve future value initiatives, and identify team and individual achievements that should be recognized.

Benefits, risks and costs

Benefits

There are several benefits to using the PROGRESS Cycle to deliver the Progress Definition. These include:

- a focus on Business Resilience in addition to delivery of initiatives enabling continuous improvement of resilience;
- a realistic assessment of challenge in addition to opportunity and alignment enabling clear decisions about viability;
- clear identification of the value initiatives that need to be delivered urgently and those that can be done at a slower pace to balance resources and workloads;
- implementation of the PACE Culture to enable teams, which releases Elevated Energy;
- a final review against the portfolio prior to release of value initiative outputs to live use, which avoids duplications or lack of demand.

Risks

As with any change there are risks to implementing the PROGRESS Cycle. These include but are not limited to:

- Resistance to change may prevent the elements being implemented. Support, training and coaching can mitigate this risk.

- Lack of understanding of the elements or activities may mean they are implemented inappropriately. Training or coaching can mitigate this.
- Lack of support within the organization to provide inputs to undertake the assessments appropriately would need to be mitigated by the Business Resilience Owner facilitating senior support.
- Lack of an appropriate Progress Definition could mean that assessments are not accurate, which would need to be mitigated by the Business Resilience Owner and Progress Master working together to ensure the Progress Definition is adequate.

Costs

Costs will vary depending on the organization and scope of value initiatives. The costs should reduce over time as learning and improvements are embedded to the processes and practices, as well as improving Business Resilience.

Summary

The PROGRESS Cycle enables progress through the implementation of rigorously assessed and tested value initiatives, delivered by self-managed collaborating teams, utilizing experiential and empirical learning. The cyclical nature of this domain leads to a continuous stream of improvements introduced by the organization responding to its Evolving Vision and requirements or the external environment pressures. The deliberate and purposeful nature of these efforts ensures that they produce meaningful contributions to the organization's Progress Definition, which, in turn, improves the organization's Business Resilience Profile.

QUESTIONS TO THINK ABOUT

- What types of value initiatives should be included in a PROGRESS Cycle; how long should a PROGRESS Cycle last and when is it completed?
- Who decides which value initiatives should be explored and which should be progressed to development during a PROGRESS Cycle?
- Who would decide on the speed of value initiatives within the PROGRESS Cycle?

References

Agile Business Consortium (2014a) *Agile Project Management Handbook v2.0*, Agile Business Consortium

Agile Business Consortium (2014b) *Agile Programme Management (AgilePgM®) Handbook*, Agile Business Consortium

Agile Business Consortium (2017) *Culture and Leadership: The nine Principles of agile leadership*, cdn.ymaws.com/www.agilebusiness.org/resource/resmgr/documents/whitepaper/the_9_Principles_of_agile_le.pdf (archived at https://perma.cc/MA8W-8WVR)

Agile Business Consortium (2018a) *AgileDS Digital Services Handbook*, Agile Business Consortium

Agile Business Consortium (2018b) *Development Matrix for Agile Culture*, cdn.ymaws.com/www.agilebusiness.org/resource/resmgr/documents/templates/agile-consortium-culture-dna.pdf (archived at https://perma.cc/4WTG-ECAA)

Assentire (2021) *Accelerating Collaboration Field Book*, https://issuu.com/assentire/docs/collaboration_field_book_v18_23_mar (archived at https://perma.cc/7A5J-79LV)

AXELOS (2010) *Management of Value*, The Stationery Office, London

AXELOS (2011) *Management of Portfolios (Managing Successful Portfolios)*, The Stationery Office, London

AXELOS (2015) *PRINCE2 Agile*, The Stationery Office, London

AXELOS (2017) *Managing Successful Projects with PRINCE2*, The Stationery Office, London

Cambridge Dictionary Online (2021a) 'Process', Dictionary.cambridge.org, dictionary.cambridge.org/dictionary/english/process (archived at https://perma.cc/XJU5-WVMR)

Cambridge Dictionary Online (2021b) 'Practice', Dictionary.cambridge.org, dictionary.cambridge.org/dictionary/english/practice (archived at https://perma.cc/H9LH-MLEW)

Emmott, R, Siebold, S and Murphy, F (2021) EU reaches deal on Belarus economic sanctions, according to Austria diplomats, *Reuters*, 18 June, www.reuters.com/world/europe/eu-reaches-deal-belarus-economic-sanctions-according-austria-diplomats-2021–06–18 (archived at https://perma.cc/CT8G-NW97)

IBM Corporation (2011) *Disciplined Agile Delivery: An introduction*, 1 January, www.agilealliance.org/wp-content/uploads/2016/01/Disciplined-Agile-Delivery-RAW14261USEN.pdf (archived at https://perma.cc/6YA5-6FD9)

Jenner, S (2012) *Managing Benefits: Optimizing the return from investments*, The Stationery Office, London

Larman, C and Vodde, B (2021) *Large Scale Scrum (LeSS): Overview*, less.works

Mann, T (2021) Process Iceberg Organization model explained, *People Alchemy*, www.alchemyassistant.com/topics/YUMf9x6HAnHxu4bB.html (archived at https://perma.cc/25GB-35J9)

Moitra, D and Ganesh, J (2005) Web services and flexible business processes: Towards the Adaptive Enterprise, *Information & Management*, https://www.sciencedirect.com/science/article/abs/pii/S0378720604001338 (archived at https://perma.cc/DFW2-29ZG)

Project Management Institute (2017) *A Guide to the Project Management Body of Knowledge (PMBOK Guide)*, Project Management Institute, Newtown Square

Scrum.org (2021) *What is Scrum?*, Scrum.org, www.scrum.org/resources/what-is-scrum (archived at https://perma.cc/4B95-96ZJ)

Sirkin, H, Keenan, P and Jackson, A (2005) The hard side of change management, *Harvard Business Review*, hbr.org/2005/10/the-hard-side-of-change-management (archived at https://perma.cc/AP9K-KJ92)

Sowden, R and Cabinet Office (2020) *Managing Successful Programmes*, The Stationery Office, London

Stolyarov, G and Balmforth, T (2021) Backlash over Minsk incident takes Belarus airline to the brink, *Reuters*, 28 May, www.reuters.com/business/aerospace-defense/backlash-over-minsk-incident-takes-belarus-airline-brink-2021–05–28 (archived at https://perma.cc/2S2P-MXN7)

Sutherland, J and Scrum Inc. (2021) *The Scrum At Scale® Guide: The definitive guide to the Scrum@Scale framework*, www.scrumatscale.com/scrum-at-scale-guide-online (archived at https://perma.cc/Z8U4-7P2K)

Wood, G (2021) The Ryanair hijacking pierced the delusion of flight, *The Atlantic*, 28 May, www.theatlantic.com/ideas/archive/2021/05/belarus-ryanair-hijacking/619028 (archived at https://perma.cc/YQ2H-R3SR)

08

PURE Business Resilience implementation strategies

Purpose

The purpose of the Business Resilience strategies is to identify how best to implement Business Resilience. PURE strategies provide alternative ways to implement some or all of the framework, comprising five domains, in which the Principles and Roles support the Progress @ Pace 8-4-8 Model. Whichever strategy is chosen, implementation needs to enable Business Resilience objectives and benefits to be realized, as outlined in earlier chapters. Once the implementation approach has been agreed by stakeholders, and the framework adopted and/or adapted, organizations will be able to make sustained progress. All Business Resilience implementation strategies provide an opportunity to adopt, adapt and continuously improve the Business Resilience Framework.

Introduction

Leaders at all levels look for practical ways to set goals and get things done, in response to requests for better products, services, processes and practices. When exploring Business Resilience, organizations will set objectives and focus on Principles and Roles, and how these enable business functions, culture and progress to flourish. These ideas should be reflected in the Evolving Vision of the organization and Progress Definition(s). Leaders must ensure sufficient clarity of communication to convey not only Business Resilience objectives, when it will be improved and what new capabilities will be embedded, but how it will be done and why this work will contribute to vision.

Business Resilience and communication

Answering why Business Resilience will be improved enables teams to connect Principles with purpose; business leaders can then communicate what the organizational benefits of resilience Principles are to staff, stakeholders and customers. Answering how Business Resilience will be improved engenders believability in the chosen strategy. Once Good Alignment between Business Resilience objectives and goals of internal teams is established, the challenge of getting started on strategy implementation becomes very attractive rather than daunting. Attention moves on to consideration of how best to achieve Business Resilience. Organizations define meaningful goals related to output and business results and teams become highly energized to achieve them. Most importantly, momentum builds as believability extends more widely among stakeholders that sustained improvements to practices and processes can be implemented (Beckhard and Harris, 1987).

Getting started

Initial implementation of a framework for Business Resilience presents a dilemma because the very thing practitioners would want to use (the Progress @ Pace 8-4-8 Model within the Business Resilience Framework) will not be available until strategy implementation is under way. So to get started, it is assumed that a development, project or progress team will work collaboratively under senior leadership, using the high-level roadmap with milestones (later in this chapter) to plan and schedule the work.

After initial implementation, work would typically be completed within PROGRESS Cycles. From the second cycle onwards, operational and development work should include delivery of the existing products and services, plus continuous improvement of the Business Resilience Framework.

The strategy commences by gaining agreement with senior stakeholders on the need and the compelling benefits of Business Resilience; this is called 'adopting Business Resilience'. A target goal for Business Resilience is shared with development and delivery teams, engaging them in the future framework. Following agreement, a strategic approach to implementing the Business Resilience Framework is selected that builds upon the existing organization environment, taking advantage of embedded development practices and processes. (Alternatively, organizations may wish to explore in-house ways to realize resilience Principles – as discussed in the exploratory strategy, below.)

Senior stakeholders and the development and delivery teams will prioritize work to be done to create a Business Resilience Framework on the basis that it not only delivers immediate benefits, but will build RESILIENCE Foundations, a PACE Culture and PROGRESS Cycle to deliver sustainable benefits, whatever the VUCA situation. As improvements to the framework are realized, organizations will become more adept at improving domain elements, and in turn, delivering better outputs and outcomes from initiatives within the portfolio.

The approach through which the Business Resilience Framework is adopted is determined by assessing the benefits that could be available to the organization, the current organization status and the delivery confidence of senior stakeholders, and the costs and risks of implementation. The PURE strategy options for moving forward are:

- Progressive – organizations build resilience from their existing processes and practices to achieve a target Business Resilience Framework standard.

- Urgent – organizations implement the entire standard Business Resilience Framework.

- Responsive – organizations add/substitute Business Resilience Framework elements to address identified weaknesses in organizational processes and practices.

- Exploratory – organizations explore Business Resilience, formulating their own methodology based only upon Business Resilience Framework Principles; the methodology and Business Resilience Framework are tested against the organization's Business Resilience objectives.

Implementation of the Business Resilience strategy will ensure that the organization's functional capabilities (RESILIENCE Foundations), its people (PACE Culture) and ability to adapt and improve its portfolio (PROGRESS Cycle) succeed where others fail in similar business situations; and whenever possible, the organization can take advantage of VUCA disruptions to deliver more customer value and make progress at pace.

Vision of Business Resilience

Clarifying and communicating the organizational resilience vision is an essential foundation element. This is a key anchor for the introduction of the Business Resilience Framework because the 22 elements of the framework define a strategy for how to realize resilience, and are inherent within a new or adapted operating model itself. Its introduction and operation is a responsibility of everyone in leadership positions, throughout the five levels of the organization. However, following a decision to adopt the framework, clarifying and communicating the vision becomes more challenging, because the Business Resilience Framework or elements will be improved (and therefore changed) regularly. So, as the processes and practices of the Business Resilience Framework are adapted to become more resilient to changing environments, this evolution of the 5 domains and 22 elements will impact the definition of progress and work of individuals, teams and partner organizations.

VISION FOR BUSINESS RESILIENCE

An organizational vision of Business Resilience could be expressed in many ways; one may be: 'a sustainable capability to connect with customers, apply professional practices and deliver solutions leading to a brighter future for all in a global digital but volatile and uncertain economy'.

Ultimately, organizations succeed because they build and sustain relative competitive strength, typically by investing in learning, innovating and testing portfolio ideas. Often there are drivers of success, where the purpose and value of individual adaptations are clear, and resilience is delivered. On other occasions, however, a lack of clarity of the vision results in confusion or indifference.

In some sectors, where Business Resilience exists, businesses have been able to demonstrate significant progress where others have been conspicuously unable to do so. A good example of this situation can be seen in the 'low-cost carrier' segment of the European airline business, which took place in the very challenging market conditions of the 2020/21 pandemic.

BUSINESS RESILIENCE ENABLES PROGRESS

Wizz Air (the Hungarian budget airline, established in 2003) provides an excellent example of steady growth in aircraft, routes and bases through a financial crisis, travel restrictions and lockdowns. A very strong financial base enabled Wizz Air to enter the 2020 pandemic with €1.6 billion in cash and the lowest unit costs in the European airline industry (Loh, 2021); this enabled Wizz

Air to make progress during the pandemic, since airports and suppliers were keen to work with them at a time when competitors were almost non-existent, or simply unable to function normally in the market. Building up cash savings in preceding years therefore enabled Wizz Air to succeed where others had failed or were failing.

Wizz Air therefore used their pillars of organizational strength to make remarkable gains in market share, a very considerable achievement in the airline industry. Additionally, prior to the pandemic, by actively engaging supply chain partners and communicating to them the importance of being financially competitive, Wizz Air managed to consolidate a leading market position in Central and Eastern Europe and carry 34 million passengers in 2019, mainly by investing in newer aircraft, lowering unit costs, increasing margins and competitiveness.

As is clear from the Wizz Air example above, it is critical that all stakeholders understand the motivation for action on Business Resilience throughout the lifecycle – communicating why it is important for organizations to compete in good times, and how to prepare to connect and collaborate effectively in challenging times. With this vision securely in place, the Progress Definition for expansion was laid and implemented in differing phases over the business lifecycle.

This example demonstrates the benefits of organizations understanding and keeping focused on their Progress Definition to achieve competitive advantage. While other airlines struggled to compete or maintain untenable market positions, resilient organizations were able to take advantage of adverse market conditions, building better networks and customer relationships, repositioning themselves for improved market conditions in the years ahead. Wizz Air demonstrates the benefits of adapting the organization, products and services to realize their vision and Progress Definition as a 'low-cost carrier'.

Value proposition of implementing Business Resilience

Senior management need clarity about the value proposition posed by Business Resilience – in particular, how much additional resource is required and how long will it take to deliver value?

To get started, practitioners should reference the role descriptions for Business Resilience Owner, Progress Master and Initiative Leaders, identifying existing resources who could fulfil the activities and duties shown to establish the framework and then to operate it. It is challenging to complete a comparative assessment of the Business Resilience Framework and current organization practices and processes, identifying overlaps and gaps. The benefits from realigning practices and processes will be assessed and then activities listed to complete the implementation. It is recommended that the work is estimated and prioritized, costed and risk-assessed using a time-boxed format. A best practice approach would be to use BRIT workshops (discussed in Chapter 5).

Typically, the Business Resilience Owner might consider developing an outline 100-day Business Resilience implementation plan including Roles, tasks and outcomes to deliver more business value, whether products or services, processes or practices across the organization's network. This would be a practical approach to implementing better Business Resilience, based upon existing practices and processes and the Business Resilience Framework.

While the Business Resilience value proposition will be organization-specific, and subject to unique factors, an assessment of the level of challenge, opportunity and alignment, including the benefits, costs and risks, should always be undertaken. This will enable a prioritized list of elements, if not adopting all, which, if improved, would make a positive impact on the organization's ability to make sustained progress. Further, the assessment should be extended across the five levels of the organization to 'right-size' the organization's Business Resilience programme, ensuring investment in individual resilience initiatives are balanced and, where possible, integrated with ongoing work across the portfolio.

The Business Resilience Owner will be assisted by the Progress Master to complete a costed schedule for the Business Resilience implementation outline plan. This should specifically include options to resource the plan from existing or, if necessary, external resources.

Business justification and resilience value model

When communicating the need for Business Resilience, a business justification case could be used; it should contain reasons for selection of the preferred approach to introduce Business Resilience, which must deliver more value to customers or users than current arrangements. The justification should address each of the four PURE strategic approaches of:

- Progressive – a bottom–up approach starting with the existing people, processes and practices and adapting them to progress toward the Business Resilience Framework.

- Urgent – a top–down approach to adopt the standard Business Resilience Framework in a single PROGRESS Cycle, replacing current ways of working.

- Responsive – a bottom–up approach starting with the existing processes and practices, adding or supplementing Business Resilience elements to enhance people, processes and practices, improving resilience by modifying current organizational ways of working.

- Exploratory – a bottom–up approach in which organizations explore Business Resilience ideas with partners, identifying resilience objectives and developing an in-house methodology based upon Business Resilience Principles to achieve resilience objectives.

The business justification would typically show the benefits, costs and risks of implementing viable Progressive, Urgent, Responsive and Exploratory approaches, with minimum and maximum variations shown, in addition, for the preferred approach. This follows discussion with stakeholders on actions required to achieve the target level or objectives for Business Resilience, and with the exploratory strategy, a comparative assessment with the Business Resilience Framework.

Viable approaches should be assessed in the context of gaps between the organization's current and target Resilience Profiles, evolutionary vision and sensitivity to the organization's challenge level and opportunity. Whichever approach is preferred, it must contribute to achieving resilience objectives or improving one or more of the eight RESILIENCE Foundations, four PACE Culture or eight PROGRESS Cycle elements, in addition to offering affordable, efficient and effective implementation.

A record of findings of the resilience value model is included, which provides an emotional cross-check for the rational decision to adopt Business Resilience in the business case. It confirms the level of stakeholder support for the preferred approach to Business Resilience implementation. It is best done independently by a Progress Master or Resilience Professional, familiar with the Progress Definition goals. The five levels of the organization should be consulted when gathering opinions for the resilience value review.

A typical 'resilience value review' would be conducted in a BRIT workshop, gathering subjective scoring and noting observations. At the end of the workshop the facilitator should ensure the leader has information on:

- positive and negative stakeholder perspectives of options, and the 'preferred' approach;
- insights gathered from internal and external network partners regarding options;
- project team or Progress Master's assessment of stakeholder passion, capability and value for all options, including the 'preferred' implementation strategy.

The combination of business justification case and resilience value review assists leaders (or if appointed a Business Resilience Owner) to make the right investment decision to adopt the Business Resilience Framework. If authorized, the preferred option will be implemented, in accordance with resilience objectives and strategy.

Adopting and adapting Business Resilience

Adopting Business Resilience

Adopting Business Resilience provides a confirmation that the organization intends to implement Business Resilience. There is a clear priority for improving Business Resilience as a strategic direction for enhancing and sustaining the organization. At this point the organization has committed itself to Business Resilience, although how this should be done and what is involved has yet to be fully explored.

Following a detailed presentation of the standard Business Resilience Framework (BRF) by a Progress Master or Resilience Professional, senior management will have carefully reviewed how the 5 domains and 22 elements of the framework work together and the Progress @ Pace 8-4-8 Model will enhance progress.

Senior management should conclude that the benefits of using the Business Resilience Framework would add value to the organization and that the costs and risks of implementation are acceptable.

Adapting Business Resilience

Adapting Business Resilience means adjusting the standard Business Resilience Framework elements to the target organization framework; or alternatively, it is adding Business Resilience elements into organizational processes and practices to become more resilient.

As previously outlined, adapting Business Resilience can use one of the PURE strategies (Progressive, Urgent, Responsive and Exploratory), depending on the preferred approach:

- Progressive involves adopting the standard Business Resilience Framework and adapting it to include existing organizational processes and practices before tailoring the framework to the organizational vision of Business Resilience.
- Urgent is to install the standard Business Resilience Framework with minimal tailoring to existing organizational Roles, processes and practices names and tools.
- Responsive involves continuing existing organizational processes and practices, including prioritized Business Resilience Framework elements, with lean tailoring of them.
- Exploratory involves a project team developing an in-house Business Resilience methodology from resilience Principles to meet organizational resilience objectives and performing comparative testing with the Business Resilience Framework.

PLUG AND PLAY

A cornerstone of making progress to improve Business Resilience at pace is the concept of plug and play. The design of the Business Resilience Framework is modular and therefore elements can simply be plugged into the relevant part of the framework and put into play for the organization. This concept is especially useful when undertaking initial implementation and identifying the existing practices that already align to the framework and so can simply be plugged in. The processes and practices may already exist or can be developed to align to the framework, which are then ready to plug and play in the next version of the framework.

Following adoption of Business Resilience, adapting starts with identifying any existing processes and practices that would improve the standard BRF or identifying BRF elements that would enhance existing processes or practices. The adapting approach is to use or extract priority existing processes or practices, where possible to do so, although it is recognized this may not be possible where they form part of integrated systems. Where it is not possible, it is necessary to identify if 'make or buy' options are available. If either approach is possible, or in the case of standard BRF elements items, the relevant items should be assembled as modules, and tested for functionality.

The modules will then be refined to the target Business Resilience Framework, including any role descriptions or tools, to deliver both Business Resilience and sustained progress. These can then be plugged into an organizational Business Resilience Framework or enhanced organizational processes and practices. Further refinement can be completed in subsequent PROGRESS Cycles, following operational use (or playing of modules) to provide functional and organizationally consistent processes, practices or elements to enhance resilience. This plug-and-play functionality also supports further adapting and tailoring, which can bring about improved ease of use or additional application benefits within the organization's Business Resilience environment.

PLUG AND PLAY

An example of the plug-and-play concept is an organization that already utilizes tailored agile and linear project and programme management methods to deliver initiatives Rapidly or more slowly; these can be plugged into the Rapids and Lagoons element of the PROGRESS Cycle as they are ready to play. They would identify agile methods for Rapid and linear for Lagoon initiatives.

Four approaches to strategy implementation

Organizations will have many reasons to become more resilient; it could be a management response to market changes in supplier or buyer behaviour that has impacted the portfolio, or influences in the wider socio-economic environment brought about by governments or natural disaster. In these circumstances, organizations may face new challenges, raising awareness of increasing VUCA conditions in their business environment. Depending on embedded processes and practices, portfolio history, current financial status and the consequences of volatility, organizations will have differing insights into the importance, urgency and scale of Business Resilience needed to provide sustainable progress.

The selected implementation strategy for Business Resilience will enable senior management teams to implement the most viable approach to achieve objectives. In anticipation, it is expected that a Resilience Professional will have presented the senior management team with essential information on Business Resilience: what is in scope, the benefits of using it in practice and indicative costs and risks of implementation approaches. In the case of the exploratory strategy, this will include a comparative assessment of the in-house methodology and the Business Resilience Framework.

Once the Business Resilience strategy is authorized, an initial task would be to refine indicative information provided in the business case, developing planning estimates, eg beneficial impacts of adopting of Business Resilience, time, cost and risks of implementation, and metrics. This will pave the way for the senior management team to authorize a budget to implement the Business Resilience initiative and establish one of the team as the Business Resilience Owner.

Progressive approach

The progressive approach (Figure 8.1) implements the Business Resilience Framework over several PROGRESS Cycles, initially introducing priority elements of the Business Resilience Framework to the whole organization or to specific departments, divisions or business units within it. This approach could target elements where progress can be made at the fastest pace or where departments or divisions of the organization have the greatest need. In a progressive approach, the organization will develop an organization Business Resilience Framework adapted to the needs of the organization, integrating effective processes and practices already in place using plug-and-play modularity of the framework reflected in the 22 elements of the standard design.

Implementation is based upon the roadmap and milestones plan. The progressive approach will have a bespoke implementation plan. Priority processes, practices, elements or tools in the standard Business Resilience Framework design are used to create the initial organizational Business

FIGURE 8.1 Progressive approach to strategy implementation

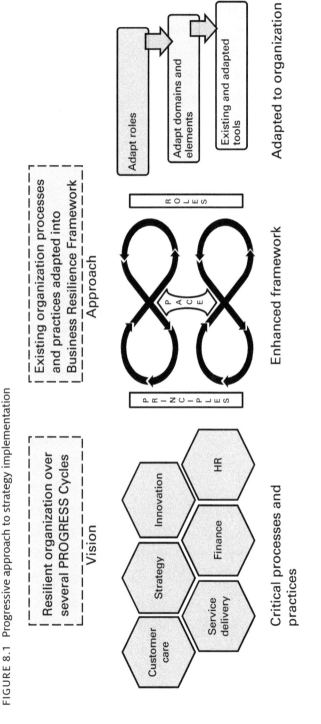

Vision

Resilient organization over several PROGRESS Cycles

Approach

Existing organization processes and practices adapted into Business Resilience Framework

Adapted to organization

Critical processes and practices

Customer care

Strategy

Innovation

Service delivery

Finance

HR

Enhanced framework

ROLES

PACE

PRINCIPLES

Adapt roles

Adapt domains and elements

Existing and adapted tools

Resilience Framework. Realization of the implementation plan is included in the Progress Definition once the PROGRESS Cycle is established to commence continuous improvement. The learning from this cycle will inform prioritization of the next adaptations required to the framework and future value initiatives; these initiatives will be reflected in updates to the Progress Definition for each subsequent PROGRESS Cycle.

The progressive approach is most appropriate where organizations have existing processes and practices; these can be adapted and included in the organization Business Resilience Framework. In this situation it is important not to discard established routines that are effective but to build on them and enhance processes and practices to improve the resilience level of the organization. It is recommended that the progressive approach is used in most situations, to improve success and reduce risk. As the organization implements the Business Resilience Framework, further changes in the environment are to be expected, requiring further adaptations; subsequent value initiatives will be included in the Progress Definition of the future PROGRESS Cycles.

Urgent approach

The urgent approach (Figure 8.2) involves the whole organization adopting the Business Resilience Framework in a single PROGRESS Cycle, using the

FIGURE 8.2 Urgent approach to strategy implementation

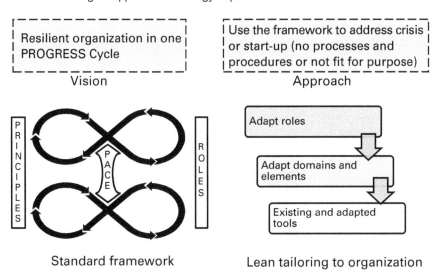

roadmap and milestones. Organizational imperatives may require lean tailoring of domains, elements or tools in the Business Resilience Framework; however, this should be minimal, such as changing names. The urgent approach encourages business-critical processes and practices to be identified and tailored to fit into the framework as part of the initial implementation. Initial implementation is done using the roadmap and milestones plan.

Once the initial framework has been implemented, subsequent improvements would be implemented in PROGRESS Cycles as value initiatives. The focus remains on new ways of working in the organization, with lean tailoring of processes and practices.

This approach is most appropriate for a start-up organization where standard processes and practices are not yet in place for the organization. It may also be useful where the organization is at a crisis point, with practices and processes that are no longer fit for purpose and needs wholesale change in order to succeed.

Responsive approach

The responsive approach (Figure 8.3) is used where the organization is not ready to adopt the whole Business Resilience Framework, but would find some domains, elements or tools within the framework useful. An example could be taken from the RESILIENCE Foundations domain, where an organization wishes to introduce the Network Collaboration element without the requirement to implement other elements. Perhaps it is a standout priority? Perhaps it is affordable? Perhaps it can be promptly tested before other framework elements are introduced? Perhaps it is simply an opportunistic situation that can be delivered within a timeframe with acceptable costs and risks? Any of these considerations may provide a good reason to use the responsive approach.

The responsive approach is most appropriate where the organization needs to respond to an anticipated external opportunity or threat. The responsive approach may provide an opportunity for teams, departments or business units to introduce elements of the standard Business Resilience Framework alongside or instead of existing processes and practices, in a way that is seen as beneficial, or functionally useful, to the organization and its customers or partners, eg where a head of business unit or department has the autonomy to adapt processes and practices, to sustain success.

FIGURE 8.3 Responsive approach to strategy implementation

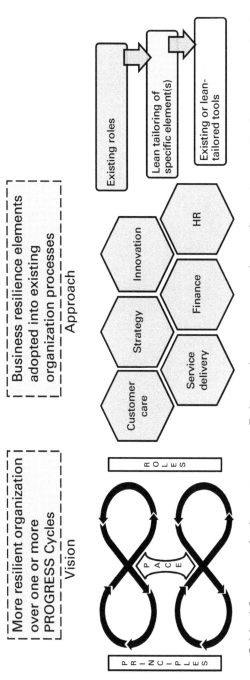

The purpose is to enhance existing processes and practices, not to replace current ways of working or to introduce organization-wide change. It should clarify the limits of changes and how pioneering elements could deliver value, energize teams and improve organization Business Resilience.

The responsive approach is most likely to be used for exploration, discovery and learning about Business Resilience. Indeed, it may be an ideal strategy for senior management to test key aspects of the Business Resilience Framework. Most likely outcomes are to continue with the responsive strategy or migrate towards a progressive approach in the future.

RESPONSIVE APPROACH

An example would be that an organization seeking benefits from strengthening existing functional competences of partnering may wish to use the Network Collaboration element within the next PROGRESS Cycle to demonstrate improvement by measuring business and resilience results. The recognition of customers and suppliers as network partners with agreed collaboration areas will improve success. Impacts could be confirmed with the Business Resilience Profile for the Network Collaboration element, providing confidence to the organization.

Exploratory approach

FIGURE 8.4 Exploratory approach to strategy implementation

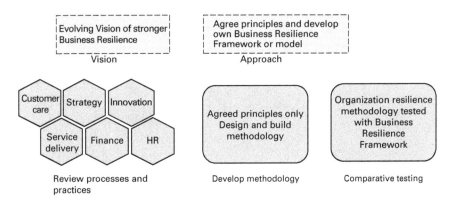

A project team is established. Organizations engage leaders/network partners to explore Business Resilience and formulate their own methodology based only upon Business Resilience Principles. The exploratory strategy (Figure 8.4) provides a ground-floor opportunity for leaders and partners to be engaged and learn together from the ground upwards.

EXPLORATORY IMPLEMENTATION

The exploratory approach would benefit considerably from establishing a series of BRIT workshops (see Chapter 5) supported by Resilience Professionals, to share practical experience and provide assistance with adapting frameworks, new designs, tools and templates.

A vision for Business Resilience will emerge from organizational analysis and discussion, and then the objectives, scope and scale of work envisaged will become more evident, as the impact on critical processes and practices is evaluated. Organizational Business Resilience objectives provide the basis of testing. A comparative test should be completed of the in-house methodology and Business Resilience Framework. Benefits, costs and risks are assessed against organizational Business Resilience objectives, and a decision taken to proceed with the preferred option.

If selected, a trial of the in-house Business Resilience methodology should be planned and tested in a pilot scheme(s) before a wider initiative is established. Ideally, the approach should be piloted at business unit or department level to ensure there is proof of concept at a significant level, prior to wider implementation, over several business cycles.

The exploratory strategy is an unconstrained approach. It will enable the organization to build stakeholder support, but, understandably, it will make progress at a slower pace than implementing the Progressive, Urgent or Responsive strategies, linked to the Business Resilience Framework.

The exploratory approach is most appropriate where organizations have embedded processes and practices that are difficult to adapt, or they have invested in adjacent concepts such as 'business continuity systems', where bespoke interfaces might need to be created or considered. In both instances, making collaboration time available is essential to building a strong organizational mandate for resilience or partnership relationships. A further instance is where the organization has a strong ethic of internal development, and exploratory approaches, designs and implementations are simply preferred.

Whichever PURE strategy is selected for implementation, the purpose is to achieve Business Resilience objectives and enhance progress at pace. In all cases, users will be able to benefit from best practices and tools, improving productivity of development and de-risking the portfolio, whatever the VUCA conditions. Central to selecting the right approach is to engage stakeholders, providing options to achieve the benefits of Business Resilience and the likelihood of realizing the Evolving Vision of the organization.

It is recommended that the progressive strategy is used in most situations, to balance time and cost, improve success and reduce risk. The urgent strategy is undoubtedly of great value in a crisis, where immediate action is essential, or opportunistically in start-ups. Responsive strategies are clearly ideal for established organizations where an existing weakness has been identified and must be resolved at pace. The exploratory strategy makes sense where stakeholders prefer in-house solutions and must be fully engaged, support confirmed and benefits proven in pilot settings, prior to rollout of a wider Business Resilience implementation.

Roadmap to adopt and adapt Business Resilience

A high-level perspective, or roadmap (shown in Figure 8.5), outlines five milestones that would be needed to implement a strategy for Business Resilience (Figure 8.6). Consideration should be given to all milestones to gain understanding of the potential scope of implementing Business Resilience. Then the preferred approach of Progressive, Urgent, Responsive and Exploratory can be identified and an outline plan developed of how Business Resilience is to be implemented.

Strategy implementation milestones:

- Adopted Business Resilience as a standard, a framework to get things done in a professional way. The senior management team decides based on the level of challenge, opportunity and alignment to the organizational vision of the Business Resilience Framework. (Not used in the responsive approach.)

FIGURE 8.5 Milestones to adopt and adapt Business Resilience

| Introduce Business Resilience | 1. Adopted Business Resilience | 2. Profiled and mapped to existing processes | 3. Selected approach (PURE) | 4. Adapted priorities and quick wins | 5. Implemented resilience priorities |

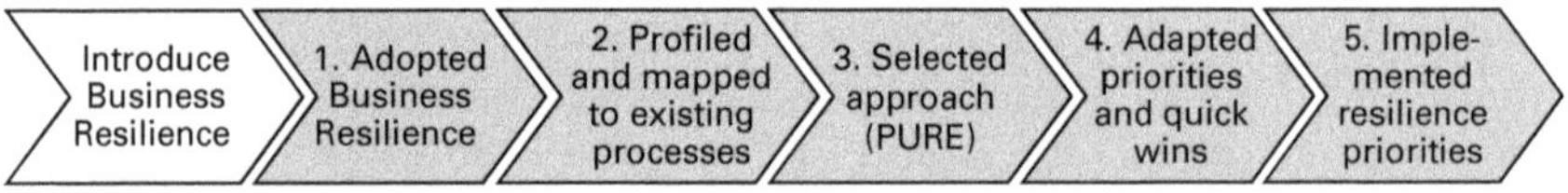

- Checked current levels of organizational Business Resilience, mapped to target and measured gaps. This is done using the Business Resilience Profile, identifying the target resilience level and measuring the differences. (Not used in the urgent approach.)

- Evaluated and selected strategic approach, which is affordable, beneficial and implementable. The approach decision and estimated implementation schedule will reflect 'as is' organization capabilities, as Business Resilience is not completed, indeed little may yet be in place.

- Identified quick wins, established Business Resilience priorities and adapted domains or elements. Following the selected approach, an organizational Business Resilience Framework or elements are designed and will contain the initial implementable elements and forms a backlog; options are proposed that are subject to assessment and approval of the business justification. (Not used in the urgent approach.)

- Plug and play for gaps, piloted/tested adapted elements, completed to Progress Definition. The implementation plan is delivered with the rate of progress determined by organizational capacity, capability and commitment. Once the initial implementation is completed, the Resilience Profile can be repeated to identify future improvements.

The roadmap milestones provide high-level guidance for the implementation, which would ideally be completed using capabilities and tools shown in the Business Resilience Framework; but clearly these assets have yet to be put in place. Thus, the initial adoption of Business Resilience will need to be completed without this. The organization will make best use of existing processes and practices to complete this initial implementation.

The milestones required for each approach are shown in Figure 8.6. It can be seen that the urgent approach does not use milestones 2 or 4, as the decision is to adopt the whole framework in a single cycle. The responsive approach does not use milestone 1, as there is not a decision to work toward adoption of the Business Resilience Framework but to implement elements.

Milestone 1 activities: Adopt Business Resilience

Senior management should invite a representative audience of all five organization levels to a presentation of the Business Resilience Framework. The purpose would be to secure understanding with indicative benefits and costs. A decision conference could be used to support this process, organized by a Progress Master or Resilience Professional. At conclusion of this milestone (Figure 8.7), senior management will have reached a consensus on the desirability of implementing Business Resilience within the organization.

FIGURE 8.6 Strategy implementation approaches and milestones utilized for each approach

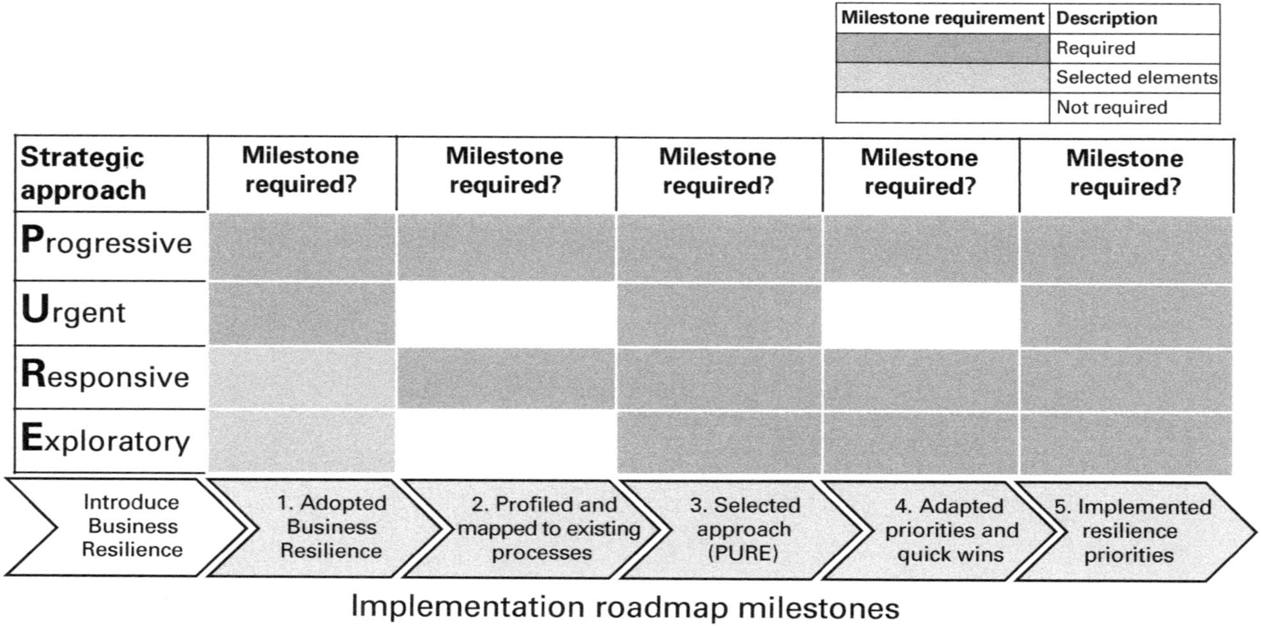

Strategic approach	Milestone required?	Milestone required?	Milestone required?	Milestone required?	Milestone required?
Progressive					
Urgent					
Responsive					
Exploratory					

Milestone requirement	Description
	Required
	Selected elements
	Not required

Introduce Business Resilience → 1. Adopted Business Resilience → 2. Profiled and mapped to existing processes → 3. Selected approach (PURE) → 4. Adapted priorities and quick wins → 5. Implemented resilience priorities

Implementation roadmap milestones

FIGURE 8.7 Output of milestone 1

Milestone 1 is not required for the responsive approach as there is a decision only to implement certain elements of Business Resilience.

Milestone 1 output is the decision to implement Business Resilience.

Milestone 2 activities: Identify the gap to the target resilience level

In working towards milestone 2, an evaluation is needed of the extent to which current practices and processes provide or support Business Resilience and progress within the organization, and where they are falling short. Current resilience should be measured using the Resilience Profile, and target Resilience Profile levels are established for the 22 elements of the Business Resilience Framework. Using the Resilience Profile scores, mapping to the target Resilience Profile can be completed. At this point, gaps become visible and then value initiatives designed to close them.

Milestone 2 (Figure 8.8) is not required in the urgent approach as the whole Business Resilience Framework is being adopted, so all elements are being implemented. In the exploratory approach, the gap is to organizational Business Resilience objectives.

Milestone 2 output is a package of value initiatives to close the gap between current and target levels of resilience to address priority elements.

Milestone 3 activities: Select approach

In milestone 3 (Figure 8.9) the Business Resilience Owner will address four high-level questions:

- Should the organization urgently implement the off-the-shelf Business Resilience Framework?

FIGURE 8.8 Output of milestone 2

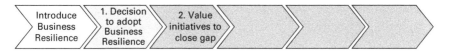

- Should the organization adapt the standard Business Resilience Framework supplemented by current ways of working?
- Should the organization introduce Business Resilience elements (only) into existing organizational processes and practices?
- Should the organization explore an in-house Business Resilience, starting from Principles only?

Answers will determine a preferred way forward using one of the PURE strategy implementation approaches:

- Progressive: adapt the standard model incrementally towards the organizational vision.
- Urgent: Business Resilience Framework: adopt the model off-the-shelf with minimal tailoring.
- Responsive: adapt elements from the standard model, to enhance organizational processes and practices.
- Exploratory: working from Business Resilience Principles, explore own methodology using best practices and tools, with comparative testing of Business Resilience Framework.

Each has distinct merits due to current organizational status, VUCA environment or ease of implementation. Nonetheless, if Progressive, Urgent, or Exploratory approaches are chosen, the initiative teams will benefit from the modular design of the Business Resilience Framework, enabling elements to be adapted or created, adding or replacing them within the framework, or existing processes and practices, to realize a bespoke solution optimizing value to the organization.

Selection will have depended on many factors within the organization and the environment in which it operates or wishes to operate in the future. Therefore, this is a good time to ensure that the benefits, costs and risks of each approach are clear. Strongly held views on an emergent preferred option might divide stakeholder opinions, so it is important that facilitated discussion focuses objectively on planned outcomes, ie Business Resilience and the likelihood of achieving progress upon implementation. Ultimately, stakeholders across the organization at all levels will want to be convinced by a fair and balanced discussion of the pros and cons of each strategy implementation approach, and belief that it can realize the vision for Business Resilience.

FIGURE 8.9 Output of milestone 3

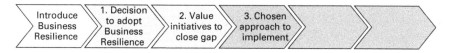

Milestone 3 output is a chosen implementation approach.

Milestone 4 activities: Quick wins and adapt priorities

Depending upon the selected approach, organizations will focus upon:

- Progressive: adopting and adapting the standard Business Resilience Framework to existing organizational processes and practices to deliver the organizational vision.

- Urgent: adopting and adapting the standard Business Resilience Framework with minimal tailoring.

- Responsive: adapting existing organizational processes and practices to include elements shown in the standard Business Resilience Framework with lean tailoring of elements.

- Exploratory: exploring in-house ways to realize Business Resilience, based upon the Principles only, with the organization and partners focusing on opportunities to create pragmatic improvements, such as extending business continuity to address Business Resilience.

In the progressive strategy, the key tasks are to identify robust processes or practices within the organization that already align to the framework. Where available, Resilience Professionals will want to build business justification based upon realizing an agreed vision of Business Resilience.

In the urgent strategy, the key tasks are to adopt the standard Business Resilience Framework, with minimal tailoring, to ensure Business Resilience is installed promptly in the organization. Resilience Professionals ensure benefits are realized in short timescales, ideally one PROGRESS Cycle.

In the responsive strategy, the key tasks are to identify high-priority elements from the standard Business Resilience Framework to add to processes or practices within the organization and possibly delete underperforming processes and practices. Resilience Professionals focus on risk management.

In the exploratory strategy, the key tasks are to identify areas of vulnerability using risk assessments, propose in-house approaches to realize Business Resilience consistent with the Principles by making best use of in-house processes and practices within an in-house implementation methodology, which has been subjected to a comparative Business Resilience Framework assessment.

In all approaches, it is essential to gain agreement and to communicate a schedule for progress through the roadmap milestones to complete this journey. When using the Business Resilience Framework, it is likely to need some adapting to implement it in the organization. If further refinement of new processes and practices is needed, or existing processes and practices require adapting, additional value initiatives can be added, or items added to the backlog. How much and which elements require adapting is influenced by the approach taken and the quality of existing processes and practices in the organization. Chapter 11 provides more details of how to refine the organization Business Resilience Framework.

Milestone 4 (Figure 8.10) output is an initial Business Resilience Framework. It will be:

- Progressive: an integration of existing practices and processes to improve resilience.
- Urgent: an immediately implementable Business Resilience Framework.
- Responsive: a package of Business Resilience Framework elements.
- Exploratory: an in-house design for Business Resilience methodology based upon the Principles.

In all cases, a solution will be ready for implementation, at the required level within the organization.

Milestone 5 activities: Implementation

This is the point at which all the preparation really takes shape and the organization can work towards their Evolving Vision and Progress

FIGURE 8.10 Output of milestone 4

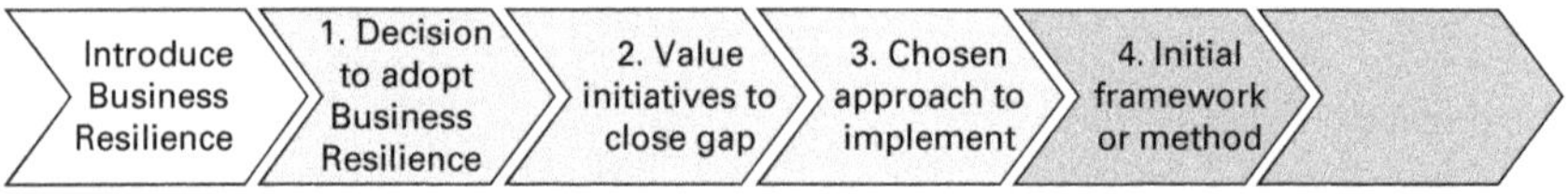

FIGURE 8.11 Output of milestone 5

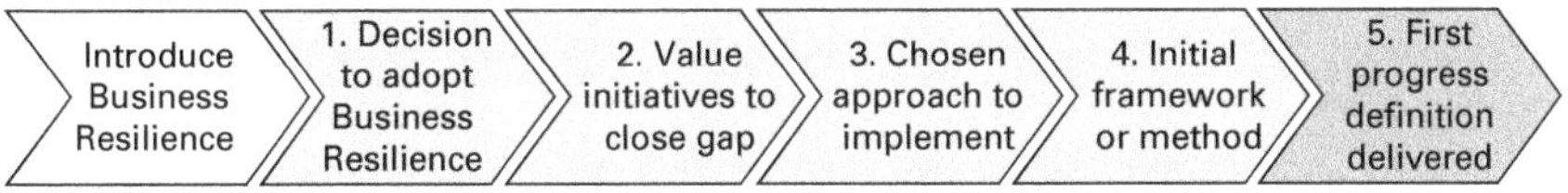

Definition(s) where they have adopted the Business Resilience Framework, or elements or Principles, and want to make progress (Figure 8.11).

The principle of building on existing good practices is fully utilized in the progressive and the responsive approach, where the organization's existing processes and practices provide the major input, with improvements gathered from the Business Resilience Framework. Only when using the urgent approach should organizations go straight to the solution, which essentially comprises pre-formed elements; this may be perfect for organizations in crisis or start-ups. The responsive approach enables Rapid progress to address a resilience element of concern, whereas exploratory strategies focus on building in-house methodologies, strengthening stakeholder commitment.

As work progresses towards completion of milestone 5, it will be necessary to test and approve the functionality and ease of use of all elements within the new organizational Business Resilience Framework or enhanced processes and practices. This is to confirm the 'play' capability of all modules to be plugged in to create the new working environment.

Milestone 5 output is achievement of the initial Progress Definition for Business Resilience.

Adaptation will be an ongoing process as the VUCA environment, socio-economic conditions and technology factors change. Where adopted, each subsequent PROGRESS Cycle provides an opportunity to review the organizational Business Resilience Framework in Success and Learning. Step 8 may suggest further adaptation(s) to be implemented in later cycles, which will increase effectiveness and therefore the level of Business Resilience and sustained progress at pace.

10 aspects of strategy implementation for tracking

As implementation strategies get under way, Business Resilience Owners are responsible for the following aspects being tracked and acted on by members of initiative or project teams:

- business benefits are clear to all stakeholders, including staff, partners and customers;

- maintenance of business justification using a roadmap and milestones during the current business or PROGRESS Cycle;

- practitioners' knowledge of compelling reasons for adopting Business Resilience (business case);

- understanding of the PURE the strategies – Progressive, Urgent, Responsive and Exploratory – and the Evolving Vision for migration towards an organizational or standard Business Resilience Framework, Business Resilience objectives or enhanced processes and practices;

- backlog reviews or gaps to realization of the next version of Business Resilience in operational practice, reflected in the Progress Definition of the PROGRESS Cycle, including dependencies between adapted domains/elements and existing process and practices;

- identification of resources for bespoke Roles required to improve the 22 framework elements; monitoring the level of stakeholder commitment to embracing the PACE Culture and PROGRESS Cycle; prepared learning or training programme to engage new and existing people;

- identification of efficiencies across the five levels of the organization; cost–benefit assessments of hiring additional Roles or adding responsibilities to existing Roles (eg PMO, transformation or change teams who could contribute to Business Resilience and progress);

- adoption of Business Resilience at organization, department or division level, domains at team level, and elements at individual level; ensure availability of Business Resilience vision and framework ('to be') and the current ('as is') version, which is visible;

- preparation of next business justification case for continuous improvement as a resilient organization; prioritized actions to install domains or elements of standard Business Resilience or current processes and practices to form organization Business Resilience Framework;

- use Resilience Profile to monitor effectiveness of Business Resilience domains and elements of the organization framework and model, and target levels of the next iteration.

The Business Resilience Owner ensures measures are established and tracked; the Progress Master facilitates collection and collation of data provided by the Initiative Leader for the implementation of the Business Resilience strategy.

Continuing improvement of Business Resilience

The scope of continuing improvement work should be defined as follows:

- domains: improvements to the framework domains so that it can support the Evolving Vision and, in turn, customer value and Business Resilience;

- elements: improvements from the five framework domains that need to be put into live operation, achieving the organizational Progress Definition for this cycle and improving the Resilience Profile (see Chapter 10); prioritized incremental improvements in development and delivery of products, services, processes or practices.

With the Business Resilience Framework implemented to the level set out in the first Progress Definition, the strategy is to realize Business Resilience incrementally through functional working, strengthening organizational culture and progress capability. This is done by addressing priority processes and practices identified for improvement in the Resilience Profile, or priority elements to be drawn down from the standard Business Resilience Framework. These are added to the Progress Backlog for regular review and development of priority items.

For organizations adopting the progressive approach, Business Resilience will involve mapping current priority processes and practices to the Business Resilience standard, and adding back modules from existing process and practices to form an organizational Business Resilience Framework. Progress is made with using the first version of the organizational Business Resilience Framework, which provides the next roadmap for continuous improvement, using the Progress @ Pace Model.

Complementary improvements

Continuing improvement work is prioritized where commercial benefits from better products, services, processes or practices within the portfolio are complemented by additional resilience benefits arising from improvements in the 5 domains or 22 elements. Nonetheless, most organizations will need to invest in commercial opportunities as the highest-level priority. Investing separately in domains and elements of the organization Business Resilience Framework or Progress @ Pace 8-4-8 Model architecture is also desirable, where organizations have the resources to do so.

Following completion of the implementation roadmap and milestones, under the progressive or urgent approaches, the Business Resilience

Framework will be in operational use. As the organization moves forward through successive periods, individual organizations will take the opportunity to invest in the framework. They will be cognizant of VUCA environments, current organizational capacity and the challenges or opportunities that face them, refining the framework regularly, in a way that fits into their own business cycles. When circumstances are favourable, they will invest.

Existing elements can be slotted in or out of the architecture and, depending upon the value of predecessor processes and practices, prior elements will be retained or adapted. The 'plug and play' design aspect provides key support to incremental improvement and iterative development, making adapted modules capable of being implemented at pace, in addition to being able to respond to customer needs. The Business Resilience Profile is used prior and post development to provide a measurable indicator of progress, and its pace. Thus, implementing resilience strategy has the potential to improve organizations' business lifecycles.

On completion of one business cycle, the next future state or Progress Definition is implemented, so the organization can benefit from better creation of customer products and services, and/or company processes and practices, together with improvements to Business Resilience.

When implemented, the 8-4-8 Model is evolutionary, so it is possible to make migration towards the future state an iterative process, with incremental releases as improvements within the framework or 8-4-8 Model design emerge and are adopted. Revisions and updates to the framework and model are expected to be implemented regularly by the Progress Master, acting in agreement with the Business Resilience Owner, who is responsible for ensuring improvements to resilience secure business benefits too.

In short, once Business Resilience Owners have adopted and implemented a Business Resilience Framework, improved organization performance should follow regularly. Organizations become a great place to work, with purposeful leadership spread throughout all five levels of the organization.

Migration to the vision or future state

While the current desired vision might never actually be reached due to changing VUCA conditions and the need for continual evolution of the organization and partnerships, a future state of some sort will be realized. Upon completion of an improvement cycle, as a consequence of enhancing RESILIENCE Foundations, developing a PACE Culture and making the

PROGRESS Cycle more economic, efficient and effective, Business Resilience will be much enhanced. This is the business value of working towards such a vision, a goal with potential for network-wide benefits arising from exploring the vision and achieving the primary objective of implementing an enhanced Business Resilience Framework.

The organization would measure its success in adopting Business Resilience using the Resilience Profile tool, which enables domains, elements and tools to be scored on a five-point scale (see Chapter 9) and completed at regular intervals. Business resilience should be measured against profile targets, which are identified in the Progress Definition.

Bringing this process to life are the Business Resilience Owner, who is responsible for creation of the organization as an Adaptive Enterprise, together with specialist Roles, called Progress Masters, who facilitate work and support initiative owners, who may already be experienced working on agile or linear projects. Collectively, these Roles provide the guiding force to succeed. In addition to their success in making incremental improvements are opportunities for learning, as shown in the PROGRESS Cycle; this learning is what powers new initiatives, which will initially be placed on the organization backlogs, for further consideration, development and implementation.

In the context of migrating to a future state, feedback to the Business Resilience Owner of items that might impact the 'Evolving Vision' (within RESILIENCE Foundations) is expected, and a new version of the vision may then emerge. Feedback would be completed at the end of the PROGRESS Cycle. Depending on the scope of the initiative, it may impact all or part of the organization as progress work can be authorized at any of the five levels (individual, team, department or business unit, organization or network level). The organization would agree when the Evolving Vision should be re-versioned and released, which would normally be at the end of a business cycle or prior to authorization of the next PROGRESS Cycle; ongoing initiatives would be reviewed for 'great alignment'; new initiatives would be subject to the new version of the vision. This activity is aligned to the organization's continuing improvement principle.

Practical examples of strategy implementation

Practical ways to implement RESILIENCE Foundations elements

RESILIENCE Foundations define the horizons of the organization, while building robust capability and capacity to realize sustainable returns; the eight elements of foundations enable growth of a dynamic organization (PACE) Culture from which creation and maintenance of customer value is assured by commitment to right-paced delivery and progressive portfolio evolution and the PROGRESS Cycle.

Implementation strategy examples for the eight elements of RESILIENCE Foundations are shown below:

- **Regulatory and Governance:** clarify industry standards and the alignment of organizational policies to them, using auditable practice from which learning and improvement takes place. Implementation example: develop governance handbook, based upon industry standards and good business practice; obtain external accreditation, review at regular intervals.

- **Evolving Vision:** a series of incrementally better organization design ideas where people collaborate within social and technological future environments to deliver benefits for all. Implementation example: engage creative project team to develop vision concepts; test with target focus group audiences; select preferred concept for internal/external communications.

- **Sustainable operations:** adaptable, digital and modular operational capability supporting lean practices with refined tools for the implementation of learning within networks. Implementation example: develop operations practices and processes using open systems architecture and modularity; subject to compliance review; review at regular intervals.

- **Innovation and Risk:** balancing the desire for portfolio innovation with resource availability from an enlightened value perspective on technological and financial risk assessment. Implementation example: conduct portfolio items age review; establish comparison with competitors; use Innovation and Risk tools to balance investments; review at regular intervals.

- **Leading and Influencing:** understanding and inspiring others; creating belief in a future where organization brand values and positioning reflect the aspirations of the network. Implementation example: conduct organizational energy review across five levels; minimize negative/maximize positive influences; cross-check to industry attitudinal survey data.

- **Enterprising Investment:** how to attract talent and investment into the organization by building believability in next steps and sharing the benefits of vision realization. Implementation example: review time to recruit and time to market data and compare with realization of investment results; identify and remove bottleneck throughout the lifecycle.

- **Network Collaboration:** a spirit of collaboration and partnership, built upon application of an agile culture, where facilitation of stakeholders, testing and customer value predominates. Implementation example: conduct portfolio collaborations review; establish comparison with competitors; introduce/use tools to accelerate collaboration; review at regular intervals.

- **Evolutionary Portfolio:** an abiding belief in market focus, digital by design and modularity combine to deliver lifecycle desirability with confidence to pivot due to VUCA conditions. Implementation example: conduct portfolio items review, using a multidimensional tool to establish product comparisons and evaluate portfolio and competitor positions.

Business resilience Owners will lead on strategy implementation, with Progress Masters and Initiative Leaders for each domain, collaborating to review 'as is' practices and processes, agree and prioritize gaps to the 'to be' model. Following approval by the Business Resilience Owner, the vanilla Business Resilience Framework will have been introduced and feedback from the organization and network partners captured following presentation. Initiative Leaders will then commence steps to implement or improve existing processes and practices within each of the domain elements. Implementation will be prioritized by the Business Resilience Owner in the first instance, although once THE Model is implemented, reference can be made to the Progress Definition. And once improvements have been made, these should be subject to internal audit with lessons ensuring components within each of the eight foundation elements evolve and remain valid. It may therefore be appropriate for a Progress Master to advise internal audit on this work.

Practical ways to implement PACE Culture elements

Collectively, the four PACE drivers work together to provide adaptability within an organization culture, generating passion or Elevated Energy for innovation. Considered individually, these four elements are the drivers of the PACE Culture: successful organizations find smart ways to invest in the following:

- **Purposeful Mindset** creating a sense of individual self-worth and belief in the value people bring to the organization in delivery and development Roles at all levels, and partnership networks, through better understanding of ambition, behavioural preferences and psychological defence.

Implementation example: engage a Resilience Professional to introduce purposeful (or growth) mindset; add practitioner (SME) to initiative and apply tools; use findings to address people challenges.

- **Application of tools:** exploration and evolution of the right tools for digital transformation, human systems and technological innovation. The resulting effectiveness, efficiency and economy of tools should be addressed from an outcome perspective of collaborative delivery of customer value. Implementation example: review digital transformation toolkit; examine technologies needed to enable profitable growth; define success criteria and measures; prioritize and implement plan.

- **Capability and Skills:** ensuring the right capabilities and skills are sought, taught or learned so teams will feel proud of their performance, starts with understanding 'why' we do things, as well as 'how' to do them. Skills certification and aligning of competences focuses on better capability. Implementation example: review skills gaps and time to recruit or train new capabilities; identify Initiative Leader resources needed; check alignment to Progress Definition; prioritize and implement.

- **Elevated Energy:** by focusing on customer relationships and agreeing priorities, individuals feel part of a team, where 'we can!', achieving visible increments and supporting collective wellbeing. Cross-checking organizational motivation results in redirecting effort towards more positive energy. Implementation example: engage organizational energy specialist; take sample tests in teams; review data and compare with expectations; retrain and remove barriers to success.

Business Resilience Professionals will not only learn capabilities and how to optimize tools, but the skills to adapt the organization under VUCA conditions. Underpinned by a Purposeful Mindset towards self, customer needs/feedback and team lessons, Initiative Leaders and Progress Masters create a culture of confidence to embrace adaptability. The PACE Culture builds on the RESILIENCE Foundation elements, whether in adapting operations or responding to the development challenges of Innovation and Risk.

Once the PACE Culture is established, further development will be directed by the Business Resilience Owner, ensuring a programme of continuing professional development is in place to assist staff at levels. For example, inclusive approaches such as the champion/challenger technique ensure the four PACE drivers evolve and remain valid. In more challenging VUCA times, positive team energy enables fundamental paradigm shifts to be tested and implemented so more radical progress can be realized.

Practical ways to implement the PROGRESS Cycle elements

For an opportunity to be selected, it should be achievable, attractive and align to one of the four backlogs (product, services, practices and processes) referenced in elements 1–4 of the cycle:

- **Progress Definition:** the first element of the cycle; it forms a reference point for delivering value to both organization and its customers and defines the gap to progress target elements. Implementation example: demonstrate 'as is' compliance with resilience 8-4-8 Model, and 'to be' target using Business Resilience Profile tool; prioritize initiatives in current business cycle, create Progress Definition.

- **Recognize Challenge** from prevailing business conditions or within the business environment (measured using capacity loading, Adaptive Enterprise capability and the VUCA Storm Scale). Implementation example: identify urgency of implementation; assess spare capacity in operational and development teams; enter Adaptive Enterprise level and VUCA Storm Scale in challenge formula.

- **Opportunity Assessment:** the customer requirement or proposed opportunity (measured as a financial and non-financial benefits assessment, and value to organization levels and partnerships). Implementation example: engage stakeholders and SMEs; hold a decision conference to establish critical success factors; score and prioritize initiatives in this business cycle.

- **Good Alignment (of opportunity to Progress Definition):** the initiative owner develops a business justification case, to satisfy the requirement based upon option appraisal techniques. There are two principal concerns: (a) benefits from meeting the requirement, and (b) benefits from closing the Business Resilience gap to target (shown in Progress Definition).

- **Decision Gate 1:** completion of the first four elements provides the basis for a 'go/no go' decision at gate 1. To proceed, risk/return of opportunities must remain attractive to customers, and contribute to the Progress Definition of the organization, and ideally its partners. Qualifying opportunities are then taken forward at the right pace – through elements 5–8 of the cycle. Other options or opportunities are returned to the process and practices backlog for review.

- **Rapids and Lagoons:** initiatives are prioritized according to negotiated requirements between customer and organization resilience needs, using typically agile or traditional project methods. Implementation example: review backlogs within the business cycle; consider available capacity; identify Business Resilience option that allows the initiative to proceed at pace.

- **Enabling Teams:** initiatives are owned and executed by self-managed work teams, working in a collaboration with customers or users, through a facilitated process of iterative development. Implementation example: engage SME; demonstrate collaboration tools; customers and users pilot initiatives; refine definition of done to MVP expectations; retrain/remove barriers to success.

- **Selection and Testing** of product/service versions and variants, following quality and market or UX testing – a key part of the PROGRESS Cycle; success confirmed by customer/portfolio reviews. Implementation example: select modular designs to test PROGRESS Cycle elements early; engage users in technical testing; use 'plug and play' architecture to advance test opportunities and results.

- **Success and Learning or failure to provide learning opportunities to refine the PROGRESS Cycle;** retrospectives may lead to the adoption of new (or replacement) PROGRESS Cycle elements or refinement. Implementation example: Progress Master ensures lessons log is maintained regularly; celebrate success of created organizational Business Resilience model, developed, adapted and tested.

- **Decision Gate 2:** in developing the PROGRESS Cycle, Principles of customer value remain at the heart of the Progress @ Pace 8-4-8 Model, supported by an enterprising culture that empowers individuals, teams, business units, entire organizations and their partners to respond flexibly to ever-changing conditions. At this point, the Business Resilience Owner must answer the question of whether or not the organization Business Resilience Framework elements bring a sufficient sense of preparedness to business planning, organization and portfolio development, to deliver the products and services required, with the flexibility and adaptability needed to respond to changing economic and social conditions. Provided this condition is met, the new framework and model can be confidently adopted and released to production or in-service use.

Roles for Business Resilience strategy implementation

Business Resilience Owner – agrees the strategy implementation approach and implementation roadmap that should be used for Business Resilience.

Progress Master – leads or advises on implementation approaches, Business Resilience tools, collecting relevant data, business justification and preparing proposals for the implementation. They will advise the Business Resilience Owner on adapting the Business Resilience Framework and provide inputs to decision-making.

Resilience Professional – will advise and support the Business Resilience Owner and Progress Master on the approach that will be most appropriate for the organization. A Resilience Professional is recommended to support an organization that is implementing Business Resilience. The support could be in a coaching, training, consulting or delivering capacity.

Benefits, costs and risks

The decision to adopt, adapt and continue to improve organizational Business Resilience over a relevant planning period, possibly two or three years, is based upon a consideration of benefits, costs and risks. The contribution towards Business Resilience and progress objectives made by initiatives, reflected in the Evolving Vision and Progress Definition, is what makes portfolio investments compelling. In this context, Business Resilience can be regarded as a competing alternative along with other initiatives for new or improved products, services, processes or practices. All should be assessed in terms of benefits, costs and risks. The costs and risks will depend on the approach chosen.

Business resilience benefit measurement is difficult; this is because benefits could be derived from a range of financial, technological, physical and psychological measures, many being subjective or based upon game theory or probability. So, while a business case may provide numerical analysis, the Business Resilience Owner will need to take account of financial and non-financial considerations. Organization leaders who are passionate about customer value and committed to building staff capabilities find it attractive to work together to deliver high-priority, high-value initiatives. So, combining rational and emotional perspectives is particularly important for the

Business Resilience Owner to make correct decisions and build organizational energy and appetite for progress and success.

Financial and non-financial benefits from investing in Business Resilience are shown below:

Financial

- commercial rewards across the portfolio;
- reduction in commercial or reputational risk;
- business continuity in VUCA environments;
- sustainable cash flows throughout product or business lifecycles;
- exploration and expansion into new markets;
- increasing share values.

Non-financial

- enhancing employee security;
- a stronger organizational culture;
- a more innovative organization;
- attracting enterprising employees and partners;
- brand growth in changing conditions;
- a sense of purpose and being valued.

Most importantly, all benefits should be considered carefully, using weighting or sensitivity analysis. In a changing VUCA world with many knowns and unknowns, it is the combination of financial and non-financial benefits that is most likely to prove enduring. Sustainable outcomes then materialize: stakeholders feel valued, customers become friends and refer their clients, markets expand, share values increase, and employee security is enhanced. Further benefits flow to the organization and its partners, as brand reputations are enhanced and organizations find it easier to attract new talent.

Summary

For Business Resilience to be implemented successfully, senior stakeholders and teams must embrace it. First is to adopt Business Resilience for the benefits to the organization and second adapting a preferred approach, starting either with the standard framework or existing organizational processes and practices, and then continually improving them.

Identifying the preferred approach requires evaluation of current business benefits available from existing processes and practices ('as is'), and comparison with the potential benefits that could be available by implementing and operating the Business Resilience Framework and model ('to be'). Then a decision on the starting point for improvement must be selected; and this will be done following measurement using the Resilience Profile and identifying performance gaps between the 'as is' and 'to be' situations.

Consideration of the resilience gaps, capacity, current client or market requirements and VUCA conditions in the environment will determine the appetite of senior teams to adopt Business Resilience. If it is adopted as an organizational policy, a decision on how best to implement it will be required, adapting the resilience standard framework or existing organizational processes and practices as a baseline, and making improvements. Once adapted, the organization commences the journey of achieving organization Business Resilience, incrementally improving the framework and model through a series of progress or business cycles.

Reasons for adopting the Business Resilience Framework are to mobilize investment in five domains, leading to skilful adaptation of the standard framework, improved processes and practices, and progress at pace. By using the Resilience Profile, business results and portfolio attractiveness will improve in addition to operational efficiency and effectiveness of processes and practices for development and delivery of products and services. The overall outcome is the organization and partners should become more resilient and successful during successive initiatives, whatever VUCA conditions prevail.

MAKING PROGRESS IN TURBULENT TIMES

Resilient businesses expect changing environmental conditions, and to take advantage of them. Sometimes changes exceed expectations. For example, heroic efforts have been witnessed during the pandemic as characterized by the Covid-19 Ventilator Challenge and vaccine programme. Building upon resilient business process and capabilities, and the PACE Culture, network partners make progress more positively and purposefully, delivering value in challenging times; this was done using a robust PROGRESS Cycle, where established timescales and risk assessment methods were challenged, and great strides were made.

QUESTIONS TO THINK ABOUT

- Why might 'new ways of working' be needed to improve Business Resilience?

- What is the correct organizational level to introduce the Business Resilience Framework?

- Where does the standard framework with 5 domains and 22 elements drive most benefits for the organization?

References

Beckhard, R and Harris, RT (1987) *Organizational Transitions: Managing complex change*, Addison-Wesley, Reading, MA

Loh, C (2021) What's behind Wizz Air's Rapid expansion, *Simple Flying*, 24 July, simpleflying.com/wizz-air-Rapid-expansion (archived at https://perma.cc/3KH3-BJWR)

09

Tools for Business Resilience

Purpose

This chapter introduces tools that are specific to the Business Resilience Framework and tools that are used within specific domains, such as the PROGRESS Cycle domain. The purpose of the Business Resilience tools is to provide Resilience Professionals with a clearer indication of when action is required to implement value initiatives and more clarity on how to achieve the Progress Definition. Tools can be used in a standalone fashion, such as an indicator, or be complementary to the other tools approved by an organization. Tools should bring more focus and objectivity to Business Resilience decision-making and actions to achieve it.

Introduction

The Business Resilience Framework encourages utilization of a great variety of popular tools and best practices that will be familiar within organizations. This allows them to readily be applied using existing knowledge and expertise to improve Business Resilience. Mapping of recommended popular tools and practices is presented in Appendix B. There are, however, tools that are introduced for the first time in this text and, therefore, require a closer look; this chapter presents these tools with sufficient detail to promote understanding of the benefits and limits of their application for Business Resilience purposes, showing how these could be applied confidently alongside existing tools and best practices.

In the PACE Culture domain, the application of tools forms a specific element encouraging knowledge, exploration and adaptation of tools throughout the Business Resilience model. Once adopted, the Business Resilience

Owner will ensure sufficient funds are available and the Progress Master will take a lead role in the provision of tools training, so that tools are understood and can be correctly applied. This will improve the efficiency and effectiveness of value initiatives, and ensure indicators and information are available to support decision-making.

The main reasons for organizations applying tools within the Business Resilience Framework are to support the primary goals of improving Business Resilience by making sustained progress at pace. There are four elements of the PROGRESS Cycle leading to Decision Gate 1 (proceed to development, delay or reject the value initiative); these first steps provide a context for discussion of specific tools (Table 9.1).

The toolset in Table 9.1 is indicative because Resilience Professionals are encouraged to use the 'plug and play' technique, enabling them to select the most appropriate toolset, choosing between a new tool and an existing one, or a combination, to support Business Resilience and progress. Nonetheless, this provides the basis for consideration of how tools should be applied to enlighten and clarify decision-making and action for improvement and progress, not to overcomplicate or cause confusion within the organization.

A workflow view might reveal an organization is responding to its business environment, seeking improvements in products and services (faster, better, cheaper) or practices and processes (economy, efficiency or effectiveness). So,

TABLE 9.1 Possibilities for specific and popular tools

PROGRESS Cycle element	Tools example	Purpose	Specific or popular tool
1 Progress Definition	Resilience Profile and multi-criteria analysis (weighting, scoring, ranking)	Set PROGRESS Cycle objectives (resilience and progress)	Specific and popular
2 Recognize Challenge	VUCA Storm Scale	Understand indicator (force and direction)	Specific
3 Opportunity Assessment	Opportunity Assessment	Define realizable benefits (matched to capacity)	Specific
4 Good Alignment	Business case and resilience value	Propose for organization (rational and emotional)	Specific and popular

in referring to the above Business Resilience elements, the following activities could take place when making progress:

- Progress Definition: establish objectives.
- Status indicators: tracking and noting changes to business environment.
- Taking resilience action: development in BRIT workshops.
- Value initiative assessments reviewed: progress for action/backlog.

The types of tools brought to bear on issues or opportunities are categorized as specific or popular.

Specific Business Resilience tools:

- VUCA Storm Scale
- Adaptive Enterprise
- resilience value model
- Urgency Scale
- Capacity Scale
- Opportunity Score Scale.

In the sections below, some of these specific tools are considered from the perspective of how they enhance the decision-making of Resilience Professionals.

Specific tools for Business Resilience

The Resilience Profile

PURPOSE

The purpose of the Resilience Profile is to enable an organization to understand where it currently is, in terms of Business Resilience, and where it has gaps to its Business Resilience target levels. The Resilience Profile is assessed for each block of the Business Resilience Framework (eg RESILIENCE Foundations, PACE Culture and PROGRESS Cycle), and enables prioritization of effort for an organization looking to make maximum progress at pace under the existing conditions (see Chapter 10 for full details). The Resilience Profile provides the organization with a pathway to improve its level of Business Resilience through targeted actions based on the Resilience Profile findings.

CONTEXT

The Resilience Profile should be done initially at the start of any Business Resilience strategy implementation approach. It should also be done at the start of each PROGRESS Cycle, if it has not been done when a value initiative has been completed, to check if the initiative has had a material impact on the overall level of Business Resilience or for any of its elements. A Resilience Profile can be done at any point the organization feels a need for it, such as when conditions change significantly in, say, an organizational merger. Execution of the tool will be influenced by the process, who is invited to participate, and if weighting has been adopted, when analysing or designing presentation of findings.

APPLICATION

Chapter 10 sets out what would be seen in the organization at each profile level for each element of the Business Resilience Framework. This can be conducted by engaging Resilience Professionals to undertake an independent view, or as a self-assessment by the organization. The Resilience Profile uses a scale of 1–5 and can be undertaken for all 5 domains and 22 elements of the framework, a single element or any combination, to focus on specific areas.

The way in which the Resilience Profile will be used will depend on the organization's position on the implementation journey and the targets that have been agreed. Essentially the baseline Resilience Profile will be identified and the target Resilience Profile agreed will be overlaid to identify the gaps between them, as shown in Figure 9.1. An organization will decide the priority areas to address, either based on the largest gaps or delivering the quick wins to gain confidence of the organization, or a mix. Once the priority areas have been agreed and included in the Progress Definition, the value initiatives to address them will be identified and proceed through the PROGRESS Cycle.

The Resilience Profile can change with circumstances, and when a 'Storm' or 'Hurricane' VUCA (volatility, uncertainty, complexity and ambiguity) level is encountered, the Resilience Profile level will fall back until the organization is at its optimum Business Resilience level and it can maintain this through all conditions.

To summarize, the Resilience Profile is a data visualization tool; it provides a thought process to leaders throughout the organization: 'whatever is being faced, ask – are the RESILIENCE Foundations in place? Is a PACE Culture being built? Can the PROGRESS Cycle be delivered?'

FIGURE 9.1 Baseline and target Resilience Profiles

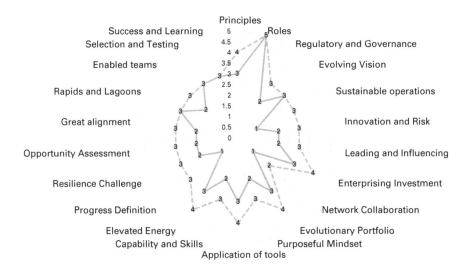

Resilience Profile elements

VUCA Storm Scale

PURPOSE

The VUCA Storm Scale is used to develop a RAG status indicator from a composite score from which a colour code is created but is not a predictive model. Its purpose is to highlight the degree of sensitivity and unpredictability in the external environment for a current PROGRESS Cycle for Resilience Professionals to take action. The VUCA Storm Score is a single indicator accounting for volatility, uncertainty, complexity and ambiguity of conditions in which the organization must make progress, alerting the organization to the overall challenge that needs to be overcome in the current PROGRESS Cycle. By extension, the VUCA Storm Score could indicate the minimum resilience level an organization would require to weather a VUCA 'storm', within a PROGRESS Cycle.

CONTEXT

Challenge to progress has several aspects, including the organizational capacity to effect change, degrees of unpredictability in the existing external environment, adaptability of the organization, and the urgency of change required. 'Recognize Challenge' in the PROGRESS Cycle has several activities covering these aspects, including VUCA sensitivity (A2.2) to address the unpredictability of the external environment. The VUCA Storm Score is an input to the Challenge Score, as a subjective measure of challenge in the current PROGRESS Cycle. Again, a Challenge Score should be viewed as an indicator, not a predictive model.

APPLICATION

The VUCA Storm Scale indicates the external environment in terms of the strength of the 'storms which need to be navigated'. According to Bennett and Lemoine (2014), the term VUCA includes the following dimensions:

- Volatility: the nature and dynamics of change, and the nature and speed of change forces and change catalysts.
- Uncertainty: the lack of predictability, the prospects for surprise, and the sense of awareness and understanding of issues and events.
- Complexity: the multiplex of forces, the confounding of issues, no cause-and-effect chain and confusion that surrounds the organization.
- Ambiguity: the haziness of reality, the potential for misreads, and the mixed meanings of conditions; cause-and-effect confusion.

Each of these aspects are assessed against the five criteria below.

Volatility (Dv)   Generally, the term means the nature, speed, volume and magnitude of change that is not in a predictable pattern. Volatility is usually associated with anything that is too fast, too slow, dynamic (ie of unstable speed), and connected to constant change, turbulence, etc. The following aspects of volatility can be subjectively assessed:

- speed of change;
- proximity of change;
- magnitude of change;
- predictability of change;
- controllability of change.

Uncertainty (Du)   The term can simply be explained as the lack of predictability in issues and events. As times are becoming more volatile, it is getting more difficult for leaders to use past issues and events as predictors of future outcome, making forecasting extremely difficult and decision-making challenging (Stevenson, 2016). The following aspects of uncertainty can be subjectively assessed:

- scarcity of past issues or events that could be used as predictors;
- challenge of forecasting (ie reliability of forecasts);
- challenge in decision-making (straightforward versus difficult);
- deficit of information to assist in decisions;
- number of stakeholders involved.

Complexity (Dc)   The term is generally used to characterize something with many parts, where those parts interact with each other in multiple ways. As John Sullivan notes (Sinar, 2013), there are often numerous and difficult-to-understand causes and mitigating factors (both inside and outside the organization) involved in a problem. This layer of complexity, added to the turbulence of change and the absence of past predictors, adds to the difficulty of decision-making. The following aspects of complexity can be subjectively assessed:

- number of components;
- number of interactions between components;
- ways in which interaction happens;
- level of technical difficulty;
- number of parties involved.

Ambiguity (Da)   The term refers to phenomena where outcomes are hazy and unclear, even when it is attempted to understand them better. It is the lack of understanding of the causes and the 'who, what, where, how and why' behind the things that are happening, and are therefore hard to ascertain. The following aspects of ambiguity can be subjectively assessed:

- lack of clarity of objectives (eg hidden agendas);
- lack of clarity on connections and impact areas;
- challenge in understanding causes of events;
- number of interpretations of information (how divided is opinion);
- challenge in understanding stakeholder relationships.

CALCULATING THE VUCA STORM SCORE

When calculating the VUCA Storm Score, the individual VUCA dimensions are summed and divided by the total number of scores provided. The subjective scores or ratings may be weighted and levels attributed to scores according to existing organizational standards and preferred scales.

For instance, a small non-technical organization promoting one product type will experience a higher level of volatility but less complexity than a large technical organization with many product types. The inherent subjectivity in this approach is similar to qualitative risk measurement; it provides an empirical way of understanding perceptions by the organization, alerting Resilience Professionals to the requirement for potential action in response to the current environment.

Following data collection, assessments use a simple five-point scale (1–5) corresponding to banded grades (very low/low/moderate/high/very high) or utilize an organizational scale to calculate a combined assessment of each VUCA dimension.

Calculation of the VUCA storm is achieved by the addition of the consensus scores of individual dimensions of VUCA, as shown in Formula 9.1.

$$\text{VUCA Storm Score} = (Dv+Du+Dc+Da)/4 \qquad (9.1)$$

where,

Dv, Du, Dc, Da = individual consensus-based VUCA dimension scores (volatility, uncertainty, complexity and ambiguity)

A more advanced approach uses the same formula plus application of customized weightings to each individual dimension and is recommended because it takes into account the organization's particular business environment. The resulting score should be rounded to the next integer and converted onto a five-point scale, where scores indicate a progressively higher level of sensitivity and unpredictability in the external environment; this could signify a minimum level of resilience the business would require when implementing value initiatives. Table 9.2 shows an example VUCA Storm Score, indicator and type.

Adaptive Enterprise (AE) scale

PURPOSE

The Adaptive Enterprise Scale measures the internal organizational capability to adapt to changes in VUCA conditions. By providing an Adaptive

TABLE 9.2 Example VUCA Storm Score, indicator and type

VUCA Storm Score	VUCA storm indicator	VUCA storm type
1	Very low	Calm
2	Low	Breeze
3	Medium	Gale
4	High	Storm
5	Very high	Hurricane

Enterprise Score as a single cumulative measure accounting for aspects of the enterprise organization, such as structure, processes, leadership and development, and customer orientation, an indicator of an organization's potential to mobilize and deliver value initiatives is provided. This score contributes to the assessment of challenge in the current PROGRESS Cycle faced by the organization.

CONTEXT

When assessing challenge to progress, the capability of an enterprise to mobilize and adapt serves as a counterbalance to the sensitivity and unpredictability of the external environment. Adaptive Enterprise capability (A2.3) shown in the 'Recognize Challenge' element of the PROGRESS Cycle undertakes this assessment; the output is the Adaptive Enterprise Score, which represents the ability to adapt to changing conditions and contributes to the calculation of the Challenge Score.

APPLICATION

The following eight dimensions could be used in assessing the Adaptive Enterprise capability:

- customer value, ie customer relevance at heart of everything organization does;

- inspirational leadership, ie visionary and inspired standards;

- energized collaboration, ie delegated authority and ownership;

- adaptive modular processes, ie sufficiency for purpose with ability to reconfigure;

- engaged partner network, ie network of empowered teams and open environment;

- innovation practices and processes, ie product, process and distribution services;
- self-organizing, ie self-organizing shared purpose with role mobility;
- growth mindset, ie openness to learning new things, continuous evolution.

Measures used to assess these dimensions can be derived from preferred organizational practices or popular best practice tools in respective areas, eg human resources management, operations and project management, strategy and innovation (Table 9.3).

CALCULATING THE ADAPTIVE ENTERPRISE SCORE

Similar to the VUCA Storm Scale assessment, measures for the individual dimensions of Adaptive Enterprise will be tailored and their levels decided based on existing organizational practice and preferred scale. The assessment may use a straightforward five-point scale (1–5) corresponding to grades of very low, low, moderate, high, very high, respectively. The calculation of the Adaptive Enterprise Score will involve an application of an arithmetic formula (Formula 9.2), or use a method based on the preferred organizational practice.

$$\text{Adaptive Enterprise Score} = (CV + IL + EC + AMP + EPN + IPP + SMO + GM)/8 \tag{9.2}$$

TABLE 9.3 Example measures for the Adaptive Enterprise assessment

Adaptive Enterprise aspect	Example measures
1. Customer value (CV)	Customer feedback/retention recommendation
2. Inspirational leadership (IL)	360-degree feedback
3. Energized collaboration (EC)	Review of authority levels
4. Adaptive modular processes (AMP)	Speed of the change process completion
5. Engaged partner network (EPN)	Engagement at five levels
6. Innovation practices and processes (IPP)	New ideas, routes and adoption
7. Self-motivated and organizing (SMO)	Staff retention/staff surveys
8. Growth mindset (GM)	Staff surveys/training/role mobility

where,

CV, IL, EC, AMP, EPN, IPP, SMO, GM = individual consensus-based AE
dimension scores

Similar to the VUCA Storm Scale assessment, the resulting score may use a more advanced method with the same formula plus the application of custom weightings to individual measures and then rounding to the next integer. Scores may be converted into a status indicator (or RAG: red, amber, green), where scores indicate progressively higher levels of capability to mobilize for and execute transformation scenarios to implement high-priority value initiatives (Table 9.4).

Urgency Scale

PURPOSE
The Urgency Scale measures the pressure to implement high-priority value initiatives in a given cycle. The Urgency Score contributes to the assessment of the overall challenge in the current PROGRESS Cycle.

CONTEXT
Along with the organization's capability to adapt and capacity to implement progress and the assessment of the sensitivity and unpredictability of the external environment, urgency is another factor contributing to the recognition of challenge to progress. Urgency of the challenge in the PROGRESS Cycle covers this assessment. Its output, the Urgency Score, represents the specific requirement or pressure to deliver specific scenarios for progress and contributes to the Challenge Score.

TABLE 9.4 Example Adaptive Enterprise Score, indicator and type

Adaptive Enterprise Score	Adaptive Enterprise indicator	Adaptive Enterprise type
1	Very low	Inert
2	Low	Aware
3	Medium	Rising
4	High	Ready
5	Very high	Spring-loaded

APPLICATION

Assessing the urgency is based on the organization's understanding of what is required to meet the Progress Definition. For instance, a global pandemic made the need to switch to homeworking immediate, whereas a financial crisis created a need to implement new rules for the global financial system with some being brought in within a year and some spanning a decade.

The Urgency Scale represents the speed at which the progress is needed. Urgency can be assigned and classified per value initiative. A five-point scale (1–5) corresponding to grades of very low, low, moderate, high and very high could be used, making it straightforward to calculate the overall Challenge Score. Table 9.5 shows example scores, indicators and types representing gradually increasing urgency levels, with examples of corresponding value initiatives.

TABLE 9.5 Urgency Score, indicator, type with description and examples

Urgency Score	Urgency indicator	Urgency type	Description	Example value initiatives
1	Very low	Back burner	Progress is made as time and resource is available or there is time from other initiatives	Internal suggestion in an area already well regarded by customers
2	Low	Normal	Time not critical to organizational success	Response to new regulations or an internally generated initiative
3	Medium	Speedy	Completion on time is important for the organization's competitive advantage	New or improved product or service introduction
4	High	Time-critical	Meeting the time goal is critical for success; any delay would mean progress failure	Technical solution is being developed by competitor
5	Very high	Blitz	Crisis events; urgent to make progress as soon as possible	Unexpected or 'black swan' event, incident or issue

Available capacity assessment

PURPOSE

The available capacity assessment represents an overall level of resource that is currently available within the organization to undertake the proposed value initiatives to deliver the Progress Definition.

CONTEXT

Available capacity is part of the calculation of the Challenge Score as there is a greater challenge if there is less capacity available. It can indicate that additional resources are required to meet the Progress Definition. This may contribute to decision-making related to urgency and can impact the level of benefits that can be achieved.

APPLICATION

There are recognized methods for measuring capacity load and those already used by the organization can continue to be used. A generic approach is for resource (workforce or equipment) utilization or productivity rate to be expressed as a ratio of committed load versus total capacity.

Assessing the available capacity depends on the internal standards of capacity loading and an agreed ranking. The capacity could use Formula 9.3 based on hours or other agreed units.

$$\text{Available capacity} = \text{total capacity} - \text{current load} \qquad (9.3)$$

The following is an example calculation of capacity score for a team of six engineers (this is scaled up for the organization) generally available to work five days a week and eight hours a day, currently engaged in a business-as-usual process consuming circa 900 hours every four weeks:

$$\text{Capacity per month} = 6 \text{ (engineers)} \times 5 \text{ (working days)} \times 8 \text{ (hours a day)} \times 4 \text{ (weeks)} = 920 \text{ hours}$$

$$\text{Current load} = 900 \text{ hours}$$

$$\text{Current load expressed as a percentage} = (900/920) \times 100 = 97.8\%$$

$$\text{Therefore, available capacity} = 920 - 900 = 20 \text{ hours}$$

$$\text{Available capacity expressed as a percentage } 100\% - 97.8\% = 2.2\%$$

The ranking will be agreed by the organization and will vary dependent on their situation. The ranks would show the following:

Available Capacity Score 1: (very low available capacity);

Available Capacity Score 2: (low available capacity);

Available Capacity Score 3: (medium available capacity);

Available Capacity Score 4: (high available capacity);

Available Capacity Score 5: (very high available capacity).

Challenge Score

PURPOSE

The Challenge Score represents an overall level of the challenge to progress the organization is facing in the current cycle. By combining the VUCA Storm Score, Adaptive Enterprise Score, Urgency Score and Available Capacity Score into a single measure, the Challenge Score provides an assessment of multifaceted business development problems and facilitates high-level decision-making for leaders working under pressure.

CONTEXT

Calculation of the Challenge Score is the final part of 'Recognize Challenge' in the PROGRESS Cycle, after the available capacity, VUCA sensitivity, Adaptive Enterprise (AE) capability and urgency of the challenge have all been assessed and scored. Its output, the Challenge Score, is the ultimate measure of the difficulties the organization would have to overcome to make progress in the current cycle and would be counterbalanced by the Opportunity Score calculated in Opportunity Assessment.

APPLICATION

Formula 9.4 is used to calculate the Challenge Score:

$$Cs = (VSs \times Us)/(AEs \times ACs) \tag{9.4}$$

where,

Cs = Challenge Score;

VSs = VUCA Storm Score;

Us = Urgency Score;

AEs = Adaptive Enterprise Score;

ACs = Available Capacity Score.

The resulting cumulative Challenge Score is expressed as a figure in a specific range or class. Table 9.6 shows example ranges, scores, indicators and types representing gradually increasing levels of challenge to progress in the current cycle.

The Challenge Score is a subjective measure of challenge in the current PROGRESS Cycle. The score should be viewed as an indicator, not a predictive model.

Opportunity Score

PURPOSE

The Opportunity Score represents an overall level of opportunity the current cycle is projected to produce in terms of benefits, value to partners of the organization, and the confidence that the progress can be delivered. By combining the benefits assessment, value to partners and delivery confidence into a single measure, the Opportunity Score provides an assessment of multifaceted business development opportunities and facilitates high-level

TABLE 9.6 Example Challenge Scores, indicators and types

Challenge Score (range)	Challenge Score	Challenge indicator	Challenge type	Description
0–5	1	Very low	Trivial	A challenge that the organization can take in its stride
6–10	2	Low	Regular	A challenge that may cause one or more parts of the organization to be under pressure
11–15	3	Medium	Significant	A significant challenge whose achievement will strengthen the organization
16–20	4	High	Drama	A very large challenge with high urgency that will test the organization severely
21–25	5	Very high	Crisis!	An overwhelming challenge with the highest urgency that could test the viability of the organization or division of the company

decision-making for leaders in the organization and its partner network, weighing up pros and cons of high-priority value initiatives.

CONTEXT

Calculation of the Opportunity Score is the final part of the Opportunity Assessment in the PROGRESS Cycle, after the benefits to the organization, value to partners and delivery confidence have all been assessed and rated. The Opportunity Score is the ultimate measure of the positive change the organization could accrue from progress in the current cycle, and the one that counterbalances the Challenge Score from the Recognize Challenge element.

APPLICATION

Calculating the Opportunity Score factors in monetary benefits to the organization, value perceived by network partners and confidence of delivery, based on a collective consideration of both the organization and partner working in collaboration.

A more advanced approach will use the same formula plus application of customized weightings to each individual dimension and is recommended because it takes into account the organization's particular business environment. The resulting score should be rounded to the next integer and converted onto a five-point scale, where scores indicate a progressively higher level of opportunity.

The weightings are developed from stakeholder opinion and, as such, are subjective values. Agreeing the weightings may be a good opportunity to further evaluate and cross-examine the organization and partner network's priorities, thereby reaching a consensus over a broader range of relevant issues.

To follow the second approach, Formula 9.5 can be used to calculate the Opportunity Score:

$$Os = Benefits \times Wb + Value \times Wv + Confidence \times Wc \qquad (9.5)$$

where

Os = Opportunity Score;

Benefits to organization = rated (1–5);

Wb = weighting applied to benefits (0–1);

Value to partners = rated (1–5);

Wv = weighting applied to value (0–1);

Confidence of delivery = rated (1–5);

Wc = weighting applied to Confidence (0–1).

The resulting cumulative Opportunity Score may be expressed as a figure in a specific range (eg 0–15, or 1 – lowest, 5 – highest), grade or class. Table 9.7 shows example ranges, scores, grades and classes representing gradually increasing levels of opportunity projected from progress in the current cycle.

BRIT workshops and the use of tools

The use of tools to assess value initiatives, and the business environment, where the status of specific indicators, eg the VUCA Storm Scale, is monitored, is undertaken to support Business Resilience. A deviation in delivery of an initiative or change to a status indicator (eg RAG colour) will be monitored by the Progress Master and reported to the Business Resilience Owner. Where such monitoring or tracking leads to a change in initiative or business environment indicator status, this may prompt the Business Resilience Owner to call a Business Resilience and initiative team (BRIT) workshop.

TABLE 9.7 Example Opportunity Scores, ranges, grades and classes

Opportunity Score (range)	Opportunity Score	Opportunity Score (grade)	Opportunity Score (class)	Description
0–3	1	Very low	Minimal	An opportunity that does not pose a good return on investment
4–6	2	Low	Modest	An opportunity with minimal positive outcomes
7–9	3	Medium	Fair	An opportunity with reasonable positive outcomes
10–12	4	High	High hopes	An opportunity promising outstanding positive outcomes
13–15	5	Very high	Treasure trove!	An opportunity promising truly unique positive outcomes

BRIT workshops provide a process and environment for the resilience team to take forward initiatives and make improvements to Business Resilience.

The specific and popular tools for Business Resilience are used to create indicators and prompt decisions by the Business Resilience Owner that action may be required; where appropriate, it will be necessary to call a BRIT workshop. Resilience Professionals will review initiatives and changes to the business environment that have resulted in changes to status indicators, with respect to progress within the PROGRESS Cycle. The BRIT members may decide to continue progress of initiatives without change, or propose changes to the Business Resilience Owner, in respect of particular products, services, practices or processes within the organization's portfolio. Such actions may involve adjustments to the design, tailoring or operation of tools or proposals to supplement or completely replace a tool. In this case, assessments of tools would form the basis of a tools initiative, with proposals scheduled for review and decisions made in the BRIT workshop to take immediate action, or place the proposal on the Progress Backlog.

Resilience Professionals should have facilitation skills for BRIT workshops, where members review, rethink and re-evaluate what has been done, or is planned, to align to the Evolving Vision and Progress Definition. This process is enhanced by using the Business Resilience Profile to focus on improvement, prioritizing enhancements across all 5 domains and 22 elements. In all cases, it is expected that tools will support BRIT workshops in the context of the Progress @ PACE 8-4-8 model.

- **On consideration of adopting or adapting Business Resilience:** when considering adopting Business Resilience, selecting one of the PURE strategies or conducting a Resilience Profile baseline or update.

- **RESILIENCE Foundations:** this domain recommends the use of BRIT workshops in each element, eg as the environment for the Evolving Vision, check Regulatory and Governance policies or to assess risk.

- **PACE Culture:** will benefit from BRIT workshops to initiate development of Purposeful Mindset, application of tools, learning to improve Capability and Skills or how to ensure working in teams leads to Elevated Energy. Academies are another tool that can provide an excellent environment to share great ideas, and stimulate excellence and recognition when optimizing the PACE Culture.

- **PROGRESS Cycle:** BRIT workshops are an important tool to improve portfolio outcomes. In addition to responding to changes, they will frequently be deployed during the PROGRESS Cycle, eg to reach consensus for Decision Gates 1 (proceed to development) and 2 (proceed to release).

In all situations, the Business Resilience Owner will want to ensure organizations can speed up the identification of realizable gains and benefits from learning opportunities using BRIT workshops.

Roles for implementing the specific tools

Business Resilience Owner – obtains organizational resources and agrees the tools to be used for Business Resilience; where appropriate, the levels to be used for the scales (such as the percentage/levels of available capacity, which rate very high to very low).

Progress Master – leads on the use of all the specific Business Resilience tools, collecting relevant data, advising on the appropriate scales, and performing the calculations. This role will advise the Business Resilience Owner on training, use of tools, interpretation of the information and value of outputs as inputs to management decision-making.

Initiative Leader – reviews information provided by tools on accepting a value initiative and future development work; makes use of the correct tools when reporting progress.

Resilience Professional – will advise and support the Business Resilience Owner and Progress Master on use of the tools. This could be in a coaching, training, consulting or delivery capacity.

Benefits, risks and costs of implementing the specific tools

The primary benefits of using the Business Resilience tools are focus, complementarity and cost-efficiency:

- The focused nature of the tools allows Resilience Professionals to plan and implement Business Resilience with higher efficiency, as opposed to scenarios where other, less targeted tools are employed.

- The complementary nature means that organizations can choose between fully embracing the Business Resilience tools or mixing it with the tools they currently use. This maximizes capability by taking advantage of tools the organization has at its disposal and only introducing new tools as needed.
- Cost-efficiency is due to the adoption being the only relevant cost, as there are no licencing fees for the tools. Organizations, therefore, can determine the required balance between focus and complementarity and concentrate on appropriate adoption that will be cost-efficient by design.

Costs

The only costs associated with the specific tools are for the training of Resilience Professionals and all those engaged in Business Resilience on the use of the tools.

Risks

Similar to other management tools, the risks with the application of a new toolset lie in:

- using wrong or incomplete data for inputs – mitigated by checking the sources and validating the data (eg by triangulation or data tracing);
- inappropriate application of the tools themselves – mitigated by provision of appropriate training or employing Resilience Professionals;
- not acting on the outputs and results in a timely and comprehensive fashion – mitigated by ensuring timescales are understood and acted on by all key stakeholders.

Summary

In the Business Resilience Framework, the central value of tools arises from provision of decision-support indicators to the Business Resilience Owner and from assistance in gathering and analysing data for tracking and monitoring purposes by other Resilience Professionals or members of initiative teams. In other words, using tools to support adoption, adaption or workflow.

It is important to be clear that the way in which tools are tailored and deployed will be for Resilience Professionals to determine, within the confines of specific organizational circumstances. What is provided in this chapter is a demonstration of how (specific or popular) tools could be used when embedding the framework or updating it during PROGRESS Cycles, in addition to managing organizational portfolios of products, services, processes and practices.

This chapter also clarifies the importance of balancing the value of tools and formulae to support Business Resilience, with the limits of gathering subjective data for management decision-making purposes. This challenge is overcome using BRIT workshops as the key professional practice in which data analysis and reported information, using specific or popular tools, is reviewed and decisions or action taken in response to changing business environments, or the need to make progress at pace within a resilient organization.

QUESTIONS TO THINK ABOUT

- Is there anything in the existing organizational toolset that already fulfils the same purpose?
- What are the potential issues and challenges with adopting new tools?
- How could we pilot the adoption of tools, such as BRIT workshops?

References

Bennett, N and Lemoine, J (2014) What a difference a word makes: Understanding threats to performance in a VUCA world, *Business Horizons*, 57 (3), pp 311–317, doi:10.1016/j.bushor.2014.01.001

Sinar, E (2013) *Are Leaders Ready for VUCA?*, drjohnsullivan.com, 15 November, drjohnsullivan.com/news-press/are-leaders-ready-for-vuca (archived at https://perma.cc/QWL4-PJ4Z)

Stevenson, H (2016) VUCA: Volatile uncertain complex ambiguous, *LinkedIn*, 21 February, https://www.linkedin.com/pulse/coaching-point-contact-herb-stevenson/ (archived at https://perma.cc/TBN7-T7U7)

10

Resilience Profile

Purpose

The Resilience Profile assesses the resilience of the organization in each of the 22 elements that contribute to the Business Resilience Framework. The purpose of the Resilience Profile is to enable an assessment of the ability of the organization to continue making progress during difficult as well as favourable circumstances. The Resilience Profile provides a focus on the areas to improve so that the organization, or part thereof, is more confident of sustained progress delivered at pace. It should also enable the areas where improvements have already been made, or have started, to be recognized, celebrated and to have a plan to protect these good practices that have been established. The Resilience Profile enables the determination of the level of Business Resilience when measured against the identified criteria. Once you've read this chapter, you can refer back to it to check each level of resilience for each element of the Business Resilience Framework as you work through the process of establishing the Resilience Profile of your organization.

Introduction

In David Hurst's book *Crisis and Renewal* (Hurst, 1995), it is acknowledged that organizations have a lifecycle and need to renew if they are to survive. The Resilience Profile helps to avoid the crisis and move directly to the renewal or evolution phase leading to growth and mature operations. Ideally, different parts of the organization will be at different phases in the lifecycle in parallel so that there is always growth and mature operating in the organization. This is important when considering what parts of the portfolio should be developed in Rapids and which in Lagoons. The Resilience Profile will assist the organization to move to a position whereby there are sufficient areas of growth or renewal to address the areas that are in decline, thus avoiding whole-organization crisis.

The Resilience Profile requires understanding of all the elements that contribute to the Business Resilience Framework to identify a level for each, in order to improve the pace of organizational progress and withstand changes to the environment.

The Business Resilience Profile is flexible and scalable so that organizations of different industries, sizes, complexity and location can all benefit from its use. It supports organizations regardless of age, maturity or other factors. The Resilience Profile provides a mechanism to assess what an organization practices against the Resilience Profile areas, reflecting the 20 elements of the Progress @ Pace 8-4-8 Model, plus the Roles and Principles. The findings, without being prescriptive, enable informed decision-making about any changes so that effective improvements can be made. It is intended to facilitate progressive incremental improvement in Business Resilience.

When to undertake a Resilience Profile

It is recommended that a baseline Resilience Profile is undertaken when starting the Business Resilience journey. The Resilience Profile should be updated each time the Progress Definition step is undertaken, although it can be revisited at any point. Any change to the portfolio or to the challenge level may require a reassessment of the Resilience Profile levels for one or more of the elements. The Resilience Profile is a good indicator of organizational fitness to face the new challenge. For this reason, some organizations will assess their Resilience Profile at regular intervals of, perhaps, every six months to continue to improve their levels of Business Resilience and make progress as an organization.

Resilience Profile levels

There are five profile levels in the Resilience Profile:

- Profile level 1 – ad hoc;
- Profile level 2 – reactive or planned in initiative(s);

- Profile level 3 – proactive or planned in department(s) – or divisions of large organizations;
- Profile level 4 – managed or planned at corporate level;
- Profile level 5 – optimized and continually improved with learning across the partner network.

Each level is explained below.

Profile level 1: Ad hoc

At the ad hoc profile level 1, the organization may have elements of Business Resilience being used. These are, however, uncoordinated and inconsistent in their application, thus missing the greater benefits that can be accrued. An example would be some development teams self-organizing using scrum while others are awaiting direction and use a range of development approaches.

The focus at profile level 1 is on compliance, as the organization has not specified how it defines or measures progress. There may be KPIs in place, target performance and a new product pipeline without a Progress Definition. This can leave the individuals and teams confused about their priorities. Are they to deliver more services, more timely responses, more services, more customers or more savings?

At profile level 1 of the Resilience Profile, there is no commitment to progress or resilience, even if there is commitment to changes that are being implemented.

Profile level 2: Reactive or planned in initiatives

At Resilience Profile level 2, the organization has a reactive response to changes in the external environment. There is likely to be a Progress Definition at local initiative or team level. For example, a team could be working to improve customer delivery times with excellent coordination within a programme, while the department has another initiative to change the customer interaction method, which is not part of the programme and collaboration does not take place.

The focus is on local delivery and the organization does not have an overarching Progress Definition that is understood at all levels. Under Calm conditions the local team coordinates to make progress with a specific initiative. As the Storm scale rises, the team can lose focus on progress and simply concentrate on survival and day-to-day delivery of business as usual. This can leave individuals within the team confused about their goal priorities.

At Resilience Profile level 2, a goal for progress is set and there may be commitment within the team. There is not wider commitment or allocation of resources to progress, although there may be a plan for change management. Progress is understood when the Storm scale is moderate, but this is lost when the Storm scale increases.

Profile level 3: Proactive or planned in departments (or divisions of large organizations)

At Resilience Profile level 3, the organization is becoming proactive about Business Resilience. It will have a Progress Definition and understand how progress is measured at departmental level. The department heads may or may not share their understanding of the Progress Definition across departments or cascade this understanding to their team leaders. Local teams will have a Progress Definition for their areas that may or may not align with the organizational definition.

The focus is on departmental delivery to meet organizational goals. There is coordination within a department, although different departments may be working differently. As the Storm scale increases, the departments increasingly compete more than collaborate. There is debate within the department regarding progress against the organizational progress plan.

At Resilience Profile level 3, goals for progress are set and the department commits to achieve progress and increase Business Resilience.

Profile level 4: Managed, planned across the organization

At Resilience Profile level 4, the organization has a clear definition of progress and how it is measured both at organizational and local levels. Progress is routinely the basis of decision-making. There is a culture within the organization that goes from the board to the individual level so that every person knows their contribution to the organizational progress plan.

The focus is on the whole organization, with good collaboration between departments as well as coordination of initiatives, processes and practices. As the Storm scale increases, the organization may find itself tending to fall back to a lower level; however, the robust Progress @ Pace 8-4-8 Model allows Rapid assessment of the new situation, reprioritization and refocusing on progress in the current Storm scale level to build or maintain resilience.

At Resilience Profile level 4, there is commitment with a plan to continue to progress. Progress is measured and achievement is recognized and celebrated.

Profile level 5: Optimized, continuously improving, shared across the network

At Resilience Profile level 5, the Business Resilience Framework is not only shared right through the organization but also across the network with the suppliers, customers, partners and internal teams all involved in ensuring delivery of customer value.

The focus is on collaboration to safeguard improvements that have already been made and continuous improvement. Improvements may be to BAU processes and practices, new product or service development or a new approach to collaboration. The whole network understands what progress means for each organization and the part they play in delivering progress to successfully develop Business Resilience, both in their own organization and across the partner network.

At Resilience Profile level 5, the organization has a commitment to progress, a plan to achieve it and sets accountability for doing so. The accountability could be by inclusion in the annual report, service user, commissioner or shareholder updates on the Resilience Profile or progress plan. It could be that progress measurement is a central element included in all reviews across the organization. Any business cases to support proposed value initiatives will need to include how the initiative contributes to organizational progress and builds resilience.

The profile levels can be tracked using a template such as the one shown in Figure 10.1.

Resilience Profile in domains and elements

Each domain and element is set out to show the expected resilience achievement at each level for the elements. Each domain has an example Resilience

FIGURE 10.1 An example of using a template to track the Resilience Profile of an organization profile

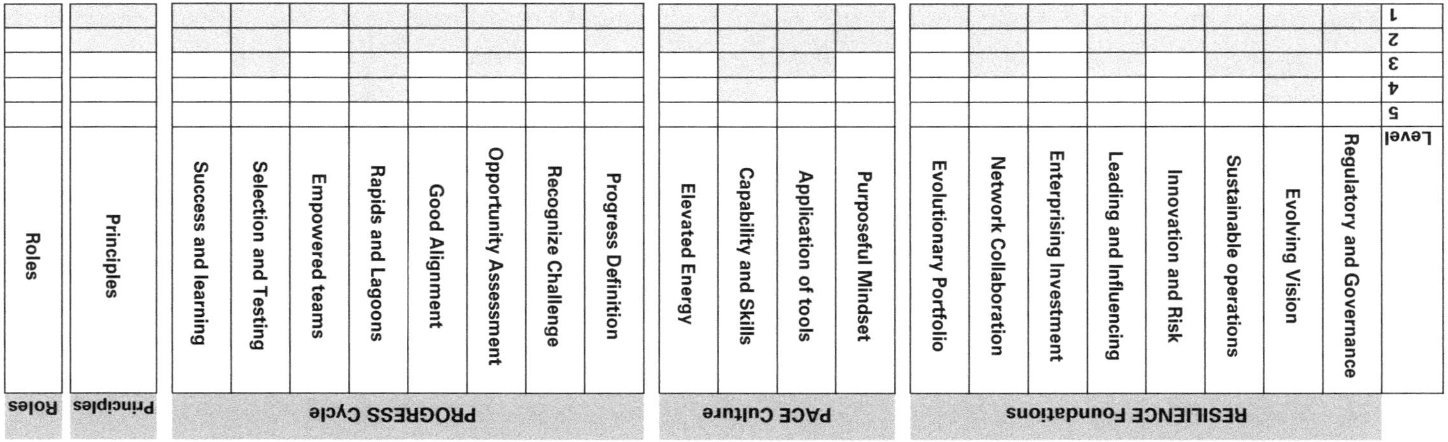

Level	1	2	3	4	5		
Regulatory and Governance							RESILIENCE Foundations
Evolving Vision							
Sustainable operations							
Innovation and Risk							
Leading and Influencing							
Enterprising Investment							
Network Collaboration							
Evolutionary Portfolio							
Purposeful Mindset							PACE Culture
Application of tools							
Capability and Skills							
Elevated Energy							
Progress Definition							PROGRESS Cycle
Recognize Challenge							
Opportunity Assessment							
Good Alignment							
Rapids and Lagoons							
Empowered teams							
Selection and Testing							
Success and learning							
Principles							Principles
Roles							Roles

Profile chart to show results. It should be noted that the type of chart can vary from a bar chart to a radial chart and different types are shown to demonstrate this. It is not expected that each domain is shown differently.

Principles profile

The Principles are assessed as a whole, since all the Principles must be in place to be effective.

- Profile level 1 – Either there are no Business Resilience Principles being utilized in the organization or there are few Principles being applied ad hoc and which may be applied by coincidence rather than to improve Business Resilience.
- Profile level 2 – There are some Business Resilience Principles being utilized in the organization, although they are not embedded or coordinated with other Principles or Business Resilience activities.
- Profile level 3 – There are some Business Resilience Principles being utilized and embedded in the organization. There may be others that are utilized but are not planned or assessed.
- Profile level 4 – There are many Business Resilience Principles being utilized and embedded in the organization. The remaining Principles are planned for adoption, and all are being assessed when undertaking business planning for the organization.
- Profile level 5 – All seven Business Resilience Principles are embedded in the organization. The Principles are shared with the partner network to enhance the resilience of the whole network.

RESILIENCE PROFILE FOR PRINCIPLES

Figure 10.2 shows an example of how an organization that has assessed the resilience status of their Business Resilience Principles, and found that they are at profile level 2, may choose to represent their findings. Examples of other ways to present findings are shown through this chapter.

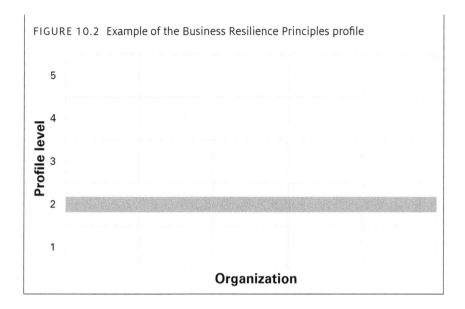

FIGURE 10.2 Example of the Business Resilience Principles profile

Roles profile

The Roles are profiled in a group as they work together effectively in a team:

- Profile level 1 – None of the Business Resilience core Roles are allocated, although some responsibilities may be undertaken by coincidence or on an ad hoc basis.

- Profile level 2 – Business Resilience core Roles are allocated without training or capability assessment of the individuals and so the outcomes are unlikely to build the resilience level desired.

- Profile level 3 – Business Resilience core Roles are allocated with training and capability assessment. The individuals may still require external support to achieve the resilience outcomes desired.

- Profile level 4 – Business Resilience core Roles are adapted and allocated with capability assessment and training. The organization understands how each role helps build Business Resilience. The organization recognizes that wide skills are needed to optimize the benefits from the core Roles.

- Profile level 5 – As profile level 4, with the additional authority to discuss with network partners the wider skills required for Business Resilience. Inspirational leadership is provided by the core Roles.

RESILIENCE PROFILE FOR ROLES

Figure 10.3 shows an example of how an organization that has assessed the resilience status of their Business Resilience Roles, and found that they are at profile level 2, may choose to represent their findings. This is an alternative to the horizontal bar chart for the Principles.

FIGURE 10.3 Example of the Business Resilience Roles profile

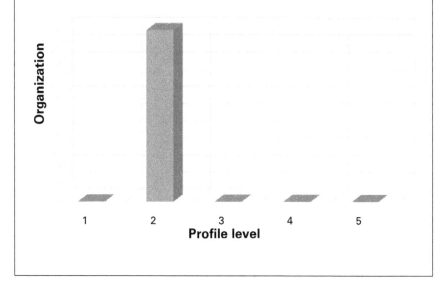

RESILIENCE Foundations profile

Each RESILIENCE Foundations element is profiled separately as they can each be improved to aid Business Resilience and actions can target one or more of the elements.

1 Regulatory and governance

- Profile level 1 – Governance is informal and not shared across all levels or parts of the organization. There is an implied or assumed level at which items are escalated and authorized. Regulatory compliance is not part of regular organizational reviews.

- Profile level 2 – Governance and regulatory compliance is documented, although this may not be known at all organization levels. Documentation may be a requirement for a contract or accreditation process. Levels of authority may be in job descriptions. Mandatory regulations may be observed.

- Profile level 3 – Governance and regulatory compliance is part of training, as appropriate, for staff at all levels. Staff are aware of their levels of authority, which items to escalate and when this is required. Recommended regulations will be observed.

- Profile level 4 – Governance and regulatory compliance is audited as part of managing the organization. Areas of poor governance or non-compliance with regulations are identified and improvements implemented.

- Profile level 5 – Governance and regulatory compliance is in place across the partner network. Network partners agree minimum compliance levels for governance and regulatory framework with actions to reach recommended levels identified.

2 Evolving Vision

- Profile level 1 – A static vision is understood at the top level of the organization, although not shared across the organization. It is not updated.

- Profile level 2 – A vision is understood at the top level of the organization and those immediately reporting to them, although this is only updated when triggered by a significant event.

- Profile level 3 – The vision is understood at divisional or departmental levels and updated at the end of each strategic plan period. It provides a sense of purpose at divisional or departmental levels.

- Profile level 4 – The vision is understood by everyone in the organization and provides a sense of purpose. It is updated annually or triggered by a significant event. Why the vision is continually evolving is understood at all levels.

- Profile level 5 – The vision is understood at all levels of the organization and across the partner network. It is reviewed regularly and as changes occur and in response to the regular review. Staff across the organization and partner network understand that the vision needs to evolve as the environment and organization evolves.

3 Sustainable operations

- Profile level 1 – There are not clear procedures in place and issues arise regularly, causing firefighting.
- Profile level 2 – Clear procedures are in place and staff have the capability required to adhere to them. Issues arise when procedures are not followed. Staff tend to have capabilities in a single area.
- Profile level 3 – Procedures are routinely followed by trained and capable staff. There is flexibility and suggestions for improvement are raised. Staff tend to be able to cover more than one area.
- Profile level 4 – Operations have modularity to adapt to meet different needs. There is use of lessons learned and best practices. Improvements are embraced by the organization and staff welcome new opportunities.
- Profile level 5 – There is flexibility of operations across the partner network. Adaptation and improvements to operations are made across the network. Staff have capabilities to adapt as required with multiple skills and knowledge areas.

4 Innovation and Risk

- Profile level 1 – Change and innovation is not welcomed by the organization. It is not understood how risk management will benefit the organization.
- Profile level 2 – Innovation and Risk management are not formalized, although some risk management and innovation activities are taking place informally.
- Profile level 3 – Innovation and Risk management strategy is in place. Innovation and Risk mitigation activities take place when time permits.
- Profile level 4 – Innovation and assessed risk-taking to enhance or exploit opportunities are welcomed. Innovation and Risk management strategy, standards and practices are in place. Innovation and Risk management activities take place regularly within the organization.
- Profile level 5 – Innovation and assessed risk-taking are welcomed across the partner network. Innovation and Risk management activities take place regularly. Staff are encouraged to have innovation time – to choose what they work on. The actions are coordinated across the partner network.

5 Leading and Influencing

- Profile level 1 – Some individuals exhibit some leadership and influencing capabilities by demonstrating standards, characteristics and behaviours to engender trust and unity. There is some communication of the vision, values and links to the Progress Definition. Leadership uses charisma as the primary tool.

- Profile level 2 – Some teams or Initiative Leaders create an environment that encourages high performance and empowers team members to reach their full potential. Leadership uses appropriate styles.

- Profile level 3 – Exhibits leadership capabilities with the right characteristics and behaviours. Appropriate leadership styles are used to gain and maintain trust, confidence, commitment and collaboration of others to ensure continued progress. Development encourages experience and knowledge-sharing.

- Profile level 4 – Management and working style of the organization demonstrates leadership attributes at all levels within the organization. Encourages open discussion so that any difficulties or challenges are identified and addressed. Inspires through standards, modesty, Calm and giving credit to others.

- Profile level 5 – The partner network working style demonstrates leadership attributes of profile level 4. Desirable behaviours are role-modelled consistently. Successes at all levels are attributed to those who have contributed and failures are owned by the leaders, with learning captured for the future.

6 Enterprising Investment

- Profile level 1 – There is no investment in people, talents, tools or assets and the organization does not attract any investment from others.

- Profile level 2 – There is some investment in people and talents, with minimal investment in tools or assets, although the organization does attract some investment from others. The organization starts to have some attraction for others to invest.

- Profile level 3 – There is reasonable investment in people, talents and tools or assets. Reserves of the organization are low, although it does attract investment from others.

- Profile level 4 – There is good investment in people, talents, tools and assets of the organization that attracts investment from others. The organization has reserves that are adequate for their anticipated needs.
- Profile level 5 – There is significant investment in people and talents with sufficient investment in tools or assets across the partner network and it is very attractive for others to invest in the organization. Organizational reserves are healthy for future anticipated and unknown needs.

7 Network Collaboration

- Profile level 1 – Members of the organization tend to work alone and where possible do not collaborate. They align to personal objectives. There is a 'silo' approach.
- Profile level 2 – Staff members are working in self-selected groups that may or may not align to the Progress Definition for the department or organization. There is a group approach more than team.
- Profile level 3 – There is collaboration within single departments or divisions. Collaboration is aligned to the departmental Progress Definition or objectives. There is a 'team' approach, albeit limited to the department or division.
- Profile level 4 – There is cross-departmental collaboration within the organization that supports the Progress Definition for the organization. There is a 'team' approach across the organization.
- Profile level 5 – There is collaboration across network partners that aligns to the Progress Definition for the organization and is also shared with partners. There is a 'team' approach across the partner network.

8 Evolutionary Portfolio

- Profile level 1 – The portfolio of products and services remains fixed, with minor changes that are considered to be in line with the static vision.
- Profile level 2 – The portfolio is reviewed when the strategic plan is reviewed, with updates to current products that target and are promoted to the same customers.

- Profile level 3 – The portfolio is reviewed when the strategic plan is updated, with new products that are linked to the current portfolio and promoted to current customers. The portfolio is reviewed annually against the current customers and demand.

- Profile level 4 – The portfolio is reviewed regularly against current customer feedback and market demand. The portfolio is amended and updated at agreed review periods. The reviews are risk-assessed, including updates to current products and new products when appropriate.

- Profile level 5 – The portfolio is reviewed regularly with network partners versus feedback from current customers, potential customers and market intelligence. The reviews are risk-assessed and updates are made as frequently as needed, which include diversification when appropriate.

RESILIENCE PROFILE FOR RESILIENCE FOUNDATIONS

Figure 10.4 shows an example of how an organization that has assessed the resilience status of all eight of their Business RESILIENCE Foundations may choose to represent their findings. This provides an alternative to the bar charts for the Principles and Roles domains.

FIGURE 10.4   Example of the RESILIENCE Foundations profile

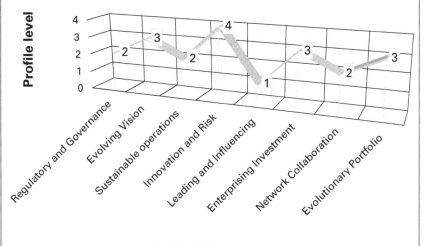

RESILIENCE Foundations elements

PACE Culture profile

Each PACE Culture element is profiled separately as they can each be improved to aid Business Resilience and actions can target one or more of the PACE Culture elements.

1 Purposeful Mindset

- Profile level 1 – There is an overall fixed mindset whereby the staff feel they cannot change and the organization or team should utilize the talents they have, without understanding the purpose and vision of the organization.
- Profile level 2 – There are pockets of growth mindset that believe change is possible but are inhibited by an overall fixed mindset. A disconnect is likely between what is stated by the organization and the policies in place.
- Profile level 3 – There is a balance between growth mindset and fixed mindset. Some policies support the growth mindset, such as development opportunities, while others implement a fixed mindset. Customer value is stated as important.
- Profile level 4 – There is an overall growth mindset within the organization or team. There is encouragement for assessed risk-taking, collaboration across teams and admitting errors. Organizational policies support the growth mindset and adding customer value.
- Profile level 5 – There is an overall growth mindset that encourages collaboration across organizational boundaries and the partner network, trying new strategies to move forward effectively. Adding customer value is at the heart of everything, whatever the VUCA Storm Scale.

2 Application of tools

- Profile level 1 – There are a few basic tools available, while most things are undertaken manually or using a system that uses off-the-shelf products, such as a calculator or word processing.

- Profile level 2 – Some more advanced tools are available to undertake tasks to make them more efficient, more effective, more economical or a combination of these, such as Excel or PowerPoint. Staff are insufficiently trained to benefit the organization from greater use.

- Profile level 3 – Advanced tools are available for most tasks but not all the staff have training to fully utilize their functionality, or have the training but do not always apply the tools. Many tasks could be undertaken more efficiently.

- Profile level 4 – Advanced tools are available and staff are trained to use them. Tools are utilized for most tasks that are commonly undertaken. Learning is captured for smarter future ways of working. Tools enable collaboration within the organization (or part thereof).

- Profile level 5 – Sophisticated tools are available and staff are adequately trained so the tools are utilized for all tasks that are common and for many less routine ones. Learning is captured and shared across the partner network to collaborate more effectively across boundaries.

3 Capability and Skills

- Profile level 1 – There is a shortage of capabilities and skills in most areas of the organization. Fifty per cent or more of the people have a skills gap when compared with the required capabilities for the role.

- Profile level 2 – There are significant capabilities and skills gaps that are not adequately covered by temporary or contract staff. Adding customer value is not identified as being important in the capabilities and skills required.

- Profile level 3 – Areas of capabilities and skills gaps where there are shortfalls are adequately covered by temporary or contract staff. Customer value is acknowledged but the focus is on simply delivering what is required more than the customer value created by the delivery.

- Profile level 4 – Most people in the organization have sufficient capabilities and skills for their current role and understand where the other skills are available to link with to deliver. Capabilities and skills are considered in relation to adding customer value.

- Profile level 5 – Most people offer more capabilities and skills than are required for their current role, thus providing flexibility to cover other Roles. There is a focus on the importance of adding customer value and utilizing capabilities and skills across boundaries and the partner network.

4 Elevated Energy

- Profile level 1 – Corrosive energy – this is seen in high levels of anger and conflict, actively hindering changes and innovations. Corrosive energy is negative and can cause progress to stop or regress.
- Profile level 2 – Resigned energy – this is seen in people who are performing only to the minimum standard required and are mentally withdrawn from their organization. There could be pockets of comfortable or productive energy.
- Profile level 3 – Comfortable energy – this is seen in a relaxed atmosphere where people understand what they are doing and where they fit. They prefer to maintain the status quo more than changes, which may cause them to be unsure. There could be pockets of productive energy.
- Profile level 4 – Productive energy – this is seen in people looking for new opportunities and taking decisive action to make progress because they care deeply about the success of the organization. They have a high emotional investment in the organization.
- Profile level 5 – Productive energy with inspirational leadership across the partner network – there is excellent leadership through inspired standards. It focuses on customer needs, collaborative working and inspiring teams and individuals to achieve continual renewal.

RESILIENCE PROFILE FOR PACE CULTURE

Figure 10.5 shows an example of how an organization that has assessed the resilience status of each element of their PACE Culture may choose to represent their findings. It is another visual presentation that can be utilized.

FIGURE 10.5 Example of the PACE Culture profile

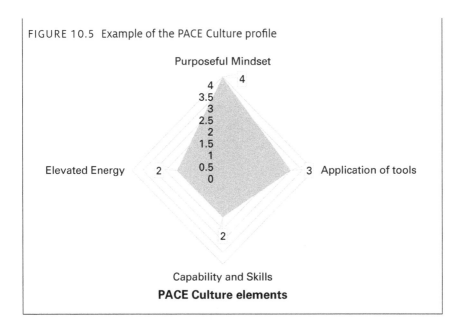

Purposeful Mindset

4
3.5
3
2.5
2
1.5
1
0.5
0

Elevated Energy   2   Application of tools   3

2

Capability and Skills
PACE Culture elements

PROGRESS Cycle profile

1 Progress Definition

- Profile level 1 – There is no definition of progress or vision for the organization. A Progress Definition could be present at team level.

- Profile level 2 – A definition of progress is present, although this is not used when cascading objectives through the organization. A Progress Definition could be present at department level.

- Profile level 3 – A definition of progress is present and shared through the organization. The Progress Definition is only updated when required. A Progress Backlog is in place.

- Profile level 4 – A definition of progress is central to the organization's operations, development and innovation. The Progress Definition is updated regularly and collaboratively, with a roadmap in place for the organization.

- Profile level 5 – A definition of progress is shared across the partner network and updated whenever there is a trigger event in addition to regular review. Network partners provide input to the Progress Backlog and the roadmap.

2 Recognize Challenge

- Profile level 1 – When a trigger event takes place, the recognition of the challenge is ad hoc and reactive based on the individuals involved.
- Profile level 2 – When a trigger event takes place, the recognition and analysis of the challenge is dependent on teams utilizing tools and techniques from their experience.
- Profile level 3 – When a trigger event takes place, there is recognition and analysis of the challenge based on the internal capacity of the organization to respond. Some elements of external and internal analysis may be utilized.
- Profile level 4 – When a trigger event takes place, there is recognition of the challenge and analysis of both the internal and the external factors that impact the ability of the organization to respond.
- Profile level 5 – When a trigger event takes place, the recognition of the challenge and analysis of the internal and external factors, including the partner network, is undertaken.

3 Opportunity Assessment

- Profile level 1 – The assessment of opportunity is based on benefits identification for each initiative, which is done without reference to a Progress Definition or other initiatives.
- Profile level 2 – The assessment of opportunity is based on the expected benefits and costs of undertaking the initiative without reference to other initiatives.
- Profile level 3 – The assessment of opportunity is based on benefits, costs and the value to customers of the organization with assessment.
- Profile level 4 – The assessment of opportunity is based on benefits, costs, value to the customers and the level of confidence in delivery by the organization.
- Profile level 5 – The assessment of opportunity is based on benefits, costs, value to the customers, the level of confidence in delivery by the organization and value to the partner network.

4 Good Alignment

- Profile level 1 – Initiatives are implemented that appear to provide benefits but without prioritization or alignment to the Progress Definition or team objectives.

- Profile level 2 – Initiatives are implemented that are aligned and prioritized in line with team objectives without alignment to the Progress Definition.

- Profile level 3 – Initiatives are implemented that have alignment to and are prioritized against departmental or divisional objectives but are not checked for alignment to the organizational Progress Definition.

- Profile level 4 – Initiatives are implemented that are aligned and prioritized in line with the organizational Progress Definition.

- Profile level 5 – Initiatives are prioritized and aligned to the organizational Progress Definition and network partner Progress Definitions.

5 Rapids and Lagoons

- Profile level 1 – Initiatives are implemented without allocation to a Rapid or Lagoon approach.

- Profile level 2 – Initiatives are implemented based on a backlog that contains all proposed initiatives.

- Profile level 3 – Initiatives are assessed and categorized for delivery using a Rapid or Lagoon approach.

- Profile level 4 – Initiatives are assessed and categorized for delivery using a Rapid or Lagoon approach. Separate Rapid and Lagoon backlogs are prioritized for their contribution to the organizational Progress Definition.

- Profile level 5 – Initiatives are assessed and categorized for delivery using a Rapid or Lagoon approach. The Rapid and Lagoon backlogs are prioritized for their contribution to the organizational Progress Definition and reprioritized regularly.

6 Enabling Teams

- Profile level 1 – Implementation of initiatives is undertaken by groups of people who may not have a shared vision or objective. There is a willingness of individuals to accept tasks that they are allocated.

- Profile level 2 – Implementation of initiatives is undertaken by teams being formed for each initiative. There is an understanding in the team of what they need to achieve and a willingness to take responsibility for delivery of the specified requirements of each initiative.

- Profile level 3 – Implementation of initiatives is undertaken by teams who not only are aware of what is needed but also learn from their individual experiences, providing a willingness to challenge requirements if the team identifies a better way to implement or to gain benefits, contributing to the Progress Definition.

- Profile level 4 – Implementation of initiatives is undertaken by teams who are aware of what is needed and learn from their collective experience. They collaborate, together and with other areas of the organization. There is a willingness to identify appropriate tools and methods for each initiative as well as challenging the specifications.

- Profile level 5 – Implementation of initiatives is undertaken by self-managed teams who identify their tasks and responsibilities according to the needs of the initiative they are delivering. The team has an adaptability to change and leads their own innovation and learning, including from the network partners.

7 Selecting and testing

- Profile level 1 – Deliverables are tested for functionality on an ad hoc basis. Testing criteria are created when development is under way (or completed), based on individual views.

- Profile level 2 – Deliverables are tested for functionality and compliance with industry or organizational standards. Testing criteria are created when development is agreed, based on standard checklists.

- Profile level 3 – In addition to the profile level 2 factors, the deliverables are also tested for market readiness. Testing criteria are agreed early to include market readiness.

- Profile level 4 – In addition to the profile level 3 factors, the deliverables are also tested for user acceptance. Testing criteria are agreed early to include user acceptance.

- Profile level 5 – In addition to the profile level 4 factors, the deliverables are tested for the impact on the Progress Definition, including any relevant network partners, to feed into Success and Learning. Testing criteria are created based on the Progress Definition.

8 Success and Learning

- Profile level 1 – Development of the next initiative follows immediately that one is completed. Success is delivery of the initiative and learning is with the individuals who have undertaken the tasks.

- Profile level 2 – Benefits are measured when initiatives are delivered or when identified in a benefits review plan. Success is seen when benefits accrue and learning is shared within the development team.

- Profile level 3 – Initiatives have a portfolio review prior to release. Benefits are measured according to a realization plan. There is ad hoc learning from experience within the relevant department.

- Profile level 4 – Initiatives have a portfolio review prior to release. Benefits are tracked. There is recognition of success within the organization and learning from experience is shared across the organization.

- Profile level 5 – Initiatives have a portfolio review prior to release. Benefits are tracked and measured. There is recognition of success across the partner network and learning from experience is shared and implemented, where relevant, across the partner network, in addition to internally.

RESILIENCE PROFILE FOR PROGRESS CYCLE

Figure 10.6 shows an example of how an organization that has assessed the resilience status of each element of their PROGRESS Cycle may choose to represent their findings.

FIGURE 10.6 Example of the PROGRESS Cycle profile

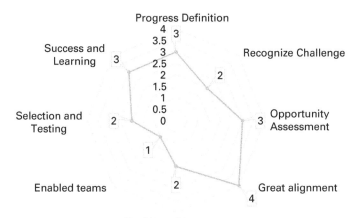

PROGRESS Cycle elements

FIGURE 10.7 Example of the overall Resilience Profile as a bar chart

All Resilience Profile elements

The profile scores for each element of the resilience framework can be reviewed separately or combined to show the overall level and pattern across all 22 elements. An example overall profile is shown in Figure 10.7 as a bar chart.

Figure 10.7 shows each element of the resilience framework and facilitates decisions on whether to focus on raising the Business Resilience level across all elements, only the lowest, or those that have the greatest gaps. Focus could also be given to a single domain, such as the PACE Culture, to enable other areas to progress more Rapidly once this is improved.

An example of the profile displayed as a radar diagram is shown in Figure 10.8. The organization can choose to identify a specific shape and size for the radar diagram.

Each element of the resilience framework that is improved will contribute to an overall improvement in Business Resilience, with the greatest improvement being seen by improvement across all the domains and elements.

It should be noted that as the VUCA Storm Scale increases or the Adaptive Enterprise Score reduces, the overall resilience level can reduce. This is because the Business Resilience Framework elements can be impacted by either the external or internal environments.

FIGURE 10.8 Example of the overall Resilience Profile as a radar diagram

All Resilience Profile elements

INCREASING THE RESILIENCE PROFILE FOR PACE CULTURE

A family-run medium-sized organization was acquired by a global company that required the organization to adopt the global processes and practices. This meant that the staff who had been very close to their customers and were used to being kept up to date with progress direction and proposed changes felt alienated, without a sense of purpose and unused to the tools they were expected to use. This reduced their energy levels, which had previously been high.

The organization realized that the PACE Culture elements needed to be addressed and so they appointed a new divisional leader who kept the staff more informed about direction and facilitated a closer relationship with the customers. Training support was given for the new tools and staff felt more empowered and regained a sense of purpose. This, in turn, elevated their energy levels and enabled the organization to make progress by cross-selling the global company products and services to the existing customers of the acquired organization.

Resilience Profile improvement

Organizations that are continually learning seek to improve their processes, practices and culture to enhance their overall performance in a changing and increasingly competitive environment. Repeatable, reliable results depend on individuals or teams with a proven track record. Long-term success through continual progress and Business Resilience requires consistency across individual, team, departmental, organizational and network levels of the organization.

Using resilience profiling, the approach to improvement would be formed following consideration of the Resilience Profile baseline, establishment of next-level targets and prioritization of domains or elements. This work would be initiated by the Business Resilience Owner and facilitated by the Progress Master, using a BRIT workshop. Participation would depend on the scope of the value initiatives (domains and elements) and the organization levels required to realize resilience improvement targets in the organization. The output of the BRIT workshop would be placed on the Progress Backlog for consideration in the next Progress Definition.

Accountability

If Business Resilience is to be effective and enable a network, organization, department or team to develop Business Resilience so that it can make progress, whether in a global crisis or a boom time, there needs to be a commitment to the result, in line with the Principles. Thus, the Resilience Profile provides accountability by measuring the baseline and remeasuring at intervals to identify the progress already made and the areas to work on next.

Accountability helps to reach goals, whether it be in the office or at the gym. A study conducted by the American Society for Training and Development, now the Association for Talent Development (Hanke, 2018), found that those who planned how they would achieve a goal, made a commitment to someone, and then set an accountability appointment with that person reached the target 65 per cent of the time, much higher than for those who simply plan to achieve it. Accountability is incorporated within the Resilience Profile by having the baseline profile. This is used and updated when the Progress Definition is updated, there is a change to the challenge level or at regular intervals.

Roles for resilience profiling

Business Resilience Owner – is responsible for ensuring the Resilience Profile is undertaken and authorizes actions as a result.

Progress Master – is responsible for undertaking the Resilience Profile or working with a Resilience Professional to do so. They advise the Business Resilience Owner and work with the Initiative Leader(s) to implement any actions authorized.

Initiative Leader(s) – are responsible for implementing actions authorized as a result of the Resilience Profile.

Resilience Professional – can aid the organization by undertaking a Resilience Profile as a baseline or working with the Business Resilience team to interpret the results and identify actions that will improve the resilience level of the organization.

Benefits, costs and risks

To optimize the benefits, the Resilience Profile should be a tool that is used regularly to facilitate a continuous improvement (or Kaizen) approach and benefits from the theory of marginal gains (Harrell, 2015), which are more effective at maintaining the momentum of progress and Business Resilience than an urgent approach to improvements, which can meet significant resistance or simply fade away after the initial introduction.

The key benefits to reviewing the Resilience Profile level and improving it in an organization are that they:

- provide a baseline for discussion about which elements are to be prioritized to improve Business Resilience;
- inform the process of adapting the Business Resilience Framework to the organizational situation;
- enable improvements to be visible and celebrated;
- enable specific areas of an organization to assess their levels against those of the whole organization.

Increasing the resilience level of the organization will improve the return on investment of the organization, in line with the findings for project management in *Quantifying the Value of Project Management* (Ibbs and Reginato, 2002). This is also the basis of the Unilever improvement in return to shareholders under the leadership of Paul Polman, which has resulted in Business Resilience that has ensured growth during the 2020 pandemic despite difficult conditions.

The way to solve the riddle of seemingly competing requirements in organizations is to understand the value that is significant to customers. If the organization is able to move up the Resilience Profile levels, productivity can be improved by working on the areas that deliver more customer value, thus reducing wasteful effort in the organization.

Costs

There is a cost to undertake the Resilience Profile. This cost can be minimized by utilizing information already collected in the organization, as far as possible. The costs may be greater if external Resilience Professionals are used to undertake the assessment and deliver a report with recommendations for priority actions to bring about Business Resilience improvements. Using professionals may save money through their expertise. Whether the assessment is undertaken internally or using external support, the costs should be exceeded by the benefits of an increased level of resilience that results from the improvements made in response to the Resilience Profile findings.

Risks

The risks associated with measuring the Resilience Profile of an organization are closely linked to the understanding of the purpose of the profile.

If the profile is misunderstood as a measure of performance, there is a risk that the individuals or teams will perceive the profile as a threat to their position or reputation, which may impact motivation and, in turn, performance.

If the team assumes the Resilience Profile results identify where their focus should be, there could be a loss of focus on delivering customer value.

If the organization concentrates on improvements to single elements of the framework in isolation, there may be reduced benefits of utilizing all the Principles of Business Resilience.

FOCUS CAN BE DIVERTED

For example, an organization that has a Resilience Profile assessment that shows that their innovation score is very low may focus so much on innovation of new products or services that their existing product portfolio is not adequately supported.

Summary

The Resilience Profile creates a baseline understanding of the level of resilience and the resilience level that the organization wishes to achieve over what period of time. A realistic plan to improve resilience can then be put in place.

QUESTIONS TO THINK ABOUT

- When would it be of benefit to undertake a baseline Resilience Profile in your organization?
- Is there a domain that you feel that a Resilience Profile will assist in the identification of areas to prioritize?
- How will you ensure the purpose of the Resilience Profile is understood and not seen as a measure of staff performance?

References

Hanke, S (2018) Three steps to overcoming resistance, *Forbes Coaches Council*, 14 August, www.forbes.com/sites/forbescoachescouncil/2018/08/14/three-steps-to-overcoming-resistance/?sh=1a1765df5eae (archived at https://perma.cc/R39Z-PAV9)

Harrell, E (2015) How 1% performance improvements led to Olympic gold, *Harvard Business Review*, 30 October, hbr.org/2015/10/how-1-performance-improvements-led-to-olympic-gold (archived at https://perma.cc/SQF7-EWJ7)

Hurst, D (1995) *Crisis and Renewal: Meeting the challenge of organizational change*, Harvard Business School Press, Boston

Ibbs, W and Reginato, J (2002) *Quantifying the Value of Project Management*, Project Management Institute, Newtown Square, PA

11

Adapting the Business Resilience Framework

Purpose

The purpose of adapting the standard Business Resilience Framework to the needs and practices of the organization is to ensure that the framework is more productive at embedding and facilitating sustained progress. Once an organization decides to adopt the Business Resilience Framework, adapting will enable this to be used in the most effective way for the organization and to build on the existing processes and practices in place with which staff are familiar.

Adapting and embedding

Adapting Business Resilience is making or adjusting the standard Business Resilience Framework elements to the target organization framework or model; or alternatively, it is adding Business Resilience elements into organizational processes and practices to become more resilient.

Embedding is defined, in Business Resilience, as setting the (adapted) Business Resilience Framework processes and practices firmly within the organization to ensure they are used.

It is recommended that the Business Resilience Framework is adapted to the organization and this organization Business Resilience Framework is embedded through training and operational adoption at all levels of the organization.

What can be adapted?

All the domains of the Business Resilience Framework can be adapted, except the Principles. It is because the Principles underpin Business Resilience and must be in place for Business Resilience to be effective. The domains of Roles, RESILIENCE Foundations, PACE Culture and the PROGRESS Cycle can all be adapted to the needs of the organization and existing effective processes and practices. If a business continuity plan is available within the organization, this may be a good starting point to adapt to be able to meet one or more of the Business Resilience Framework elements. There could be parts of a business continuity plan that are a useful 'plug and play' starting point.

Adapting Principles

The Principles underpin the framework and can be used to judge whether Business Resilience is being implemented effectively, whether using the Progress @ Pace 8-4-8 Model or another approach. The Principles must be in place for the organization to achieve sustained progress delivered at pace; therefore, they are not adapted. The way in which the Principles are implemented may vary, but they must be present so that a Resilience Professional can recognize them and advise on how to further strengthen the organization's Business Resilience. If an exploratory approach is used to implement Business Resilience, the Principles must be able to be demonstrated if the organization is to achieve sustained progress.

FIGURE 11.1 Business Resilience Framework

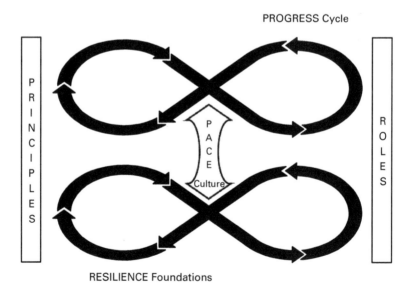

Adapting the Roles

The Business Resilience Roles are all required within the organization, although the titles and exact responsibilities can be adapted. It is unlikely that there will be an existing role with the title of Business Resilience Owner, although there are some chief resilience officers in place. The Progress Master role will often be taken on by someone in the organization who is in the project management office (PMO), transformation, organization development or change team. Each role should be considered in terms of the responsibilities and decisions on adapting based on where the responsibilities should be placed. This is, in part, based on the levels of authority that are available within the organization's corporate governance and the extent to which the PACE Culture is embedded. In some situations, it will be most appropriate to bring in external skills (Resilience Professional) until the organization has sufficient experience and competence in Business Resilience. These can support and coach the internal team to build new capabilities.

Adapting the RESILIENCE Foundations

Each of the RESILIENCE Foundations elements will need different capabilities, skills and tools to be utilized. It is likely that organizations will have some or all of the RESILIENCE Foundations elements in place to some degree, and so the way in which they are adapted will depend on the baseline Resilience Profile scores that show the size of gap to being effective for Business Resilience. An example would be the RESILIENCE Foundations element of 'Enterprising Investment'. The finance function of a small organization may be focused on ensuring the accounts are documented appropriately. When the wider RESILIENCE Foundations Enterprising Investment areas of attracting investment, business cases and moving beyond controlling budgets are implemented, the organization will need processes, practices and staff whose focus is not only internal but also external across its partner network.

Adapting the PACE Culture

Adapting the PACE Culture elements will mean that each PACE element should be defined to align to the long-term vision or Progress Definition of the organization. This means that the organization needs to decide what their Purposeful Mindset should comprise to achieve the vision or long-term

Progress Definition. Is the purpose simply to complete work? Is it to innovate new services for customers? Is it to excel at one thing? Is it the wellbeing of employees and customers? This can then lead to adapting the application of tools, such as an innovation workshop, that should be applied, and the Capability and Skills that are needed to deliver the innovation identified. In turn, the Elevated Energy may need to be increased to deliver the innovation for sustained Progress @ Pace. Adapting the PACE Culture is likely to change continuously; as the organization becomes more resilient, the PACE Culture will change with it.

Adapting the PROGRESS Cycle

The PROGRESS Cycle elements will be adapted to utilize any process or practices, tools and techniques that already exist in the organization and are effective, efficient and economical to use. Organizations are likely to have elements of the PROGRESS Cycle in place, and the baseline Resilience Profile will show which steps have the greatest gaps. When considering the Rapids and Lagoons step, the programme or project management approach used is most likely to already be established based on which method is best suited to the organization or division. Indeed, more than one method may be used where the organization is undertaking value initiatives in different parts of the organization.

ADAPTING TO 'PLUG AND PLAY' EXISTING PRACTICES THAT ARE WORKING

For example, a nuclear decommissioning organization has Lagoon value initiatives for the decommissioning and storage of the nuclear material that use linear project methods, while the IT department of the same organization has Rapid value initiatives that will use iterative or agile project methods to deliver the IT value initiatives.

Adapting the terms or language

The elements of the standard Business Resilience Framework use terms and language that can be adapted so that they are easier for the organization to adopt. This is true whether translating into a language or using terms that the organization already uses. The Business Resilience core Roles are a good example, where the role of Initiative Leader is likely to be project or programme sponsors or managers in an organization. The most important thing when adapting the terms used in the Business Resilience Framework is that the terms are used consistently across the organization and that everyone in the organization understands what they mean.

ADAPTING THE LANGUAGE OR TERMS

An example is in Decision Gate 1 of the PROGRESS Cycle. If the organization already has a process to approve value initiatives that has another name, such as final investment decision, this name can be used, if the objectives of Decision Gate 1 are achieved. Adapting the terms may identify some amendments to processes or practices to improve the resilience of the relevant element.

Approaches to adapting the Business Resilience Framework

The approaches to adapting the Business Resilience Framework can be the same as those used for creating a strategy to implement Business Resilience for the whole organization. These can be Progressive, Urgent, Responsive or Exploratory (PURE approaches, see Chapter 8). For the progressive approach, the adapted processes and practices can be implemented at one or more levels of the organization. For the urgent approach, it is likely that the standard Business Resilience Framework will be implemented, and elements adapted following initial implementation. In the responsive approach, one or more elements of the framework can be adapted for embedding at any time. In the exploratory approach, the organization will create its own model based on the Principles but may adapt some elements following implementation. Thus, all approaches are likely to take an incremental approach to adapting and embedding the organization Business Resilience Framework.

Plug-and-play practice

The plug-and-play practice is recommended to be used when adapting the Business Resilience Framework. Plug and play means that where the organization has a process or practice that undertakes one or more activities that are required for that element of Business Resilience to be fulfilled, it can simply be 'plugged in' to the framework and 'played' as part of operating the processes or practices to be used. The modular design of the framework facilitates this approach and fits with the principle of 'change is certain, but progress is not'. Plug and play is used for the progressive and responsive implementations. Urgent and exploratory approaches could use plug and play following the initial implementation.

NOT BUILDING ON THE EXISTING PROCESSES AND PRACTICES

A global delivery organization engaged a large consultancy to advise on tailoring their project and programme management methodology based on standard recognized methods. The consultancy spent time to understand the existing processes and practices and then developed the tailored approach with a new full organizational method that was supported by templates, procedures and training. The organizational context was that the individuals who were delivering projects and programmes were already overstretched and delivering projects and programmes that were broadly achieving the organization's objectives. The new methodology first tranche of training was undertaken and met a great deal of resistance due to the volume of changes required to the existing processes and practices with which the overstretched staff were familiar. The staff continued to use the existing standard methods and the organization did not reap the benefits expected from this initiative.

The learning points from this are that the organization had decided on an approach without considering the principle that change is certain and progress is not. The level of change that could be absorbed by the organization had not been sufficiently assessed and the risks then outweighed the benefits, meaning that the costs were not recovered.

Steps to adapt the Business Resilience Framework to an organization

Adapting should always begin with where the organization is currently. This will highlight any areas that are already effective and that may need to be adapted to deliver sustained progress. The steps below provide an example approach to adapting the Business Resilience Framework:

1 Profile the current situation – to create a baseline.

2 Identify the organizational context for Business Resilience.

3 Review the existing processes and practices.

4 Identify the elements, process and practices that are priorities to be adapted.

5 Create the Progress Definition and priorities for Business Resilience.

6 Implement the adapted Business Resilience Framework elements and test.

7 Embed the adapted Business Resilience Framework.

8 Review adapting for implementation and continuing improvement.

1 Profile the current situation

The current situation is the starting point for adapting the framework. The current resilience level will be identified by the baseline Resilience Profile (see Chapter 10). The baseline profile is needed to define progress in the PROGRESS Cycle or milestone 1 of the implementation roadmap. This baseline can be utilized to prioritize those areas that will be adapted, in milestone 4 of the roadmap or in the 'Success and Learning' element of the PROGRESS Cycle following initial implementation. This could be by adapting those areas that have the smallest gap and so add value quickly, or by targeting the areas with the largest gaps as these have the greatest need.

Output – baseline Resilience Profile of organization.

2 Identify the organizational context for Business Resilience

The organizational context should be considered when adapting. The context will include the organizational need or appetite to adopt Business Resilience, the capabilities, skills and resource availability to undertake the processes and practices of Business Resilience and the market drivers that will be satisfied by implementing the Business Resilience Framework. This 'as is' context will influence the prioritization and resource availability for the value initiatives to adapt the Business Resilience Framework. This could utilize 'Recognize Challenge' in the PROGRESS Cycle.

Output – organizational context identified.

3 Review the existing processes and practices

Adapting the standard Business Resilience Framework elements should always build on what is working. Existing processes and practices should be reviewed against the Resilience Profile to identify which areas of the Resilience Profile are already supported with appropriate processes and practices to deliver the target level of resilience. These processes and practices will simply be migrated as part of the adapted organizational Business Resilience Framework. An example will be an existing business justification case that can be used when assessing initiatives in 'Good Alignment' of the PROGRESS Cycle.

Output – existing processes and practices identified that meet the requirement for Business Resilience.

4 Identify the elements, processes and practices that are priorities for adapting

Following the review of existing process and practices, elements that need to be adapted for the Business Resilience Framework will be identified. The modular design of the framework enables the 'plug and play' approach to adapting elements and then plugging them into the framework.

PRIORITIZING ELEMENTS THAT REQUIRE LEAST EFFORT WHERE THERE IS LITTLE RESOURCE AVAILABILITY

For example, where the organizational context has little resource availability for Business Resilience, the adapting will be constrained so that adapting elements that require least effort for the most effect will be prioritized. This exercise could include a value initiative to engage a Resilience Professional or Progress Master to deliver some 'benefits of Business Resilience' sessions to help the team to understand why the effort to adopt and adapt Business Resilience will benefit both them as individuals and the organization.

Output – elements identified that need to be adapted.

5 *Create the Progress Definition and priorities for Business Resilience*

When creating the Progress Definition, value initiatives that are targeted to improve the Business Resilience Framework should be included. This can be done by adapting or implementing processes and practices based on the priority areas identified by combining the baseline Resilience Profile with the organizational context and review of existing processes and practices. In this situation the value initiatives related to adapting should be placed on the Progress Backlog in the PROGRESS Cycle for consideration with any other items on the backlog.

Output – Progress Definition and prioritized value initiatives to adapt
Business Resilience.

6 *Implement the adapted Business Resilience Framework elements and test*

Initial implementation will use approaches shown in Chapter 8 and should test the adapted elements. The PROGRESS Cycle is used to implement value initiatives to adapt the elements, after initial implementation. These will be assessed for the level of challenge, opportunity and alignment before a decision is taken to develop the adapted organization Business Resilience Framework, or elements. The scope of the adaptations will be balanced with other organizational commitments and resource availability. Once the adapted organization framework, or element(s), has been developed, it will be checked against the Business Resilience Principles and the Progress Definition as well as the value initiative quality criteria in Selection and Testing. Once it is confirmed as ready for release, the organizational context will be reviewed again in Success and Learning, prior to release for use.

Output – an organizational Business Resilience Framework or element(s)
adapted and implemented.

7 *Embed the adapted Business Resilience Framework*

Once the adapted elements have been implemented, they need to be embedded in organizational processes and practices or the effort will be in vain. Each strategy implementation approach will have a different approach to embedding. For the urgent approach, a value initiative would be developed to embed the lean tailored framework across the organization. In a progressive approach, new processes and procedures would be adapted and embedded incrementally by initiative(s) or department(s). This could result in overlap between the standard and adapted versions but avoids existing initiatives changing during development. The responsive approach would mean that one element is adapted at a time to see a gradual increase in Business Resilience. The exploratory approach will embed the practices aligned to the Principles.

This is in line with the principle that resilience can be at the most appropriate pace, whether fast or slow; indeed, varying the pace may be necessary for differing organizational levels or business divisions.

8 Review adapting for implementation and continuing improvement

Using a progressive approach, the organization will implement incrementally. As additional elements or domains are implemented, a review of those already introduced should check they remain effective, efficient and economical for the organization's current situation. The framework may be implemented in one division with a focus on logistics and is now being rolled out across another with a focus on production, meaning the adaptations should be reviewed to ensure they remain appropriate. The Resilience Profile (see Chapter 10) can be used for this review.

An urgent approach should periodically review the embedded framework to improve its effectiveness. A responsive approach should review to check if adaptations are needed to the elements implemented or if additional elements should be adapted and embedded. An exploratory approach will review the Principles to check if processes or practices could be aligned more closely.

For all approaches, each time Success and Learning in the PROGRESS Cycle is undertaken, the organization Business Resilience Framework, or elements, should be reviewed. Continuous improvement includes adaptations to further improve Business Resilience for the organization.

Output – continuous improvements to Business Resilience Framework elements identified.

Roles for Business Resilience Framework adaptation

All the core Business Resilience Roles will be involved in adapting although the Progress Master (or Resilience Professional) will be the primary role as they have the most expertise:

Business Resilience Owner – this person is responsible for authorizing the initial baseline Resilience Profile and leads initial prioritization of Business

Resilience value initiatives to add to the Progress Backlog. The Business Resilience Owner will authorize release to live use of the adapted version of the organizational Business Resilience Framework. They are responsible for ensuring reviews take place for continuous improvement.

Progress Master – this will be the primary role involved, as they have expertise in the Business Resilience Framework. They are responsible for undertaking or facilitating the Resilience Profile, review of existing processes and practices, and advise on prioritization of the value initiatives to add to the Progress Backlog. They are then responsible for facilitating the development of the elements to be adapted with the Initiative Leader(s).

Initiative Leader – the Initiative Leader(s) is responsible for developing and implementing the new processes and practices and rolling them out across the organization or division, to deliver Business Resilience improvement.

Resilience Professional – this role will be involved in any or all of the steps of adapting. They have expertise to advise the Business Resilience Roles or can undertake these Roles to adapt the elements, processes or practices.

Benefits, costs and risks

Benefits

The key benefit of adapting the Business Resilience Framework is making it easier to deliver sustained Progress @ Pace, whatever the business environment. The benefits of adapting include:

- Speed – the embedding of the Business Resilience Framework will be faster if the staff of the organization are able to build on the processes and practices that are already familiar and work.

- Minimized changes – if there are existing processes and practices that can be adopted as a part of the organization Business Resilience Framework, there are fewer changes that would be required and this would make the implementation or improvement of Business Resilience less disruptive.

- Less resistance – if the staff understand that any processes and practices that are adapted are only the ones that have been identified as a priority and will make the organization more resilient, there will be less resistance to the adaptations being introduced.

- Progress continuity – more effective embedding means that whatever the socio-economic environment, the organization will continue to deliver customer value and take opportunities to build Business Resilience.

- Return on investment – using terms, processes and practices that are best suited to the organization will enable the resilience levels to improve more quickly and the organization will be able to enjoy more success and return on the investment.

Costs

The costs of adapting will depend on the approach to implementing the Business Resilience Framework and the Capability and Skills available internally. There is time and effort involved to adapt to the organizational context and embed.

A progressive approach can assess where the greatest payback will be achieved and prioritize these elements. These elements will start to pay back and so will reduce the costs of the next elements to be adapted.

An urgent approach incurs the highest costs as it will require an organization-wide rollout, training and support.

The responsive approach is clearly lowest cost as it only adapts elements of the Business Resilience Framework.

Risks

There are risks associated with any value initiative and these should be assessed using standard risk assessment approaches. There are some risks that are specific to adapting the Business Resilience Framework, or elements. The risks may influence which strategy implementation approach is chosen. The risks include, but are not limited to:

- Lack of support of either senior management or staff undertaking the practices may lead to the adapted organizational Business Resilience Framework, or elements, not being embedded once developed, leading to wasted effort and little change.
- Staff responsible for adapting may not have sufficient understanding of the existing processes and practices or, alternatively, the Business Resilience Framework to provide the most appropriate adaptations, resulting in additional confusion.
- Too many adaptations at the same time may overload the organization and risk business as usual, leading to no take-up (highest risk with an urgent approach).

- Some parts of the organization may not see why or how the adapted processes or practices will benefit them and so will not implement them if it is possible to avoid doing so, resulting in more indifference (higher risk with urgent and responsive).

- PROGRESS Cycle adapting could divert focus to Business Resilience more than adding customer value, because staff want to see simple straightforward ways ahead.

- If the PACE Culture has a high Resilience Profile score, the risks will be lower than an organization with a low score. Thus, the PACE Culture domain could be a good starting point when adapting and embedding.

- Cognitive biases may diminish the pace and effectiveness of adapted processes by reducing the objectivity of review and updates, leading to reduced resilience.

Summary

The standard Business Resilience Framework is designed to enable organizations to adopt the framework quickly and effectively. Organizations that then adapt the framework to their specific situation and context will benefit from faster implementation with less resistance and greater return on investments through being able to achieve sustained progress delivered at pace. Adapting the Business Resilience Framework may continue through PROGRESS Cycles until adopting is complete. It will then continue with the Evolving Vision for the organization.

QUESTIONS TO THINK ABOUT

- Are there processes or practices that already exist within the organization that can be used to 'plug and play' during the Business Resilience implementation?

- Are there elements of the Business Resilience Framework that your organization will benefit by adapting for smooth implementation?

- What level of adaptation should be undertaken prior to commencing a Business Resilience implementation and what should be done as continuous improvement?

12

Insights from the front line

Purpose

The purpose of the insights shared in this chapter is to demonstrate how the Business Resilience Framework could be implemented in practice to improve the resilience of an organization. In each of the insights, an organizational situation is highlighted and the actions taken are described, together with alignment to the Business Resilience Framework or 8-4-8 Model elements. These connections confirm the practical relevance of this approach, and the potential for improvement in a diverse range of organizations and industries.

Each insight follows a similar structure, although the contents vary in length due to data availability; each insight addresses a different industry or sector, and the information provided is based upon publicly available information or personal experience. Public sector and commercial organizations have been selected, as well as different sizes of businesses, from SMEs to publicly quoted organizations. To the largest extent possible, the impact of actions taken, as well as the outcomes, are shown so that it is clear how Business Resilience has been affected.

Readers are encouraged to consider how, possibly as a Resilience Professional, the framework, model, tools and techniques in this book could be used to accelerate Business Resilience and realize benefits for all stakeholders engaged at different organizational levels: individual staff, teams, departments or business units, the organization as a whole and its customers, partners or investors.

There are many great success stories in Business Resilience, and the authors have selected a diverse range in the insights considered below; all provide opportunities to learn from recent events. They also provide inspiration, justification and guidance for this fresh approach, in which people and capabilities are central to organization culture, and technologies combine to form Adaptive Enterprises, which continually update themselves to deliver more customer value.

Introduction

Consider what is needed as a typical starting point for today's organization, before turning to the insights. Many businesses are already invested in digitalization, flat structures, lean processes and just-in-time management. Are everyday activities driving progress for customers and themselves? Can they help to create the right response in VUCA conditions, taking advantage of the opportunities posed by low-touch economies or virtual working environments?

Professionals in product and service design, execution, in sales or customer service, in client-side or home-based advisory teams should ask how to take advantage of challenging conditions. Is BAU transformation to a more dynamic enterprise already under way, or is innovation not vision-led?

The Business Resilience Framework addresses these concerns, engaging staff and customers in common endeavour, to create value and business success. The strategy is to identify and measure current practices, clarifying what is good, and what is not, in current socio-economic or market conditions. Our goal is to ensure businesses and network partners are able to act from a customer value perspective, to realize possibilities and create better relationships, whatever the VUCA environment.

Organizations that become Adaptive Enterprises enjoy a clear sense of purpose; they deliver more customer value; their partnerships develop more capability; the teams feel proud of their achievements. These sentiments provide the organizational energy of Business Resilience, a critical component to survival and prosperity that is reflected in each of the five insights shown below.

Insight 1: Lincoln Electric – Big business in specialist manufacturing

This insight is provided to illustrate the application of the Business Resilience Framework to strategy implementation in organizations; all content is adapted from published information.

Industry and organization

Since 1895, Lincoln Electric has been the world leader in the design, development and manufacture of arc welding products, automated joining, assembly and cutting systems. Their products are used across multiple industry sectors in over 160 countries. The company has 55 manufacturing locations in 18 countries and in 2020 generated $2.7 billion in revenue (Lincoln Electric Company, 2021a).

Situation

The rise of the digital age and dot-com bubble had swayed professionals towards digital Roles, which had left a lower number of people with an interest in the field of welding and hence perhaps a reduced talent pool to choose and train from. Lincoln Electric therefore sought to ensure ongoing and ever-improving operational excellence by building a succession pipeline rather than recruiting senior leaders from other industrial sectors, which has its own challenges due to the highly technical and specialized nature of the welding industry. In addition to functional expertise and management qualifications, the successors of senior Roles should have accumulated knowledge and experience in welding, company products and organizational culture if they were to lead and succeed in their senior Roles.

Desired outcome

Lincoln Electric have stated that their goal is 'to ensure a strong succession pipeline and ample development opportunities for advancing skills, knowledge, and expertise to prepare employees for bigger career opportunities and challenges ahead'.

Obstacles to success

There was difficulty in finding well-trained functional experts, especially welders, technical sales representatives and researchers who had knowledge of welding processes, consumables and equipment to the desired level.

There was difficulty in attracting and recruiting new talent in an era where the dot-com boom was pulling a considerable amount of talent towards digital jobs that were more highly paid.

What had helped before

The four core elements (Lincoln Electric Company, 2021b) of the incentive management system had worked well in the past, and continued in portions of their North and South American operations as well as in China. The system – which resulted in a diverse and highly engaged organization – consisted of the following elements and augments solid foundations for succession-building:

- Pay for performance: employees maximize their earnings through piece-work compensation.

- Guaranteed employment ['No lay-off policy']: eligible employees will not be laid off in an economic downturn.

- Profit-sharing: eligible employees received an annual, merit-based profit-sharing bonus.

- Open door policy: informal executive access and an official advisory board comprising employee representatives meeting regularly with the CEO to foster open communication.

Actions

Awareness was created in the welding industry about the Roles. Skills development was promoted with training at different levels to different age groups. Career prospects were demonstrated to attract quality personnel (Lincoln Electric Company, 2021c). This meant investing in people to ensure a strong succession pipeline and ample development opportunities to advance skills, knowledge and expertise to prepare employees for bigger career opportunities ahead. A search of the Lincoln Electric website reveals that some of the programmes that were implemented to achieve this included 'formal leadership, management and professional development programs, tuition reimbursement for external accredited programs, mentoring, self-guided online courses, instructor-led programs, and special project and rotational assignments that can lead to extensive global exposure'.

Outcomes

The company now has an abundant global supply of available trained talent at all levels and across the disciplines, including apprentices, who can lead and deliver Business Resilience value initiatives either in business-as-usual or stormy VUCA environments without needing time to understand the company culture, products and welding, because they are already part of the company.

Impact

As a result of building resilience in the talent pool, in the US the company will benefit from the \$2 trillion investment programme announced by the US president in March 2021 (Tankersley, 2021). This is because all the infrastructure development projects will require joining and cutting machines and special welding consumables, which will be sourced from within the US, where the company has its head office and production facilities. The company will also benefit globally because of the expected investments by governments to promote a V-shaped recovery after Covid-19, where demand recovers Rapidly and the skills needed are secured by the strong succession pipeline.

Business Resilience domain and elements

The Business Resilience Progress @ Pace 8-4-8 Model contains three domains, and this insight demonstrates the value of careful attention to many of the elements within them, ensuring Lincoln Electric is still vibrant after more than a century:

- RESILIENCE Foundations: This insight demonstrates an Evolving Vision to respond to changing circumstances, support for sustainable operations by creating a strong succession pipeline, undertaking Enterprising Investment in the development of talent, and Leading and Influencing to deliver the value initiative – which are all elements of RESILIENCE Foundations.
- PACE Culture: The process for creating awareness, talent acquisition, training and retention demonstrate a Purposeful Mindset, application of tools, development of Capability and Skills and Elevated Energy – which are elements of the PACE Culture.
- PROGRESS Cycle: The definition of progress in terms of recruiting and training talent at all levels, recognition of the challenge of a shortage of successors, Good Alignment with the company's goals Enabling Teams to be ready to lead and deliver initiatives, and Success and Learning to improve on what's already been achieved are elements of the PROGRESS Cycle.

These elements are also critical within the Business Resilience Framework, containing the five domains, and these actions to improve the organization's resilience have ensured Lincoln Electric is in an excellent position to emerge from the pandemic stronger than at the start of this most challenging period in its history.

Insight 2: London Heathrow Airport – Big business in travel infrastructure

This insight is provided to illustrate the application of the Business Resilience Framework to strategy implementation in organizations; all content is adapted from published information.

Industry and organization

Heathrow Airport is one of the world's busiest airports and models a small city in complexity and traffic, with over 76,000 people working on a given day facilitating travel needs of 80 million passengers headed towards 200 destinations in 84 countries (Microsoft, 2019).

Situation

There is a great deal of manual work resulting in huge amounts of paperwork and repetitive tasks needing to be carried out by humans. This creates a lot of potential to optimize operations through digitization of repetitive tasks.

Desired outcome

Digitize operations to automate workload and save working hours, reduce manual paperwork and accelerate processing for travellers, as well as store sensitive information in a secure and information assurance compliant manner.

Obstacles to success

Not many in-house software packages were in use and hundreds of developers were required to work for years to deliver automation of envisaged processes.

What had helped before

Microsoft Office 365 was introduced for front-line workers at Heathrow in an initiative towards digitization. Some employees had found it useful and explored it further to see what other benefits they could derive from it.

Actions

An employee explored MS PowerApps within MS Office 365 and developed the first proof of a concept mobile app for 'Language Book', which was followed by low code development of 29 more apps by Heathrow's first-line employees, all of which used Microsoft Power Apps to turn thousands of processes into apps without requiring hundreds of developers and years of work.

Outcomes

Elimination of 75,000 pages of paperwork and reduced data entry by nearly 1,000 hours each year, hence efficient operations and significantly reduced costs.

Business Resilience domain and elements

The Progress @ Pace 8-4-8 Model contains three domains. This insight demonstrates how attention to many of the elements within the model has ensured Heathrow Airport has been able to greatly improve operational efficiency, reducing repetitive tasks at a time when employee expectations of work were migrating towards higher-valued work and experiences:

- RESILIENCE Foundations: This insight demonstrates an Evolving Vision to automate processes, support for sustainable operations by saving person hours, undertaking Enterprising Investment by utilizing Microsoft Office 365, and Leading and Influencing to deliver on the automation initiative are all elements of RESILIENCE Foundations.
- PACE Culture: The process of exploring MS Office 365, conceiving and developing apps using MS Power Apps to automate processes demonstrate a Purposeful Mindset, application of tools, development of Capability and Skills, and Elevated Energy – which are elements of PACE Culture.
- PROGRESS Cycle: The definition of progress in terms of automation of processes, recognition of challenge to digitize processes without developers, Enabling Teams to conceive, develop and deliver the app by first-line staff, Good Alignment with overall goals of the airport, and Success and Learning to develop more apps by learning from the success of already developed apps are elements of PROGRESS Cycle.

This insight demonstrates it is possible to make a good contribution to Business Resilience, at all levels of the organization, and that task-oriented efficiency improvements can make a useful difference to operational duties in large organizations, improving positive energy among staff.

Impact

This insight demonstrates improved efficiency at the airport, raised capability level of first-line employees, potential to automate future bottleneck, repetitive, time-consuming processes, reduce costs and limitless possibilities that can be driven by the users themselves without dependence on development.

Insight 3: Software Italiano – SME in software development

This insight is provided to illustrate the application of the Business Resilience Framework to strategy implementation in organizations; all content is adapted from published information or experience.

Industry and organization type

Software Italiano is the fictitious name of a European commercial high-tech company developing software products for the autonomous/driverless car market and facing growth issues typical of SMEs going through a Rapid scale-up phase.

Situation

Software Italiano began as a start-up exploiting the intellectual capital created by one of its founders seven years ago. In those years, the business has gone from just two employees to nearly fifty developers organized in five teams working on a variety of linked projects. The teams have historically enjoyed broad independence in the choice of tools and working practices to produce their deliverables. As a result, the workforce employed a mix of approaches and instruments to plan, develop and deliver their products, which made it difficult to coordinate work across teams and maintain its transparency organization-wide. This in turn led to frequent delays, higher production costs, and poor customer satisfaction in projects where several interdependent teams were involved. The situation got worse a year ago, when Software Italiano became a subsidiary of a much larger organization that had plans for a significant increase of activity in the autonomous/driverless car market space. Facing the imminent scale-up, Software Italiano realized it could no longer afford its former inefficiencies and had to come up with better ways of organizing its production process.

Desired outcome

Software Italiano required a significant adjustment of its operations, with the chief objective being a unified production process (practices and tools) and streamlined communications organization-wide across interdependent teams. Primary benefits of this adjustment would be the minimization (and, potentially, complete elimination) of delays in handovers between interdependent teams and the associated cost-efficiency and higher customer satisfaction.

Factors impeding progress

Since its inception, Software Italiano has grown steadily, but with no clear vision or specific growth targets in sight. Projects were created based on opportunities originating outside the organization and realized with the method of choice of the teams tasked with the delivery and based predominantly on the said team's preferences. There was also little concerted effort to monitor best industry practice and tools and adopt them appropriately and consistently across the organization.

What had helped before

Attempts were made in the last year to gain familiarity with popular project and product delivery approaches and to select an appropriate software tool to support those approaches from among the most well-known candidates. This led to a better awareness in the organization about the options available and limited adoption of select tools for team communication and collaboration, distributed software development and version control, and continuous deployment and integration. This also highlighted the importance of a single company-wide production process and single set of software tools to integrate and automate it.

Actions

Progress Definition was achieved through the following value initiatives:

- identification of the project and product delivery best practice to improve the Software Italiano production process;
- redesign of the Software Italiano production process and broader DevOps-based operating model taking advantage of the best practice identified;
- identification of a software tool best suited to support the Software Italiano improved production process and operating model;
- adoption of the tool organization-wide.

Outcomes

The following outcomes were generated in the first PROGRESS Cycle:

- organization-wide awareness and confidence in applying agile project and product delivery methodologies, such as AgilePM and Scrum;
- integration of relevant agile practices in the redesigned Software Italiano production process;
- pilot implementation of the redesigned process in the GitLab environment for a single team.

The second run through the PROGRESS Cycle delivered the following additional outcomes:

- rollout of the redesigned process across the company;
- increased confidence in the leadership that Software Italiano would be able to meet the projected increased demand for its services from the parent organization.

Business Resilience domains and elements

Many Business Resilience elements are at play here. This has enabled Software Italiano to greatly improve operational flexibility, lower unit costs, improve customer satisfaction, and migrate towards their vision of production at scale:

- RESILIENCE Foundations: Sustainable operations – the objective was to create an adaptable operational capability supported by lean (agile) practices enabling the organization to scale its operations up and down as necessary.

- PACE Culture: Purposeful Mindset – the move towards a more flexible operating model was both disciplined and deliberate, aligning the newly developed capabilities with the evolved organization's vision of operating at scale and with cost-efficiency and greater customer satisfaction.
- PACE Culture: Understanding application of tools – tools identified as suitable to support the improved operating model became the means of 'building, adapting and innovating working solutions' for Software Italiano on the organization level.
- PROGRESS Cycle: Progress Definition – the realization of progress entailed gradual refinement of the objectives and required several iterations through the PROGRESS Cycle, resulting in the achievement of both short- and long-term impacts on the Business Resilience of Software Italiano.

Impact

The immediate effect of the progress achieved was higher customer satisfaction and greater cost-efficiency for the organization achieved through higher-quality, more predictable and faster product releases. The longer-term impact was the increased flexibility of the company's operating model. Thus, together, the above aspects have increased Software Italiano's Business Resilience.

Insight 4: UK university – Medium business in higher education

This insight is provided to illustrate the application of the Business Resilience Framework to strategy implementation in organizations; all content is adapted from published information or experience.

Industry

The Covid-19 crises severely affected the educational industry worldwide, which is one area that cannot afford to fail, even under severe VUCA disruptions. This insight is on a UK university that adapted processes to enable them to be resilient, survive and thrive.

Situation

When the Covid-19 pandemic was declared in March 2020, the UK – along with most countries around the world – went into lockdown and people had to stay at home. The lockdown was introduced to stop the spread of the virus, save lives and protect the National Health Service from being overwhelmed. University staff and students could not attend teaching, learning or assessments. This was a black swan VUCA disruption (see Chapter 3) and something universities had no plan in place to cope with.

Desired outcome

Universities needed to continue progressing students through their degrees, align to the university quality assurance standards and follow course validation guidelines, as well as provide a good student and staff experience. They had to recruit, teach and assess students. Student accommodation, working environments, access to technology and student welfare had to be taken care of. Good online, hybrid and blended learning, where students engage and learn, was required. Online staff meetings and exam boards were another necessity to succeed.

Obstacles to success

The main problem was how to make the transition: identifying and procuring the required technology, transitioning to online teaching and meetings, and managing changed processes. Staff and students without experience of online learning were resistant to the change. Some were exhausted and burned out so did not welcome online learning and meetings. Some students disengaged, for many reasons. Students were isolated in their accommodation, which made it difficult to focus, they were paying for accommodation they could not leave and they felt lonely.

Lessons from previous experience

Universities had already been conducting some online hybrid (blended) learning due to large classes. Classes are taught in one classroom while simultaneously being streamed to another class. Online meetings had taken place with international partners. Students who could not attend their vivas could do this online in some cases. Student and staff welfare and engagement processes were in place. This experience was invaluable in designing the value initiatives to respond to Covid-19.

Actions

The university leadership set up emergency planning for operating features, online teaching and assessment, and disinfecting rooms. On top of this, the UK government updated their rules and policies continuously every few weeks and the university had to keep up to date. During the period from March to September 2020, only online teaching took place. New timetabling and bookings had to be created to take into consideration online teaching and spreading out the teaching, as it is very difficult for students and staff to spend a long time online. From September to December 2020, the university was a hybrid of online and face-to-face in-class teaching. During the hybrid teaching, the face-to-face in-class teaching required students to observe social distancing rules, where people must have a 2-metre gap between them. Classes had to be repeated to accommodate the numbers. In January 2021, just when people were expecting to be going back to normal, a new variant resulted in a new full lockdown. During the period of January to August 2021, fully online teaching resumed. In addition, new examination processes had to be put in place to cope with online examinations. Students were given a 24-hour window to do the online exam, which meant that the exams had to be adapted as an open book exam. There were many students with mitigating circumstances, which meant the processes were reviewed. The university had to invest in the appropriate technology to manage the online processes.

Outcomes

The university has successfully run online courses following investment. Staff and students engaged with the online learning have been able to participate and complete assessments.

The timetabling team have managed to organize constantly changing teaching times and room bookings as required to enable the online and face-to-face teaching.

The university has set up online conferencing facilities to organize student recruitment open days. This was for students interested in applying to learn about the courses and facilities, and discuss their questions and concerns with course directors.

Hybrid or blended teaching was implemented successfully. Teaching was done in a classroom with socially distanced students in-class, face-to-face, while simultaneously running the online teaching for students who could not attend.

Staff successfully held online weekly meetings to keep up to date and alleviate staff concerns. Senior staff confirmed the changing governance and policies and then cascaded this to the heads of departments and other staff. All student assessment and progression boards were successfully completed so students could progress to their next year and achieve their final degrees. Instead of graduation ceremonies, online congratulations by the university teams were recorded for graduating students.

Research supervisions, conferences, seminars and meetings continued to be run successfully online. MSc and PhD viva exams were successfully completed online. New PhD students have even enrolled and started their courses during this period.

The student wellbeing service and student union contacted students online and were available to help students who might be having a difficult time.

Business Resilience domain and elements

The university response to the Covid-19 crises has demonstrated most of the elements of the Business Resilience Framework. Throughout this period the senior management and staff held many workshops, which could be adapted and improved to BRIT workshops.

RESILIENCE Foundations were demonstrated as below:

- Regulatory and governance clarified continuously changing organizational policies developed to align with government policies and advice. However, this was constrained to ensure courses continued to align to the required standards.
- Evolving Vision through a series of incrementally better organization design processes to allow people to collaborate with the online tools to deliver benefits for students and staff.
- Sustainable operations enabled adaptation of operational capability to support the processes and online tools to continue business processes to progress students through their degrees.
- Innovation and Risk was implemented through identifying and innovating processes and choosing the appropriate tools, taking into consideration resource availability, improved value, and technological and financial risk assessment.
- Leading and Influencing permitted understanding, inspiring and supporting the people, creating belief in a future where values and positioning reflect the aspirations of the university.

PACE Culture is demonstrated below:

- Purposeful Mindset created awareness and purpose through senior staff meetings and cascading the information, action points, policies and advice to all staff and students.
- Application of tools meant that the right tools were chosen with training for online learning and meetings.
- Capability and Skills were developed through training, experience and support.
- Elevated Energy was particularly important, with long periods of time on screens draining energy. Procedures restricted time on screens and the number of meetings were reduced. There were shorter teaching periods and more breaks. Elevated Energy resulted.

PROGRESS Cycle is demonstrated below:

- The Progress Definition with value initiatives was clear and specified by the university.
- 'Recognize Challenge' and 'Opportunity Assessment' were undertaken to understand the balance between challenge and opportunity.
- Good Alignment with the university goals in the Progress Definition was quickly confirmed.
- Rapids and Lagoons established that the value initiatives were Rapids and a real map to progress increased the level of activities.
- Empowered teams were enabled through good communication and training to be ready to lead and deliver the initiatives supported by the university leadership.
- Selection and Testing of the right tools, policies and procedures included the user experience and market acceptance of these approaches.
- Success and Learning improved on what had been achieved and were documented and stored to be reused in future similar situations.
- As the university reverted back to all face-to-face in-class teaching in September 2021, new regulations and policies were adopted and the number of emergency processes were reduced, the university could work as 'business as usual' in a Lagoon. The university achieved sustained progress delivered at pace, as it has more options for students and the online offering has strengthened its position in the market.

Impact

Blended learning was already part of the university strategy but would have taken several years to implement to a good standard. However, due to the immediate needs generated by the Covid-19 crisis, there was accelerated learning and implementation of the technology and process. The fast response to the Covid-19 crisis has given the university confidence in their ability to respond to a crisis and they will continue developing improved blended learning and online meetings.

Staff can continue to work from home online when it is preferred to do so, and hot-desking can be introduced to alleviate pressure on room spacing.

The number of students enrolling on courses remained stable during the Covid-19 period, which has meant the university has not suffered financially.

Insight 5: Luxury brand – A niche business within the automotive industry

This insight is provided to illustrate the application of the Business Resilience Framework to strategy implementation in organizations; all content is adapted from published information.

Industry

Few industries have been impacted more than auto manufacturers since 2010 – climate change, the Covid-19 pandemic and financial crises are just the most recent VUCA arrivals in an ever-changing business landscape, where relentless competition and technological innovation are ongoing. Despite these most challenging conditions, a handful of automotive brands have endured for more than a century, demonstrating unparalleled Business Resilience. This insight focuses on one of them, Aston Martin, and its remarkable crusade to survive and thrive.

Situation

Despite a very strong image as a modern, exclusive sports car brand with a unique heritage, instantly recognized around the world, when the Covid-19 pandemic was declared in March 2020, Aston Martin had already endured a challenging environment since the financial crisis of 2008, and it quickly faced a collapse in sales and profits due to lockdown. By early 2020, the share price had plummeted over 90 per cent from its 2018 IPO. The company and its investors faced a brutal onslaught. Crisis and renewal has been a signature feature in Aston Martin's history, and private equity partners had supported the company from flotation. A clear vision and leadership was now paramount, with sufficient resources and team commitment to make progress critical. Believability was key, and the new chairman, Lawrence Stroll, has invested over $1 billion and brings a great track record in growing luxury brands to the organization.

Desired outcome

'The plan was to get to 10,000 cars and 500 million in EBITDA by 2025, and the company is now fully funded to do that,' he said, referencing a commonly used way to measure profits: earnings before interest, taxes, depreciation and amortization (Aston Martin, 2021a).

The vision is to keep close to existing customers, reflecting their aspirations and values, while reaching out to new ones. Brand strength is therefore essential, and Aston Martin has enjoyed an alluring image through its connection with the James Bond movies since *Goldfinger* in 1965 (Aston Martin, 2021b). The company's relationship with EON Productions is yet another essential partnership, confirmed in their 2021 production *No Time to Die* (O'Connell, 2020).

The hoped-for outcome is to grow the business organically, modernizing its portfolio of production and bespoke models with technology partners, developing its headquarters staff, two manufacturing sites, racing team and commercial network partnerships. Most importantly, it hopes to evolve a culture of success within the new organization and socialize this spirit through brand experiences.

Obstacles to success

After 74 years of independence, Aston Martin learned to overcome resourcing and technology challenges through collaborations and partnerships; first Ford bought 75 per cent of the company in 1987, before acquiring it outright in 1994. This has enabled Aston Martin to compete in product development as a niche automotive player, developing its signature V12 engine without overwhelming costs. But such is the volatile nature of this industry that cash calls for next portfolio refresh on their automotive partners come with great regularity, leaving Aston Martin subject to acquisition and disposal. Clearly, this is a significant risk to business, in addition to economic cycles.

And today, the need for hybrid and electric power vehicles continues to pose a similar challenge.

Lessons from previous experience

Aston Martin had made forays into hydrogen and electric power, with its record-breaking Hybrid Hydrogen Rapide S (Excell, 2013) and planned Rapide E models (O'Kane, 2020). But these were concept vehicles, and practicality and costs of production simply made them unviable. More robust solutions would have to be sought and this meant reaching out to a new technology partner.

In recent years Aston Martin's share price has been on quite a roller-coaster ride since the IPO in 2018. Priced at over 12,000p per share at issue, the stock dived down to just 670p by 2020, as debts mounted due to lack-lustre sales of recent models – a 95 per cent decline in just two years! Following a script issue to shareholders in 2020 and raising additional investment, a major restructuring of the business enabled progress to be made and another recovery story for Aston Martin to begin. So, despite the pandemic, the share price recovered towards 2,000p per share by late 2021.

Actions

At the centre of Aston Martin's recovery is the chairman's five-point plan to re-energize the organization. It is interesting to consider how the Business Resilience Framework domains and elements are reflected in these actions.

- Step 1: Launching the DBX (SUV) was key, Stroll said. 'The orders are there, the customers love it,' he said. 'It's the best-looking SUV, it drives like a sports car.' Thereby entering a new market sector.

- Step 2: He brought in a new management team, led by CEO Tobias Moers, the former CEO of Mercedes-AMG and a widely respected car engineer. 'He understands this business and he's also a chief technology officer, which is rare in the business,' Stroll said.

- Step 3: Mercedes-Benz became a financial and strategic partner (at 20 per cent the second largest after the 25 per cent of Chairman Stroll). It is providing technological solutions for the production of petrol, hybrid and electric vehicles, in addition to the racing car division, deepening and broadening Aston Martin's partnership opportunities.

- Step 4: Improving the portfolio, planned product range improvements and a new hybrid model. Moers stated 'more than 10 cars' before the end of 2023; cancellation of some previous projects.

- Step 5: Finally, Stroll highlighted the launch of its Formula 1 team, which helps market the brand and develop technologies used in its mid-engine sports cars, like the Valkyrie.

The action points confirm the importance of RESILIENCE Foundations, PACE Culture and PROGRESS Cycle within the framework; nearly every element is connected to this insight, confirming its value as a planning and audit tool. The action points also confirm the complex nature of luxury vehicles goes well beyond manufacture, as 'the risks, the market, the technology – means that passion and politics are often as important a part of the story as any discussion of pure commercial success or failure' (Moore, 2013).

Outcomes

Practical outcomes will emerge from this plan: better facilities delivering inspiring designs; vehicles producing a luxury brand experience beyond travel; perhaps a feeling of 'graciously going places'. But at the core of the organization there is now a pursuit of excellence in all dimensions, including the products, the service and the public. New cars with new technologies will come forward, but the charm and sense of occasion must remain part of Aston Martin's corporate social responsibility.

Building resilience at Aston Martin has stretched many leaders, designers, production workers, sales and service staff for over a century. What is it that joins investors and customers together? Is it common values or Principles? Perhaps it is the insight of life's highs and lows, feeling a positive mindset from a journey that finds common purpose in refreshing a grand vision, where past glories and the anticipation of future success can be found. Today, the organization is about more than 'power, beauty and soul', more than branding; Business Resilience has created a feeling of connecting to life.

This sentiment is what powers the organization, what brings people together with common purpose and makes Aston Martin the most inclusive of exclusive brands, yielding a very positive reaction from would-be customers and onlookers (Moore, 2013) – something to cherish and to share. While the organization continues to execute Business Resilience in an inclusive way, investors and customers will remain loyal, and the organization will sustain its success. In the same way, Business Resilience demonstrates this commitment to people, placing PACE Culture at the heart of the model.

Strategy

The company business strategy is underpinned by brand strength and network partnerships, enabling provision of financial and technological support. In a global vehicle market where car sales are expected to grow to over 71 million automobiles in 2021, up from an estimated 63.8 million units in 2020 (Statista, 2021), Aston Martin is certainly a niche player; in 2020 it sold 1,638 vehicles and, in a typical year, sales are about 2,500 cars, or 0.02 per cent of the market, with a best-ever performance in 2005/06 when it sold just under 4,000 vehicles. The organization has an objective to achieve 10,000 sales per annum across its portfolio by 2025 (Demandt, 2021).

Business Resilience domains and elements

Many of the Business Resilience Framework domains and elements are reflected in Aston Martin's actions and business plans. It can be confirmed by mapping publicly shared implementation strategy information on their website, using elements of the Business Resilience Framework.

RESILIENCE Foundations were demonstrated as below:

- Regulatory and governance: Commitment to meet regulatory climate restrictions on sale of new vehicles is aligned with business planning to meet the market demand for sustainable new products.
- Evolving Vision: Aston Martin are seeking 'to enrich what is unique to the brand' – which they define as 'the combination of high performance and ultimate luxury together in one automobile'.
- Sustainable operations: New production systems are being developed, which are 'driven by technology, digitalization and efficient supply chains'. Aston Martin credit these systems with annual savings of 30 per cent.
- Innovation and Risk: Innovative product and process changes are being introduced to 'de-risk the business and position it for controlled, long-term, profitable growth'.

- Leading and Influencing: A new chief operation office has been established to steer transformation, under the guidance of the new CEO, who also has responsibility as chief technology officer.
- Enterprising Investment: Engaging customers with limited availability models has enabled the organization to attract substantial deposits much earlier in product lifecycles, enabling projects to be 'cash flow positive from design to the end of the product life cycle'.
- Network Collaboration: Aston Martin have extended and expanded their 'Strategic Cooperation Agreement with Mercedes-Benz AG'. This will enable Aston Martin to gain cost-competitive access to best-in-class technologies, which is critical to supporting their product expansion plans, 'especially electric and hybrid powertrains'.
- Evolving portfolio: Aston Martin expects that advances, such as their 'modular based engineering', will allow them to cut costs by using 'shared systems and components to reduce engineering complexities, resulting in cost-saving and model synergies going forward'.

PACE Culture is demonstrated below:

- Purposeful Mindset: Aston Martin strive to have a 'dynamic and innovative mind-set perceptible throughout the organization'.
- Application of tools: Aston Martin have implemented a new configurator, which aims to improve the customer experience and journey.
- Capability and Skills: The organization has recognized the value of hiring 'experienced external staff to lead powertrain and vehicle development' projects.
- Elevated Energy: Organization culture has been reinvigorated by combining brand awareness initiatives and 'leveraging the Aston Martin F1 team during 2021'.

PROGRESS Cycle is shown below:

- Progress Definition: The definition of progress provided by Aston Martin is the 'expansion of portfolio based on DBX and GT/Sports platform', which means the organization can set evolutionary objectives based upon modular engineering.
- Recognize Challenge: As a consequence of the 2020/21 pandemic, the company sought to reduce staff numbers 'through a voluntary redundancy

and early retirement programme, to enhance efficiency and reduce costs in line with lower than planned production volumes'.

- Opportunity Assessment: Changing market preferences has provided an opportunity to capitalize on the strategic partnership with Mercedes-Benz to create the 'recently launched DBX model which now accounts for 50 per cent of sales' and 'a high incremental return on investments'.

- Good Alignment: Following a difficult period of product releases, new products are both aligned to market, and the company has 'aligned production to industry standard working practices'.

- Rapids and Lagoons: Aston Martin Rapidly repositioned or re-engineered the addition of mid-engine cars, such as 'a Special mid-engine supercar (Valhalla) and a core mid-engine supercar (the Vanquish)', to enhance their portfolio.

- Empowered teams: The company has raised new finance, invested in brand and new Formula 1 business, and rationalized production 'to significantly increase productivity, through cross functional collaboration and digitalization'.

- Selection and Testing: Partnering with Red Bull Advanced Technologies resulted in fast pace testing of the 'Aston Martin Valkyrie – with innovative design and performance for a road car'.

- Success and Learning: Aston Martin adapted its new model programme, evolving its development strategy and 'optimizing the operational footprint' to deliver significant annual savings of 30 per cent.

Impact

Achieving the vision: the company message is 'to enrich what is unique to the Aston Martin brand – the combination of high performance and ultimate luxury together in one automobile'. It has set a challenging agenda, to become 'the most agile and efficient company in the luxury segment, to achieve the best outcome for the product, our customers, our investors and other stakeholders'.

A review of the organization's 2021 website (Aston Martin, 2021c) reveals a more mature, business-focused approach to sharing the vision with stakeholders and its strategy to achieve it. At the time of writing, the Business Resilience elements are clear: the primacy of investing in the brand through its partnership with EON Productions, the resurgent F1 team, more exciting halo products within the portfolio, a willingness to call out for more investment from individuals and organizations strongly aligned to the brand values, and embracing the future through enhanced technological partnerships and networks. It has certainly reached another milestone in Business Resilience in 2021.

Summary

This summary provides observations about how Business Resilience has enabled these organizations to progress, succeed and endure in VUCA environments, over the long term, together with a reflection on the prospective value of Business Resilience audits as a progressive way forward for today's business leaders.

Observations

These insights reveal the industry-wide appeal and application of Business Resilience, suggesting how the ideas contained within the Business Resilience Framework can be implemented to have a beneficial impact on organizational Business Resilience, which, in turn, places the organization in a stronger position to make sustained progress, delivered at pace, whatever the VUCA condition.

In the most challenging VUCA conditions, it is not BAU. Staff should consider not only what customer(s) want but have the confidence or passion (Elevated Energy) to ask why it is needed; this can be a key to innovation, and it is for organization leaders to support them in improving RESILIENCE Foundation elements and the value of a product, rather than simply the product or service itself.

A willingness of development teams to check why something is required, rather than simply what is needed, makes progress both easier and more worthwhile; PACE encourages customer enquiry and collaboration; real progress then results from development and testing of evolutionary solutions. PACE Culture energizes business networks and must be shared at all five levels of the organization.

Realizing plans starts with vision and engagement; it extends to all levels of the organization, and beyond into our markets. The keys to progress and success lie in understanding beliefs and behaviours that drive customer journeys, knowing why their journey matters and aligning the PACE Culture to it. These insights demonstrate that the most resilient organizations have done just that, satisfying the shared values of customers and investors over repeated PROGRESS Cycles to achieve Business Resilience, even in the most challenging of circumstances.

Further information on Business Resilience audits and the work of Resilience Professionals is available, and readers are encouraged to visit www. resilienceprofessionals.com

---

QUESTIONS TO THINK ABOUT

- What are the highest-priority domains and elements that enabled Business Resilience and progress to be made in these organizations?

- What are the most important lessons from these insights that could be implemented in your organization?

- As a Resilience Professional, could you recommend any additional actions to increase Business Resilience further and explain why these will be effective?

References

Aston Martin (2021a) Aston Martin Chairman Stroll on luxury automaker's turnaround plan: The risks are behind us, *CNBC*, 18 August, www.cnbc.com/2021/08/18/aston-martin-chairman-stroll-on-turnaround-plan-the-risks-are-behind-us.html (archived at https://perma.cc/93KV-LUB3)

Aston Martin (2021b) *Making History: The first new DB5 in more than 50 years rolls off the line as inaugural Aston Martin DB5 Goldfinger Continuation car is completed*, 24 September, media.astonmartin.com/making-history-the-first-new-db5-in-more-than-50-years-rolls-off-the-line-as-inaugural-aston-martin-db5-goldfinger-continuation-car-is-completed (archived at https://perma.cc/Y7P7-ZY2Z)

Aston Martin (2021c) *Aston Martin Lagonda: Strategy*, 18 August, www.astonmartinlagonda.com/about-us/strategy (archived at https://perma.cc/BD4G-VT6Y)

Demandt, B (2021) Aston Martin sales data and trends for the European automotive market, *CarSalesBase*, 18 October, https://carsalesbase.com/europe-aston-martin/ (archived at https://perma.cc/98GS-F8N6)

Excell, J (2013) Hydrogen hybrid Aston Martin to take to the track, *The Engineer*, 12 April, www.theengineer.co.uk/hydrogen-hybrid-aston-martin-to-take-to-the-track (archived at https://perma.cc/QRC9-YHDM)

Lincoln Electric Company (2021a) *Why LECO? Reasons to invest in Lincoln Electric*, https://ir.lincolnelectric.com/why-leco (archived at https://perma.cc/XY9F-NEC4)

Lincoln Electric Company (2021b) *Employee Engagement*, https://sustainability.lincolnelectric.com/employee-engagement.html (archived at https://perma.cc/Y6ZU-72ZT)

Lincoln Electric Company (2021c) *Developing Our People*, https://sustainability.lincolnelectric.com/our-people.html (archived at https://perma.cc/P35N-JFC4)

Microsoft (2019) *Heathrow Airport inspires employee engagement with Microsoft Power Apps*, 7 November, customers.microsoft.com/en-us/story/766053-heathrow-airport-travel-transportation-power-apps (archived at https://perma.cc/E3M4-S5JT)

Moore, J (2013) Aston Martin: 100 years, 100 stories, *Speedhunters*, 22 August, www.speedhunters.com/2013/08/aston-martin-100-years-100-stories (archived at https://perma.cc/UR6T-8SAB)

O'Connell, M (2020) *Vantage Point – Aston Martin and EON Productions unveil* No Time To Die's *newest tie-in marque*, 17 August, markoconnell.co.uk/vantage-point-aston-martin-and-eon-productions-unveil-no-time-to-dies-newest-tie-in-marque (archived at https://perma.cc/ES9B-DNG4)

O'Kane, S (2020) Aston Martin delays electric car plans after raising emergency funds, *The Verge*, 31 January, www.theverge.com/2020/1/31/21116675/aston-martin-electric-Rapide-lagonda-delay-stroll-investment (archived at https://perma.cc/Q4KM-FN8T)

Statista (2021) *Number of cars sold worldwide between 2010 and 2021*, www.statista.com/statistics/200002/international-car-sales-since-1990 (archived at https://perma.cc/D2H6-39H9)

Tankersley, J (2021) Biden details $2 trillion plan to rebuild infrastructure and reshape the economy, *New York Times*, 31 March, www.nytimes.com/2021/03/31/business/economy/biden-infrastructure-plan.html (archived at https://perma.cc/4LN4-A5CZ)

APPENDIX A: BUSINESS RESILIENCE ROLE DESCRIPTIONS

Purpose

The purpose of having the role descriptions is to enable organizations to allocate the Roles appropriately to individuals with a shared understanding of the responsibilities expected. These descriptions provide organizations with a template as a starting point for the creation of individual role descriptions that have been tailored to the specific organizational environment and circumstance. Those who are tasked with undertaking the responsibilities are able to review and ensure they have the skills and capabilities to fulfil the role.

Introduction

The role descriptions will be used to support the implementation and improvement of Business Resilience. The role descriptions cover the three core Roles and one optional role for Business Resilience. The names of each role can be adapted to the environment and organization in which they are being used (Figure A.1). It is also possible for the responsibilities to be carried out by Roles that are already in place, and some examples of Roles that can take on the responsibilities are included in each description. Others may also be appropriate. In some situations it will be suitable to appoint individuals into new positions, while in others it will be better to include responsibilities in existing positions.

The following role descriptions should be tailored to each individual and organizational business requirement. When introducing Business Resilience at a departmental or divisional level, the Roles should be reviewed to ensure they are commensurate with the level at which the implementation is being undertaken. The existing Roles that are suggested for the Business Resilience responsibilities will also need to be considered in this context. When the first Business Resilience Profile is completed, it can form an input to how the Roles should be tailored to align to the priorities identified by the profile. It is important to consider the readiness of the organization for Business Resilience and the level of Capability and Skills to undertake the responsibilities that are available.

Each role description shows the specific responsibilities and attributes that would be expected of the role. It also shows the Roles that may exist in the organization and could take on the responsibilities, if this is more appropriate.

Business Resilience team Roles diagram

Figure A.1 shows the Business Resilience core and supplementary Roles described in this appendix.

Business Resilience Owner

The Business Resilience Owner is an experienced and seasoned business leader who is watchful of external business ecosystem events. They have the knowledge and experience of best practices for Business Resilience and the ability to decide when to use which practice depending on factors such as specific scenarios, available resources, past effectiveness and industry norms. Business

FIGURE A.1 Business Resilience core and optional Roles

Resilience best practice assumes that the senior management and leadership of vigilant organizations have a built-in early warning mechanism. The warnings can be raised due to the external business ecosystem, political, environmental, social, technological, legislative or economic (PESTLE) events, and partner network or internal changes. This ensures that any alerts are recorded, analysed and allocated to relevant Roles.

Specific responsibilities

The Business Resilience Owner is responsible for:

- accountability to the leadership team for implementing and continually improving Business Resilience in the organization;
- good understanding of *Business Resilience: A practical guide to sustained progress delivered at pace*, especially Business Resilience Principles, Progress @ Pace 8-4-8 Model, tools and techniques, and Resilience Profile measures;
- ensuring that VUCA events are identified and assessed using appropriate techniques for their impact analysis;
- maintaining a high-level state of Resilience Profile to reflect the risks that must be monitored actively;
- approving relevant Business Resilience actions and allocating them as shown in the relevant chapters;
- signing off the Progress Definition (with any relevant KPIs), the Resilience Profile and decision gates 1 and 2;
- ensuring that the Progress Definition is designed to optimize value for customers and identified in consultation with relevant business functional areas so that they remain specific, measurable, achievable, realistic, relevant and time bound (SMARRT);
- selecting a Progress Master and collaborating with them on assessments of value initiatives in response to a VUCA event as soon as it is envisaged;
- establishing and maintaining RESILIENCE Foundations, embedding Business Resilience Principles across the entity (eg organization, department or division);
- establishing and maintaining the PACE Culture to ensure the organization culture supports Business Resilience;
- establishing and maintaining the PROGRESS Cycle according to the Business Resilience best practice.

Desirable attributes

The Business Resilience Owner should have attributes that include:

- inspirational leadership;
- knowledge of portfolio management, programme management and other relevant best practices;
- authority to take strategic decisions;
- conflict management, negotiation and strong people management skills;
- demonstration of the Stockdale Paradox;
- track record of converting crises into opportunities;
- high emotional quotient and open to criticism with a focus on value creation for customer and business;
- understanding of the organization's DNA;
- desire to become a catalyst for success and will not settle for anything trivial.

Organizational Roles mapped

This Business Resilience Owner role will default to one person, irrespective of the size of the organization. In small organizations, the role will mostly default to the head of the organization. In medium organizations, this role can be allocated to the head of a department, but they will have to liaise with the rest of the business functional areas to define value and progress. In large organizations, this role can be allocated to the head of a business unit who will liaise with the rest of the business entities; in public entities this role can sometimes be allocated to the chief resilience officer. Business Resilience Owners with significant experience of implementing Business Resilience can grow into Business Resilience consultants and vice versa.

Examples of organizational Roles that could have the responsibilities of the Business Resilience Owner are: head of division, head of department, head of portfolio, managing director, senior manager, C-level Roles such as chief operations officer, chief transformation officer, chief finance officer, chief executive officer, chief agility officer, chief resilience officer and chief progress officer.

Progress Master

The Progress Master is a qualified professional with demonstrable expertise in *Business Resilience: A practical guide to sustained progress delivered at pace.* They have expertise in the implementation and use of Business Resilience Principles, Progress @ Pace 8-4-8 Model, tools and techniques, and Resilience Profile measures. The Progress Master is a key link between the Business Resilience Owner, the Initiative Leaders and other areas of the organization.

Specific responsibilities

The Progress Master is responsible for:

- ensuring that sustained progress is made towards an organization's Business Resilience objectives through execution of RESILIENCE Foundations, PACE Culture and PROGRESS Cycle;
- being the subject-matter expert for implementation of the framework and can get involved in more than one Business Resilience initiative;
- ensuring that the progress of the Initiative Leader(s) and the corresponding initiative team(s) is aligned with the Progress Definition;
- using appropriate elements from the Progress @ Pace 8-4-8 Model when implementing initiatives.

Assist the Business Resilience Owner to ensure that the Progress Definition identified has the features shown below:

- the Progress Definition is aligned with the Evolving Vision;
- Progress Definition delivers benefits for the customer and organization;
- initiatives are financially viable with funds committed;
- initiatives are attractive for network partners;
- progress can be delivered using the processes and practices in place and the success and benefits can be measured.

Desirable attributes

The Progress Master should have attributes that include:

- flexibility and focus;

- being well versed in relevant best practices, eg project and programme management and risk management;
- experience of using digital tools for implementing processes;
- understanding of the business environment;
- demonstrable conflict management and negotiation skills;
- experience of managing partners, stakeholders and people;
- a promoter of leadership culture.

Organizational Roles mapped

The Progress Master can be a new role or can have the responsibilities taken on by an existing role. If it is a new role, the individual should have the attributes above. If it is an existing role, they may need training and support from a Resilience Professional until they gain experience. There can be several Progress Masters supporting a Business Resilience Owner.

Examples of organizational Roles that could have the Progress Master responsibilities include: portfolio manager, programme manager, change manager, transformation manager, operations manager, agile coach, Business Resilience manager, progress manager. With deep domain knowledge of the Business Resilience and implementation experience across various initiatives, the Progress Master can be elevated to become a Business Resilience Owner or choose to become a Resilience Professional.

Initiative Leader

This role is responsible for implementing the Business Resilience initiative(s). After the Business Resilience Owner and Progress Master have agreed the relevant initiatives in decision gate 1, the Initiative Leaders need to be appointed (if not already appointed). The Initiative Leader ensures that the value initiatives are executed according to plan using relevant best practices, technology accelerators, techniques, industry standards and relevant Business Resilience elements.

Specific responsibilities

The Initiative Leader is responsible for:

- liaising with the Progress Master to understand the context and desired goals of the value initiative;

- advising the Progress Master, if relevant, in steps 1–4 of the PROGRESS Cycle to develop the value initiative proposals, including the selection of appropriate best practices, technology products and industry standards, eg Lean, acatech Industrie 4.0 Maturity Index, PRINCE2®, MS Project, product-based planning;
- selecting value initiative team members and planning the delivery of the desired goals of value initiatives;
- managing the initiative team(s) by ensuring that effective communication channels have been established;
- overcoming hurdles during planning, execution and delivery by being a catalyst for team-building and progress;
- contributing domain expertise pertaining to the specific value initiative (eg marketing head for a marketing initiative to create awareness about a new product among existing and proposed customers);
- being a focused leader with Capability and Skills to guide the team through forming, storming, norming and performing phases and hence deliver progress;
- manage all risks and issues at team level and communicate those outside tolerances to appropriate management levels;
- benefit from and consult with advisers available for subject-matter expertise.

Desirable attributes

The Initiative Leader should have attributes that include:

- flexible and focused on delivering goals while respectful towards team members and stakeholders;
- team management including collaboration, conflict management and negotiation;
- knowledge of project/programme management and other best practices, including risk management, planning and quality;
- domain expertise for the relevant value initiative;
- high emotional quotient (or the will to improve it);
- accentuates the positive;
- courage to be honest and up front.

Organizational Roles mapped

The Initiative Leader is likely to be an existing role that is adapted to ensure an appropriate focus on Business Resilience. Only rarely would a new role be required, usually when needing to recruit an additional individual to deliver value initiatives. The Initiative Leader will have appropriate Capability and Skills in the most appropriate methods to deliver the value initiative. There is likely to be more than one Initiative Leader linking with and supported by each Progress Master.

Examples of organizational Roles that could have the responsibilities are: project manager, programme manager, initiative manager, change manager, transformation manager, department manager, heads of sales, marketing, research and others.

Resilience Professional

The Resilience Professional is a role that can be employed to assist in the implementation or improvement of Business Resilience. This role can take on the Business Resilience Owner or Progress Master role or support these Roles. If the organization is implementing Business Resilience, a Resilience Professional will enable the implementation to progress more rapidly and more confidently.

Specific responsibilities

The Resilience Professional is responsible for:

- training potential Business Resilience Owner and/or Progress Master in Business Resilience;
- coaching the Business Resilience Owner and/or Progress Master in role or being shadowed by these Roles;
- advising on the best strategy implementation approach;
- advising on and support adapting Business Resilience;
- ensuring RESILIENCE Foundations (or elements) are understood and implemented;
- supporting the PACE Culture to be developed;
- delivering the PROGRESS Cycle (or elements);

- ensuring the project management office has sufficient understanding of Business Resilience and the Initiative Leader role;
- implementing and advising on Business Resilience in accordance with best practice.

Desirable attributes

The Resilience Professional should have attributes that include:

- knowledge and experience of Business Resilience best practice;
- wider business best practice knowledge;
- excellent communication skills to assist organizations developing Business Resilience;
- experience of stakeholder engagement across organizational boundaries;
- flexibility to adapt standard practices to the organization;
- inspirational leadership;
- coaching skills.

Organizational Roles mapped

The Resilience Professional is likely to be an external role for an organization that is implementing Business Resilience. The Resilience Professional can support extending the departments or divisions where Business Resilience is implemented, or support Business Resilience being improved. Therefore, the Resilience Professional is expected to be a consultant or specialist appointed to the organization for a specific purpose.

QUESTIONS TO THINK ABOUT

- Identify some Business Resilience responsibilities of core Business Resilience Roles that are most relevant for your organization that could be added to existing Roles.
- For the responsibilities identified in the point above, what attributes are recommended for individuals who are identified to take on these responsibilities to be effective?
- Who in your organization is the most appropriate person to take on the Business Resilience Owner role to implement the Business Resilience Framework and why?

APPENDIX B: POPULAR BEST PRACTICE TOOLS COMPLEMENTING THE UNIQUE BUSINESS RESILENCE FRAMEWORK TOOLS

Purpose

Throughout the whole Business Resilience Framework, wherever possible, tools and established best practice are referenced that are not necessarily specific to Business Resilience. The purpose of this appendix is to demonstrate some examples of tools and best practices that can be utilized by Business Resilience that are mapped to the elements of the framework. In fact, as organizations have historically invested a lot of their resources into various methodologies, practices and tools to improve their performance, it is only logical to actively embrace and leverage the existing investment and expertise in achieving Progress @ Pace.

Tools and best practices

Table B.1 presents typical best practices and tools that, among others, may be used within the Business Resilience Framework.

TABLE B.1 Best practices and tools to be used within the Business Resilience Framework

P@P element	Management domain	Practice/ objective(s)	Relevant guidance/tool(s)/primary source
RESILIENCE Foundations			
Regulatory and Governance	Regulatory compliance	Industry or business-related compliance	Impey, D and Montague, N (2014) *Running a Limited Company: A practical guide on legal, accounting, tax compliance rules and implications of running a company*, Jordan Publishing, London
	Corporate governance	Standards and best practices	Empson, L (2017) *Leading Professionals: Power, politics, and prima donnas*, Oxford University Press, Oxford

(continued)

TABLE B.1 (Continued)

P@P element	Management domain	Practice/ objective(s)	Relevant guidance/tool(s)/primary source
	Accountability	Financial and management audit	Financial Reporting Council (2021) *Corporate Governance and Stewardship*, FRC, London
		Audit and desired autonomy	Financial Conduct Authority (2021) *UK Regulators, Government and Other Bodies*, FCA, London
			Murdock, H (2016) *Operational Auditing: Principles and techniques for a changing world*, CRC Press, Boca Raton, FL
	Responding to public policy	Alignment to policy	Trevor, J (2019) *Align: A leadership blueprint for aligning enterprise purpose, strategy and organisation*, Bloomsbury Business, London
Evolving Vision	Vision, mission and values		Meldrum, M and McDonald, M (1995) *The Directional Policy Matrix*, Palgrave, London
	Strategic positioning	Segmentation, targeting and positioning	Wernerfelt, B (1984) A resource-based view of the firm, *Strategic Management Journal*, **5** (2), pp 171–180
			Porter, M (1979) How competitive forces shape strategy, *Harvard Business Review*, March
			Porter, M (1980) *Competitive Strategy*, Free Press, New York
			Bowman, C and Faulkner, D (1997) *Competitive and Corporate Strategy*, Irwin Professional Publishing, Burr Ridge, IL
			Ansoff, H (1957) Strategies for diversification, *Harvard Business Review*, **35** (5)
			Kim, W and Mauborgne, R (2004) *Blue Ocean Strategy: How to create uncontested market space and make the competition irrelevant*, Harvard Business Review Press, Boston
		Alignment with customer values	Ries, A and Trout, J (2001) *Positioning: The battle for your mind*, McGraw-Hill Education, New York

(*continued*)

TABLE B.1 (Continued)

P@P element	Management domain	Practice/ objective(s)	Relevant guidance/tool(s)/primary source
			Kapferer, J (2012) *The New Strategic Brand Management: Advanced insights and strategic thinking*, Kogan Page, London
	Credibility	Stakeholder acceptance and support of the company vision	Beckhard Change Formula, in Beckhard, R and Harris, R (1987) *Organizational Transitions: Managing complex change*, Addison-Wesley, Boston
Sustainable Operations	Efficient operating model	Value engineering	Campbell, A *et al* (2017) *Operating Model Canvas: Aligning operations and organization with strategy*, Van Haren Publishing, Norwich, UK
	Adaptability and pivoting	Embedded business continuity	Forrester (2021) *The Adaptive Enterprise*
	Accessible and reliable systems		Duchek, S (2020) Organizational resilience: A capability-based conceptualization, *Business Research*, **13**, pp 215–246
			Masaaki, I (1986) *Kaizen: The key to Japan's competitive success*, McGraw-Hill, New York
	Right technologies	Technology accelerators	The Open Group (2021) *The TOGAF® Standard Overview*
			Ross, J *et al* (2006) *Enterprise Architecture as Strategy: Creating a foundation for business execution*, Harvard Business Review Press, Boston
			Accenture (2021) *Technology Vision 2021*
			Harvard Business Review (2021) The way forward with digital transformation accelerated by a pandemic, 11 January
			APMG (2021) *OBASHI® – Business and IT Management*
			TechTarget (2020) *Cloud Computing*

(continued)

TABLE B.1 (Continued)

P@P element	Management domain	Practice/ objective(s)	Relevant guidance/tool(s)/primary source
Innovation and Risk	Innovation efficiency assessment	Multi-criterial innovation analysis	Preston, J and Cooper, R (1990) Winning at new products, *Journal of the Operational Research Society*, **41** (2), p 181
			Rogers, E (1983) *Diffusion of Innovations*, Free Press, New York
	Robust and stress-tolerant systems	System testing and point of failure identification	Bank of England (2021) *Stress Testing*
	Controlled risk-taking	Risk management process	AXELOS (2021) *M_o_R – Risk Management*
			International Organization for Standardization (2018) *BS ISO 31000:2018 Risk Management*
	Inclusive decision-making	Stakeholder and network partner engagement	Reynolds, A and Lewis, D (2017) Teams solve problems faster when they're more cognitively diverse, *Harvard Business Review*, 30 March
			Bourke, J (2018) The diversity and inclusion revolution: Eight powerful truths, *Deloitte Review*, **2**
			FirstRoundReview (2021) *The 6 Decision-Making Frameworks That Help Startup Leaders Tackle Tough Calls*
Leading and Influencing	Leadership at 5 levels	Inspiring others to lead	Collins, J (2001) *Good to Great: Why some companies make the leap... and others don't*, Random House Business, New York
			Agile Business Consortium (2017) *The Nine Principles of Agile Leadership*
			Sinek, S (2011) *Start With Why: How great leaders inspire everyone to take action*, Penguin, New York

(continued)

TABLE B.1 (Continued)

P@P element	Management domain	Practice/ objective(s)	Relevant guidance/tool(s)/primary source
	Self-organization and adaptability	Empowering peers to make important decisions within their purview	Pink, D (2011) *Drive: The surprising truth about what motivates us*, Canongate Books, London
			Baumgartner, N (2020) Build a culture that aligns with people's values, *Harvard Business Review*, 8 April
	Trust and confidence	Taking care of employees as team players	Agile Business Consortium (2017) *The Nine Principles of Agile Leadership*
	Support for health and wellbeing	Developing and supporting others	Dweck, C (2017) *Mindset: The new psychology of success*, Ballantine Books, New York
			Covey, S (2008) *The Speed of Trust: The one thing that changes everything*, Free Press, New York
Enterprising Investment	Enabled external investment	Returns to business partners, shareholders and investors	Morgaine, B (2021) *11 Foolproof Ways to Attract Investors*, https://articles.bplans.com/11-foolproof-ways-to-convince-people-to-invest-in-your-business/
			Cremades, A (2018) 7 ways for entrepreneurs to find investors and raise millions, *Forbes*, 2 September
	Enabled internal investment	Efficient decisions on business cases	HM Treasury (2018) *Guide to Developing the Project Business Case*
			Boston Consulting Group (2020) *The Digital Path to Business Resilience*
	Talent nurturing	Attracting and retaining talent	McKinsey & Company (2018) *Talent Management as a Business Discipline: A conversation with Unilever CHRO Leena Nair*
			Rath, T (2007) *StrengthsFinder 2.0: From Gallup*, Gallup Press, New York

(continued)

TABLE B.1 (Continued)

P@P element	Management domain	Practice/ objective(s)	Relevant guidance/tool(s)/primary source
			WikiJob Team (2021) *The Best UK Job Boards in 2021*
	Asset management	Managing assets and resilient systems for business as usual	Woods, D and Hollnagel, E (2006) *Resilience Engineering: Concepts and precepts*, Ashgate, Aldershot, UK
			Jordan, B *et al* (2013) *Corporate Finance: Core Principles and applications*, McGraw-Hill/Irwin, New York
			Daecher, A *et al* (2019) Asset performance management: Driving value beyond predictive maintenance, *Deloitte Insights*, 26 February
Network Collaboration	Robust and secure supply chain	Achieving mutual gains for partners	Accenture (2021) *Supply Chain Disruption*
			Womack, J *et al.* (2007) *The Machine That Changed the World*, Simon & Schuster, New York
			Womack, J and Jones, D (2003) *Lean Thinking: Banish waste and create wealth in your corporation*, Simon & Schuster, New York
		Overcoming silos and barriers to collaboration	Womack, J (2015) *Lean Solutions: How companies and customers can create value and wealth together*, Free Press, New York
			Willis, R (2021) *Accelerating Collaboration Everywhere*
	Facilitated learning network	Learning organization and continued professional development	APM (2013) *Earned Value Management Handbook*
			Kearns, P (2015) *Organizational Learning and Development: From an evidence base*, Routledge, London

(continued)

TABLE B.1 (Continued)

P@P element	Management domain	Practice/ objective(s)	Relevant guidance/tool(s)/primary source
			Senge, P (2006) *The Fifth Discipline: The art and practice of the learning organization*, Random House Business, New York
	Culture of partnering	Successful partnership behaviours	Agile Business Consortium (2021) *Development Matrix for Agile Culture*
Evolutionary Portfolio	Design thinking	Developing solutions with use of case-driven approach	Brown, T (2019) *Change by Design: How design thinking transforms organizations and inspires innovation*, HarperBusiness, New York
			Goodwin, K (2009) *Designing for the Digital Age: How to create human-centered products and services*, Wiley, Hoboken, NJ
	Agile thinking	Information and technology-driven innovation	Smith, M (2020) *Agile Project Management: The Bible: How to deliver products of value with fast turnaround times: Scrum, Kanban, Lean Six Sigma, Agile*
			Schwaber, K (2004) *Agile Project Management with Scrum*, Microsoft Press
			Fujitsu (2021) *People Power Adaptive Organisations*
			Agile Business Consortium (2010) *Agile Project Management Handbook*
	Balanced and prioritized portfolio	Prioritizing programmes, projects and value initiatives	Lazar, O (2018) *The Four Pillars of Portfolio Management: Organizational agility, strategy, risk, and resources*, Auerbach Publications
			AXELOS (2011) *Management of Portfolios (Managing Successful Portfolios)*
			AXELOS (2020) *Managing Successful Programmes*

(continued)

TABLE B.1 (Continued)

P@P element	Management domain	Practice/ objective(s)	Relevant guidance/tool(s)/primary source
			Nunes, K (2020) Coca-Cola cleaning up portfolio, approach to innovation, *Food Business News*, 22 July
			Strong, C *et al* (2018) *The Lean Product Lifecycle: A playbook for making products people want*, Pearson Business, London
	Modularity and scalability	Modular design and common platforms	Baldwin, C (2000) *Design Rules: The Power of Modularity v. 1: Volume 1*, MIT Press, Boston
			Ulrich, K and Eppinger, S (2011) *Product Design and Development*, McGraw-Hill, New York
			EY (2021) *Modular Product Design: Reducing complexity, increasing efficacy*
PACE Culture			
Purposeful Mindset	Growth mindset	Belief in positive change	Dweck, C (2017) *Mindset: Changing the way you think to fulfil your potential*, Robinson, New York
	Focus on outcomes	Responsive behaviour	Covey, S (2004) *7 Habits of Highly Effective People*, Free Press, New York
	Leveraged behavioural preferences	Behavioural models	DiSC Profile of Behavioural Types and Personality Styles, in Marston, W (2014) *Emotions of Normal People*, Cooper Press
	Personal resilience	Resilience	Johnstone, C (2019) *7 Ways to Build Resilience*, Robinson, New York
			Seligman, M (2006) *Learned Optimism: How to change your mind and your life*, Vintage Books, New York
Application of tools	Leveraged technology competitiveness	Digital technology and innovation	Betz, F (2011) *Managing Technological Innovation: Competitive advantage from change*, Wiley, Hoboken, NJ

(continued)

TABLE B.1 (Continued)

P@P element	Management domain	Practice/ objective(s)	Relevant guidance/tool(s)/primary source
			Rogers, D (2016) *The Digital Transformation Playbook: Rethink your business for the digital age*, Columbia University Press, New York
	Effective business growth	Growth frameworks	Osterwalder, A (2020) *The Invincible Company*, Wiley, Hoboken, NJ
	Leveraged human capital	Human resource management	Henderson, I (2019) *Human Resource Management for MBA and Business Masters*, Kogan Page/CIPD, London
	Improved alignment of tools to customer value	Business process re-engineering	Johnston, G (2017) *Business Process Re-engineering: A simple process improvement approach to improve business performance*
Capability and Skills	Balanced interpersonal and technical skills	Continuing professional development	Bossert, O and Laartz, J (2017) Perpetual evolution: The management approach required for digital transformation, *McKinsey Digital*, 5 June
	Embedded coaching	Coaching as a process and capability	Owen, J (2013) *How to Coach: Coaching yourself and your team to success*, Pearson, London
	Alignment of skills to evolving business needs	Skills at 5 Progress @ Pace levels	Competence assessment relevant to area of work, eg APM (2015) *APM Competence Framework*
	Alignment of capability to evolving business needs	Capability evolution	Helfat, C (2007) *Dynamic Capabilities: Understanding strategic change in organizations*, Wiley, Hoboken, NJ
Elevated Energy	Energy type and level diagnostics	Positive vs negative energy	Energy profile questionnaire, in Bruch, H and Vogel, B (2011) *Fully Charged: How great leaders boost their organization's energy and ignite high performance*, Harvard Business Review Press, Boston
			Branson, R (2014) *The Virgin Way: Everything I know about leadership*, Portfolio, London

TABLE B.1 (Continued)

P@P element	Management domain	Practice/ objective(s)	Relevant guidance/tool(s)/primary source
		Motivation and culture	Sinek, S (2020) *The Energized Workplace: Designing organizations where people flourish*, Kogan Page, London
	Embedded culture of Energy Elevation	Energy built on inspiration and trust	Pink, D (2011) *Drive: The surprising truth about what motivates us*, Canongate Books, London
			Bruch, H and Vogel, B (2011) *Fully Charged: How great leaders boost their organization's energy and ignite high performance*, Harvard Business Review Press, Boston
			Bain & Company (2016) *How Leaders Inspire: Cracking the code*
PROGRESS Cycle			
Progress Definition	Strategic analysis and planning	Market environment	PESTLE, in Richardson, J (2017) A Brief Intellectual History of the STEPE Model or Framework, https://pages.gseis.ucla.edu/faculty/richardson/STEPE.htm
			Porter's Five Forces, in Porter, M (1979) How competitive forces shape strategy, *Harvard Business Review*, March
			Strategic Group Analysis, in Porter, M (1980) *Competitive Strategy: Techniques for analyzing industries and competitors*, Free Press, New York
			Critical success factors, in Yarbrough, Q (2021) What is a critical success factor? A quick guide, *ProjectManager*, 4 May
			Stakeholder Mapping, in Miro (2021) *Complete Stakeholder Mapping Guide*
		Organizational context	Resource Audit, in Chapman, R (2011) *Simple Tools and Techniques for Enterprise Risk Management*, Wiley, Hoboken, NJ

(continued)

TABLE B.1 (Continued)

P@P element	Management domain	Practice/ objective(s)	Relevant guidance/tool(s)/primary source
			Value chain analysis, in Stobierski, T (2020) What is a value chain analysis?, *Harvard Business School Online*, 3 December
			Directional Policy Matrix, in Young, L (2011) *The Marketer's Handbook: Reassessing marketing techniques for modern business*, Wiley, Hoboken, NJ
			SWOT/TOWS, in Watkins, M (2007) From SWOT to TOWS: Answering a reader's strategy question, *Harvard Business Review*, 27 March
		Strategic options	Porter's Generic Strategies, in Porter, M (1980) *Competitive Strategy: Techniques for analyzing industries and competitors*, Free Press, New York
			Ansoff Matrix, in Ansoff, I (1957) Strategies for diversification, *Harvard Business Review*, **35** (5)
			Bowman's Strategy Clock, in Bowman, C and Faulkner, D (1997) *Competitive and Corporate Strategy*, Irwin Professional Publishing, Burr Ridge, IL
			Diamond of Innovation, in Cooper, R and Mill, M (2005) *Succeeding at New Products the P&G Way: Work the innovation diamond*
			Red Teaming (Restatement and Provocation), in Hoffman, B (2017) *Red Teaming: How your business can conquer the competition by challenging everything*, Crown Business, New York
	Required benefits	Benefits management	AXELOS (2011) *Management of Portfolios (Managing Successful Portfolios)*
	Urgency for progress	Risk and return appetite	Risk Appetite Instrument, in Quail, R (2012) *Defining Your Taste for Risk*

(continued)

TABLE B.1 (Continued)

P@P element	Management domain	Practice/ objective(s)	Relevant guidance/tool(s)/primary source
	Business objectives	Target operating model	POTI Model, in Department for Business, Innovation and Skills (2010) *Guidelines for Managing Programmes: Understanding programmes and programme management*
Recognize Challenge	Available capacity for transformation	Capacity to meet CSFs	Informing Change (2017) *A Guide to Organizational Capacity Assessment Tools*
			Snowden, D and Boone, M (2007) A leader's framework for decision making, *Harvard Business Review*
Opportunity Assessment	Product innovation	Improved and new products	HM Treasury (2018) *Guide to Developing the Project Business Case*
	Services innovation	Improved and new services	McKinsey & Company (2020) *How Covid 19 has pushed companies over the technology tipping point – and transformed business forever*
	Process improvement	Empowered operational decision-taking	Partner (stakeholder) weightings in multi-criteria assessments, eg Ruangpan, L *et al* (2021) Incorporating stakeholders' preferences into a multi-criteria framework for planning large-scale Nature-Based Solutions, *Ambio*, **50**, pp 1514–1531
	Practice improvement	Managing benefits	Infrastructure and Major Projects Authority (2017) *Guide for Effective Benefits Management in Major Projects*
			Crispin, P (2018) *Benefits Maps: Painting by numbers*
Good Alignment	Business environment	Performance and quality management	Rastogi, A (2018) *DMAIC – A Six Sigma Process Improvement Methodology*
	Capability improvement	Roadmap to closing maturity gap	Chrissis, M *et al* (2003) *CMMI: Guidelines for process integration and product improvement*, Addison-Wesley Professional, New York

(continued)

TABLE B.1 (Continued)

P@P element	Management domain	Practice/ objective(s)	Relevant guidance/tool(s)/primary source
			Hedgehog model, in Collins, J (2001) *Good to Great: Why some companies make the leap… and others don't*, Random House Business, New York
	Partner feasibility	LEAN process	Johnston, G (2017) *Business Process Re-engineering: A simple process improvement approach to improve business performance*
	Customer value mapping	Value studies	Miles, L (1972) *Techniques of Value Analysis and Engineering*
Rapids and Lagoons	Portfolio composition	Balanced and up-to-date portfolio	AXELOS (2011) *Management of Portfolios (Managing Successful Portfolios)*
		Calculated risk-taking	PwC (2012) *Smart Implementation: Reining in the risk and cost of regulatory change in banking*
	Initiative prioritization	Prioritized backlog	Agile Business Consortium (2021) *MoSCoW Prioritisation*
	Initiative resourcing	Resource balancing	Carbno, C (1999) Optimal resource allocation for projects, *Project Management Journal*, 30 (2), pp 22–31
	Initiative delivery and monitoring		Landau, P (2020) Gantt Chart vs. PERT Chart vs. Network Diagram: What are the differences?, *ProjectManager*, 30 September
			Kanbanize (2021) Kanban vs Scrum: Detailed comparison
	Commercially robust evolution of portfolio	Circular economy	Kwant, C (2021) *How to Design Products for the Circular Economy?*, Modular Management
Enabling Teams	Self-managed teams	Scrum	Agile Alliance (2021) *Manifesto for Agile Software Development*
			Agile Alliance (2021) *Scrum*
	Teams and Roles	Psychographic profile	The Myers & Briggs Foundation (2021) *MBTI® Basics*
			Belbin Associates (2021) *What's Belbin All About?*

(continued)

TABLE B.1 (Continued)

P@P element	Management domain	Practice/ objective(s)	Relevant guidance/tool(s)/primary source
			True Colors (2021) Valuing Differences – Creating Unity
	Team performance	Behaviours and development cycle	Toomer, J et al (2018) *The Catalyst Effect: 12 skills and behaviors to boost your impact and elevate team performance*, Emerald Publishing, Bingley, UK
			Tuckman, B (1965) Developmental sequence in small groups, *Psychological Bulletin*, **63** (6), pp 384–399
			Erikson, T (2019) *Surrounded by Idiots: The four types of human behavior and how to effectively communicate with each in business*, St. Martin's Essentials, New York
	Facilitation of teams	Facilitation tools	Mann, T (2014) *Facilitation: Develop your expertise*, Resource Strategic Change Developers
Selecting and testing	Building, testing and integration	Increments and continuous integration	ASQ (2021) *What is the Plan-Do-Check-Act (PDCA) Cycle?*
			Green, S (2002) *Criterion Referenced Assessment as a Guide to Learning*
			TestingXperts (2020) *Integration Testing: What is, types, tools, steps to perform*
			Kazerouni, A et al (2019) *Assessing Incremental Testing Practices and Their Impact on Project Outcomes*
			Business Smart (2020) *Business Simulation Testing*
		Iterations and failing fast	Crispin, L and Gregory, J (2008) *Agile Testing: A practical guide for testers and agile teams*, Addison-Wesley Professional, New YOrk

(continued)

TABLE B.1 (Continued)

P@P element	Management domain	Practice/ objective(s)	Relevant guidance/tool(s)/primary source
			BioMed Central (2020) *Translational simulation for Rapid transformation of health services, using the example of the Covid 19 pandemic preparation*
		Regression testing	IEEE (2001) *Prioritizing Test Cases for Regression Testing*
Success and Learning	Learning organization	Systematic learning	Beckford, J (2019) *The Intelligent Organisation: Driving systemic change with information*, Routledge, London
		Progress as foremost success criterion	Champion/Challenger model, in AXELOS (2011) *Management of Portfolios (Managing Successful Portfolios)*
	Learning individual	Establishing new 'normal' and business as usual	Duhigg, C (2016) *The Power of Habit: Why we do what we do, and how to change*, Random House Books, New York
		Action-centred success	Ibarra, H (2015) *Act Like a Leader, Think Like a Leader*, Harvard Business Review Press, Boston

QUESTIONS TO THINK ABOUT

- Which of these tools are already in use in your organization that you would utilize for Business Resilience?
- Are there tools shown that would help implement Business Resilience in your organization?
- Which tools may benefit continuous improvement of Business Resilience in your organization?

APPENDIX C: MAPPING TO INTERNATIONAL STANDARDS

Purpose

The purpose of mapping the Business Resilience Framework to international standards is to provide organizations with the ability to ensure there is compatibility with the standards that are relevant to their situation. This is particularly important where there are regulatory or governance requirements for a specific standard to meet regulations or for a contract.

International standards mapped

The national and international standards and frameworks against which the Business Resilience Framework has been assessed for compatibility are:

- ISO 22316:2017: Security and resilience – Organizational resilience – Principles and attributes (International Organization for Standardization, 2017);
- ASIS SPC.1-2009: Organizational resilience: security, preparedness, and continuity management systems (American National Standards Institute, 2009);
- BS 65000: Organizational Resilience standard – guidance on achieving enhanced Organizational Resilience (British Standards Institution, 2014);
- Organizational Resilience Framework: Helping organizations to anticipate, prepare for, respond and adapt to disruptions (British Standards Institution, 2021).

Other relevant standards and frameworks

The Business Resilience Framework has also been mapped to the Business Resilience approaches that are presented by some of the global consultancies, including 'the Big Four'. This has been undertaken in the same way as the international standards.

TABLE C.1   Example of mapping to the international standards

Item in the standard	Business Resilience Framework element that is compatible with the standard item	Comment
Item one	Regulatory and governance element	Fully met by this element

In addition, the United Nations 17 Sustainable Development Goals have been assessed. The Business Resilience Framework will support each goal to be developed with resilience which, in turn, will strengthen sustainability.

How the mapping has been undertaken

For each of the standards each individual item in the standard has been assessed and the element of the Business Resilience Framework which is compatible with that item has been identified (Table C.1).

Benefits

The key benefit from using the mapping of the Business Resilience Framework to other standards is that organizations can realize the relevant international standards by implementing the framework. It provides a practical approach to demonstrating how the organization meets the relevant standard.

Where more details can be found

The full mapping of the Business Resilience Framework against each standard has been produced. This is available by contacting the authors or from www.resilienceprofessionals.com

QUESTIONS TO THINK ABOUT

- Has your organization already met any of the international standards?
- If the answer is yes, can these processes and procedures be enhanced to 'plug and play' in the Business Resilience Framework?
- If the answer is no, with which of the international standards does your organization need to demonstrate compliance?

References

American National Standards Institute (2009) *Organizational Resilience: Security, preparedness, and continuity management systems*, ASIS SPC.1-2009, American National Standards Institute, https://webstore.ansi.org/standards/asis/asisspc2009 (archived at https://perma.cc/4KMY-T566)

British Standards Institution (2014) *Organizational Resilience Standard – Guidance on achieving enhanced organizational resilience*, BS 65000, British Standards Institution, shop.bsigroup.com/products/guidance-on-organizational-resilience?pid=000000000030258792 (archived at https://perma.cc/WXA6-7MS8)

British Standards Institution (2021) *Helping Organizations to Anticipate, Prepare for, Respond and Adapt to Disruptions*, British Standards Institution, www.bsigroup.com/en-GB/our-services/Organizational-Resilience/bsi-organizational-resilience-framework/ (archived at https://perma.cc/U3HA-8DL3)

International Organization for Standardization (2017) *Security and Resilience – Organizational resilience: Principles and attributes*, ISO 22316: 2017, International Organization for Standardization, www.iso.org/standard/50053.html (archived at https://perma.cc/3QZV-LPDU)

APPENDIX D: PROGRESS @ PACE 8-4-8 MODEL

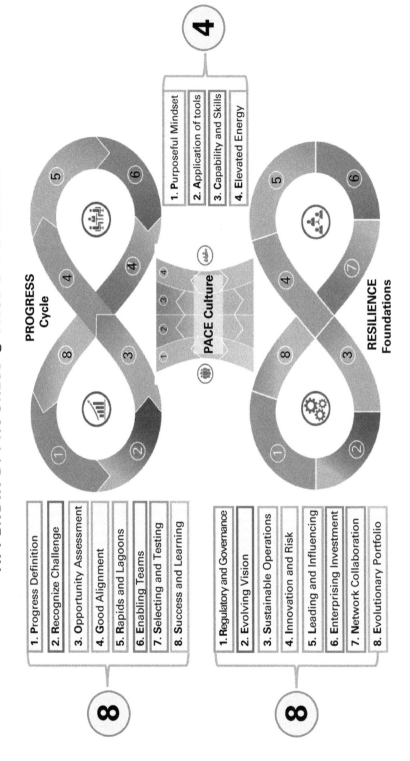

PROGRESS Cycle

RESILIENCE Foundations

PACE Culture

1. Purposeful Mindset
2. Application of tools
3. Capability and Skills
4. Elevated Energy

1. Progress Definition
2. Recognize Challenge
3. Opportunity Assessment
4. Good Alignment
5. Rapids and Lagoons
6. Enabling Teams
7. Selecting and Testing
8. Success and Learning

1. Regulatory and Governance
2. Evolving Vision
3. Sustainable Operations
4. Innovation and Risk
5. Leading and Influencing
6. Enterprising Investment
7. Network Collaboration
8. Evolutionary Portfolio

APPENDIX E: BUSINESS RESILIENCE FRAMEWORK OVERVIEW

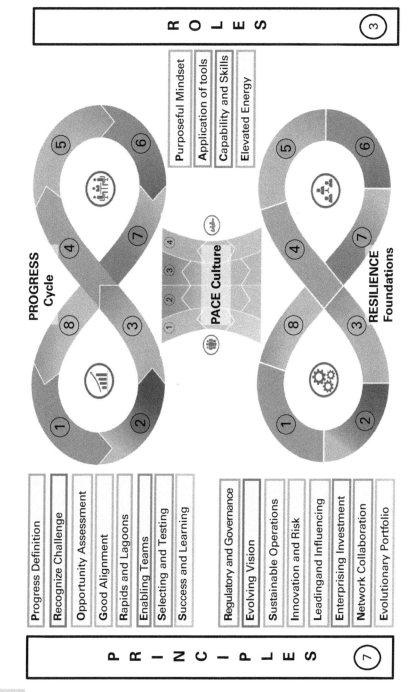

ROLES (3)

- Purposeful Mindset
- Application of tools
- Capability and Skills
- Elevated Energy

PROGRESS Cycle

PACE Culture

RESILIENCE Foundations

PRINCIPLES (7)

- Progress Definition
- Recognize Challenge
- Opportunity Assessment
- Good Alignment
- Rapids and Lagoons
- Enabling Teams
- Selecting and Testing
- Success and Learning

- Regulatory and Governance
- Evolving Vision
- Sustainable Operations
- Innovation and Risk
- Leading and Influencing
- Enterprising Investment
- Network Collaboration
- Evolutionary Portfolio

GLOSSARY

ABCDE – Adversity, belief, consequence, disputation, energization.

ACE (Accelerating Collaboration Everywhere) – An approach to understanding, improving and strengthening the bonds within dynamic professional groups.

Adaptive Enterprise scale – An instrument measuring the internal organizational capability to adapt to changes in VUCA conditions.

AE (Adaptive Enterprise) – The ability to change or adjust flexibly by altering routines and practices in response to internal and external changes.

Agile culture matrix – An instrument to help organizations understand their team's culture using five stages and seven DNA elements of cultural agility.

AgileDS – Agile framework focusing on building and delivery of digital services.

AgilePfM – An agile portfolio management framework ensuring that business change strategy remains current and under continuous review.

AgilePgM – Agile programme management framework focusing on a disciplined and flexible management of organizational change ensuring programmes capture their vision.

AgilePM – An agile project management framework focusing on using agile principles to deliver projects.

Ansoff Matrix – A tool with four strategies that can be used to help a firm plan to grow; also analyses the risk associated with each strategy.

Application of tools – A PACE Culture element that focuses on the utilization of tools for teams to build, adapt and innovate working solutions, taking advantage of opportunities to overcome challenge and satisfy customers today, while increasing Business Resilience.

Balanced scorecard – A business performance tool to implement and manage strategy, linking vision to strategic objectives, measures, targets and initiatives; balances financial measures with performance measures and objectives related to all other parts of the organization.

BM – Benefits Management.

BRIT – Business resilience and initiative team.

Business Adviser – A role that interacts with the Business Resilience roles and is responsible for advising on strategic or functional business-level matters; can be internal or external to the organization.

Business as usual (BAU) – An organization's normal day-to-day operations or steady state.

Business case – The rational basis for justifying a value initiative, based upon planned improvements to products, services, practices and processes.

Business justification case – A short-format business case that identifies a preferred option in terms of benefits, costs and risks to achieve a business goal, on the basis of rational analysis.

Business resilience – Sustained progress, delivered at pace.

Business resilience domains – Principles, RESILIENCE Foundations, PACE Culture, PROGRESS Cycle, Roles.

Business Resilience Framework – A framework with five domains – Principles, RESILIENCE Foundations, PACE Culture, PROGRESS Cycle and Roles – to build Business Resilience in organizations.

Business resilience owner – The role accountable and responsible for the adoption, implementation and improvement of Business Resilience in the organization.

Capability and Skills – A PACE Culture element that focuses on core and specialist capabilities and skills to enable teams to understand customer needs and enhance products, services, processes and practices.

Challenge formula – A tool to assess the overall level of challenge the organization is facing, based upon VUCA Storm scale, Urgency Score, Adaptive Enterprise score and Available Capacity Score.

Challenge Score – A score representing the overall level of challenge to progress that the organization is facing.

Champion/challenger technique – A technique where everyone is expected to comply with the defined process (champion) but anyone can recommend a change (challenger), which is only implemented if authorized.

Change formula – A tool to assess if organizational change will happen, eg Beckhard's formula.

CLEVER – A list of critical capabilities that aid Business Resilience and support the effectiveness of individual or team capabilities.

CPD tool – Continuing Professional Development.

Decision Gate 1 – A decision to proceed to development of the value initiative; a major milestone in the PROGRESS Cycle.

Decision Gate 2 – A decision to release the output to production or the market; a major milestone in the PROGRESS Cycle.

Diamond of innovation – A tool to position innovations by considering four dimensions: novelty, technology, complexity and pace.

DICE – A popular framework offering a statistical analysis-based method to assess the chance of successful delivery of a project.

Digital Tx – Digital Transformation.

DiSC – An assessment that examines how an individual ranks in four areas of behaviour: dominance, influence, steadiness and conscientiousness.

Disciplined Agile Delivery (DAD) – The software development portion of the Disciplined Agile Toolkit, enabling teams to make simplified process decisions around incremental and iterative solution delivery and building on the agile software development principles.

Elevated Energy – A PACE Culture element in which the energy of self-managed teams enables performance beyond that which could reasonably be expected of the individuals.

Emotional quotient – The level of a person's emotional intelligence.

Empowered teams – A PROGRESS Cycle element in which teams are self-managed, self-directed and have delegated authority to make decisions to achieve agreed goals.

Enterprising Investment – A RESILIENCE Foundations element for investment that utilizes initiative and resourcefulness.

Evolutionary Portfolio – A RESILIENCE Foundations element comprising the organization's portfolio that continues to evolve and respond, as needed, to the environment.

Evolving Vision – A RESILIENCE Foundations element comprising a vision of what an organization will achieve and how it will operate in the future, progressing from the current (as is) situation through iterations to the future (to be) desired state.

Exploratory strategy – A strategy to achieve Business Resilience through experimentation, where the Business Resilience Framework is used as a comparator approach when testing improvements.

Functional Lead – The lead for a specific functional area, eg sales, marketing or logistics, who advises the Initiative Leader and team on matters relating to this area.

Good Alignment – A PROGRESS Cycle element in which value initiatives are assessed to confirm that the selected value initiatives align well with the Progress Definition objectives of its partner network and Resilience Profile of the organization.

HRM – Human resources management.

Initiative team – A team to support an Initiative Leader to execute a value initiative.

Innovation and Risk – A RESILIENCE Foundations element that balances the desire for portfolio innovation with resource availability and assesses risk levels.

Innovation networks – A type of collaboration where firms share research and development goals related to products, services, processes or business models, and organizational wellbeing.

Kanban board – An agile project management tool designed to help visualize work, limit work-in-progress and maximize efficiency (or flow).

Lagoon – A Business Resilience value initiative that can be implemented at a slower pace.

Leading and influencing – A RESILIENCE Foundations element to inspire others and create belief in a future where organization brand values and positioning reflect the aspirations of the network.

LeSS – A framework for scaling scrum, lean and agile development to big product groups.

Lessons log – A repository for lessons that apply to this or future initiatives.

Management of value – A value management methodology that can be utilized to get the best financial and non-financial benefits from programmes, projects and portfolios.

MBTI – Myers-Briggs Type Indicator is a personality test classifying 16 personality types.

MCA – Multi-criteria analysis.

MoP – Management of Portfolios

MoSCoW – A prioritization technique for requirements that uses the levels of: Must Have, Should Have, Could Have and Won't Have This Time.

MSP® – A methodology representing a systematic approach to managing programmes of business change to achieve outcomes and realize benefits that are of strategic importance.

MoV – Management of Value

MVP – minimum viable product.

Network Collaboration – A RESILIENCE Foundations element that engenders a spirit of collaboration and partnership, both internally and externally.

Network partner – An organization's partner, eg supplier, resellers, contractor, distributor, developer, regulator, local community.

Opportunity Assessment – A PROGRESS Cycle element to understand the level of opportunity this Progress Definition presents, specifically in terms of benefits, value and how sure the organization is that it will be able to deliver.

Opportunity Score – A measure of opportunity a Progress Definition presents in terms of benefits, value and delivery confidence for the organization implementing it.

Organization Business Resilience Framework – An adaptation of the Business Resilience Framework suited to an organization's context and environment.

PACE Culture – A people-centred environment where organizations invest in four elements: Purposeful Mindset, application of tools, Capability and Skills, and Elevated Energy.

PACE retrospective – A review of what went well and what did not work, when considering how to improve organization culture.

PERMA – A model representing five core elements of happiness and wellbeing – positive emotion, engagement, relationships, meaning and accomplishments.

PESTLE – An assessment of the environment using the dimensions of political, environmental, social, technological, legislative, economic.

PMBoK – A publication from the Project Management Institute, as a resource for effective project management in any industry.

PMO – Portfolio, programme or project management office.

Porter's Five Forces – A framework for analysing the operating environment and competition of a business.

Portfolio – The totality of investment in the changes required to achieve the organization's strategic objectives, including programmes, projects and other changes.

PRINCE2 – A structured project management method emphasizing dividing projects into manageable and controllable stages.

PRINCE2 Agile – A methodology blending the flexibility and responsiveness of agile with the defined governance of PRINCE2 (see PRINCE2).

Principles – A Business Resilience Framework domain that identifies the set of beliefs that underpin the Business Resilience Framework.

Process Iceberg Methodology – A hierarchical, sequential and interdependent model to explain what happens in the group dynamics of meetings, used in facilitation.

Progress @ Pace (P@P) – The optimal development and delivery of products, services, processes and practices to realize the next Progress Definition.

Progress @ Pace 8-4-8 Resilience Model – The model comprises three domains of the Business Resilience Framework – RESILIENCE Foundations, PACE Culture and PROGRESS Cycle – to implement progress; supported and guided by the domains of roles and principles.

Progress Backlog – A collection of value initiatives that may require implementation to realize progress.

PROGRESS Cycle – A Business Resilience Framework domain comprising eight delivery elements in an infinity loop design, leading to purposeful and deliberate progress, in all VUCA conditions.

Progress Definition – (1) A PROGRESS Cycle element that defines progress in terms of improvement of organizational efficiency or outputs resulting from selected value initiatives contributing to stronger Business Resilience; (2) The output of the Progress Definition element

Progress Master – A qualified professional with demonstrable expertise in Business Resilience to implement the organization's Business Resilience strategy.

Progress roadmap – A presentation of the longitudinal view of progress for the current PROGRESS Cycle.

Progress status board – A visual tool to capture value initiative implementation status.

Progressive strategy – A strategy to achieve Business Resilience over several PROGRESS Cycles, progressively introducing elements of the Business Resilience Framework according to their prioritization level.

PSPP backlog – A backlog of initiatives relating to products, services, processes or practices.

PURE strategies – Four alternative strategies recommended to achieve Business Resilience in organizations.

Purposeful Mindset – A PACE Culture element that adapts a growth mindset to include alignment with the organization's vision and is key to developing a PACE Culture.

RAG – Red, amber, green.

Rapid – A Business Resilience value initiative that needs immediate execution.

RFE – RESILIENCE Foundation elements

Recognize Challenge – A PROGRESS CYCLE element to understand the internal and external factors that could challenge the implementation of chosen value initiatives.

Red teaming – A process in which a 'red team' plays the role of an enemy or competitor and provides security feedback from that perspective.

Regulatory and Governance – A RESILIENCE Foundations element to clarify industry standards and ensure that the organizational policies are aligned to them.

RESILIENCE Foundations – A Business Resilience Framework domain comprising eight functional elements in an infinity loop design, supporting actions and activities in the PROGRESS Cycle in all VUCA conditions.

Resilience Professional – An experienced professional with qualifications in Business Resilience, who can take the role of Business Resilience owner or progress Master or act as a consultant.

Resilience Profile – A tool to measure the level of Business Resilience of one or more elements of the Business Resilience Framework.

Resilient organization – An organization that can achieve progress in all VUCA environments.

Responsive strategy – A strategy to improve Business Resilience rapidly by introducing one or more elements of the Business Resilience Framework.

Scrum – A framework based on agile principles for developing, delivering and sustaining products in a complex environment, designed for teams of 10 or fewer members, who break their work into goals that can be completed within time-boxed iterations.

Scrum@Scale – A framework providing the structure for systems and processes to grow organically out of the unique conditions of one's organization, based on scrum, complex adaptive systems theory, game theory and object-oriented technology.

Selection and Testing – A PROGRESS Cycle element that undertakes quality testing of value initiative outputs and subsequently marks them as ready for release into production or live use.

SMARRT – Objectives defined in terms that are specific, measurable, achievable, realistic, relevant and timebound.

SPL – Strategic Project Leadership.

Stockdale Paradox – A concept postulating that productive change begins when one confronts the brutal facts, ie balancing realism with optimism .

Success and Learning – A PROGRESS Cycle element that ensures recognition of success, as a basis for energizing organizational learning and adoption of improvements.

Sustained Operations – A RESILIENCE Foundations element focused on establishing adaptable, digital and modular operational capability supporting efficient practices.

SWOT – A popular organizational analysis model looking at strengths, weaknesses, opportunities and threats.

TOGAF – The Open Group Architecture Framework.

TOWS – An extension of the popular SWOT analysis providing actionable links between the different parts of one's business and environment.

Urgency Scale – A measure of the pressure to implement high-priority value initiatives in a given cycle; contributes to the assessment of the overall challenge in the current PROGRESS Cycle.

Urgency Score – An indicator of specific requirement or pressure to deliver a Progress Definition; contributes to the Challenge Score (see Challenge Score).

Urgent strategy – A strategy to achieve Business Resilience, by adopting the Business Resilience Framework as an off-the-shelf solution, subject only to lean tailoring in the organization.

Value engineering – Value engineering is a development technique to substitute materials and methods with less expensive alternatives, without sacrificing functionality.

Value initiative – Any initiative that potentially results in the notable improvement of the organizational efficiency or outputs; contributing to the Progress Definition and Evolving Vision.

Value proposition – A proposal for an initiative to enhance benefits or reduce costs or risks associated with a product, service, process or practice.

VUCA – An acronym for volatile, uncertain, complex and ambiguous environments, which are fast-paced and unpredictable.

VUCA Storm scale – A tool to measure of the level of volatility, uncertainty, complexity and ambiguity of the external environment.

VUCA Storm score –A measure of the external environment that reflects the 'strength of the storm that needs to be navigated'.

INDEX

Page numbers in *italic* indicate figures or tables.

CPSIA information can be obtained
at www.ICGtesting.com
Printed in the USA
JSHW010024300322
24434JS00006B/20

9 781398 604643